BETA SIGMA PHI
INTERNATIONAL

Gourmet
COOKBOOK

Beta Sigma Phi

P.O. BOX 8500
1800 WEST 91ST PLACE
KANSAS CITY, MO. 64114
TELEPHONE: HILAND 4-6800

It's my personal pleasure . . .

. . . to introduce a distinctive collection of gourmet creations, each an adventure in good eating! Every entry in this exciting new cookbook may be relied upon for accuracy and taste appeal . . . because all have been successfully proven in the kitchens of members of Beta Sigma Phi.

Beta Sigma Phis are enthusiastic and inventive hostesses who love to get together. Preparing imaginative meals for friends as well as for their own families is a challenge that members meet with unmatched creativity. For this reason, you may well expect to find that the recipes gathered in this book are far from the ordinary, everyday fare.

Beta Sigma Phi, with over 200,000 members, is an international organization for women offering opportunities for friendship, development of cultural appreciation and community service. The Greek letters stand for Life, Learning and Friendship. Members believe the only right they have is the right to be useful.

Beta Sigma Phis have a vitality and love for life – and therefore, the ability to enjoy life to the fullest. They are aware young women who appreciate the beauty in the world, and have found happiness in using their energy and talents to add to that beauty. Their worthwhile community service projects include scholarships, disaster relief funds, collection of toys and clothing for needy children, fund drives for mental health clinics and the heart fund, aid for the handicapped – and so many more that it would take pages to list them all. The great joy of sincere, genuine sharing with others, and with each other, brings them satisfaction.

Members in the more than 10,000 chapters believe that when they join hands and hearts to accomplish something, a small idea can grow to produce tremendous feats. This belief was expressed in the frequent remark by the late founder of Beta Sigma Phi, Walter W. Ross, "You can do anything you dream." Beta Sigma Phis have made dreams come true time after time, not only for themselves but for others as well. The sale of this cookbook will help chapters raise funds to sustain countless beneficial projects.

Bill Ross

WALTER W. ROSS III
President
International Executive Council

© Favorite Recipes Press MCMLXXIII
Post Office Box 3396, Montgomery, Alabama 36109
Library of Congress Catalog Card No. 73-82896
ISBN 0-87197-051-1

Preface

As a homemaker, you know that families want something out of the ordinary in their meals, and so do guests. There have likely been many occasions when you have thought, "I wish there were something *different* to prepare for tonight's dinner," and you turned to your cookbook collection.

In this latest BETA SIGMA PHI Cookbook, you will find a multitude of very "special" appetizers, salads, entrees, desserts — GOURMET recipes that will delight both family and guest with the out-of-the-ordinary. Home-tested and proven successful by members of one of the largest groups of homemakers in America, Beta Sigma Phi International, recipes in this edition are practical and clearly stated, yet unique. As in the Beta Sigma Phi cookbooks that have preceded it, members have submitted their most successful recipes and have proudly signed their names to their submissions. On the basis of eating quality, originality and recipe accuracy, the very best have been chosen to appear in this edition.

Now you can draw upon the experience of some of the finest cooks anywhere . . . Beta Sigma Phis who honestly enjoy the satisfaction of preparing delicious meals for the important people in their lives. The wide variety of recipes offers food creations to challenge the experienced cook, and others that are simple enough for the novice in the kitchen.

You will find that the BETA SIGMA PHI GOURMET Cookbook is the one you will turn to when you are searching for the unusual and delicious for a special occasion, special guests — or perhaps on an impulse to do something very special for your family.

Contents

Glossary of Gourmet Terms

Everybody gets excited at the prospect of preparing a gourmet meal. But to many women, the words "epicurean" or "gourmet" suggest complicated, time-consuming recipes, foreign phrases and out-of-the-ordinary ingredients. Gourmet cooking is, however, simply a matter of careful preparation, the proper chef's tools, and patience. It is the ability to follow a recipe with the assurance that your own personal cooking skills are all that is needed to produce first-class epicurean dishes.

This cookbook is a collection of gourmet recipes for both the novice and the accomplished cook. It is written for women who love to cook and are anxious to develop new culinary talents. No matter how particular the gourmet in your family may be, this unique selection of the best Beta Sigma Phi gourmet recipes is sure to be a gastronomic success. For your convenience, we have included in the following glossary a list of cooking terms and illustrations which you may want to add to your culinary vocabulary.

Aspic Clear jelly made from a clarified chicken/fish/meat stock used with a relevant dish, as deviled eggs in aspic. Wine/liqueur may be added to the stock. If necessary, gelatin may be used to set.

Bain-Marie (au) To cook at temperatures just below boiling point in a saucepan standing in a larger pan of simmering water. Used in the oven or on top of the stove in the preparation of sauces, creams and foods which should not be cooked over direct heat.

Bard To cover lean meats with bacon/pork fat before cooking. See also **Lardon**.

Baste To spoon melted butter, fat or a liquid over food as it cooks.

Beat To mix foods or liquids thoroughly and vigorously with a spoon, whip or electric beater. If you use a whisk or fork for beating, train yourself to use the muscles of your lower arm and wrist, as they tire less quickly than shoulder muscles.

Blanch To plunge food into boiling water to soften, precook or partially cook it. Meats may be whitened in this manner. Food is blanched to remove or reduce too strong a taste, as for cabbage or onions.

Bombe A sophisticated French dessert that combines different flavors of ice cream, sherbet or ices in a special bombe mold.

Bouquet Garni Traditionally a combination of parsley, thyme and bayleaf tied in a cheesecloth bag and used for flavoring stews and sauces. Remove before serving dish.

Brine A salt and water solution used in preserving meats and vegetables.

Brioche An individual-sized sweet roll prepared from a very light yeast dough which may be hollowed out and filled with a sweet and savory sauce. Brioches may be baked in muffin cups or the traditional fluted brioche mold.

Brochette (a la) Small pieces of meat, fish or offal which are grilled with vegetables on a skewer (as for kabob).

Butter Cream which has been churned into a solid state. It may be salted or sweet (unsalted).

    Beurre blanc: A combination of butter, white wine/wine vinegar, fish stock, chopped shallots; served as a sauce over poached or boiled fish.

    Beurre manie: A combination of twice as much butter as flour worked together to a paste consistency and added in small pieces to thicken liquid (usually at the end of the cooking process).

Beurre noir: Clarified butter cooked to a deep brown, then acidulated with reduced vinegar or lemon juice. Parsley or capers may be added to this sauce which is used mainly for fish and brains.

Beurre noisette: Clarified butter which is cooked to a nut-brown color.

Clarified butter: Butter which has been heated gently until foaming. The clear yellow oil is skimmed, then strained off, leaving the milk solids behind.

Canelle knife Also called a lemon stripper, it is used most often for garnishing and food decoration.

Caramelise 1 To dissolve sugar slowly in water, then boil steadily, without stirring, to a toffee-brown color. This is used for a syrup or glaze. **2** To give a thin caramel topping on a cake or pudding by dusting the top of sweet with granulated or confectioners' sugar, and broiling slowly.

Casserole A stewpan. Also a type of meat and vegetable stew cooked in liquid slowly in an oven.

Clarify 1 To remove impurities by melting used fat (beef, poultry or bacon drippings) with one-third quantity of water, boiling, straining and cooling. When fat is set, scrape any impurities from base of cake. **2** To clear cold stock with egg whites, whisk while bringing both to a boil in saucepan, cooling and straining.

Colander A bowl shaped utensil, usually made of metal, which has perforations permitting its use as a strainer.

Compote 1 Dried or fresh fruit poached in a sugar and water syrup to which a liqueur, brandy or rum may be added. **2** A deep bowl, usually on a stem.

Concasser To chop roughly or shred coarsely.

Consomme Clear soup made from a meat stock which is concentrated and clarified before serving, hot or cold.

Court bouillon Stock made from water, root vegetables, wine or vinegar and seasoning and herbs. It is primarily used for poaching veal or fish and for use in sauces.

Croquette Most often a savory mixture shaped into rounds, balls or cones, coated with egg and breadcrumbs, and deep-fat fried and served as a main dish.

Croute A small toasted or fried round of bread, spread or topped with a savory mixture. It may also be used as a garnish.

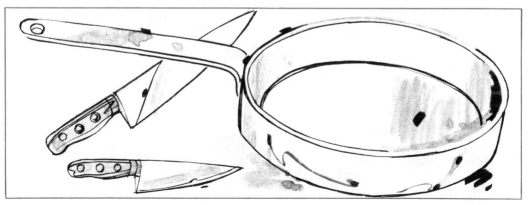

Crouton Small squares, or diced pieces of fried bread or potato to accompany puree or cream soups.

Deglaze After the removal of excess fat, stock and or wine is heated together with the flavorful coagulated cooking juices and sediments left in the roasting or frying pan. This mixture forms a gravy or sauce base.

Degrease To remove accumulated fat from the surface of hot liquids.

Degorger To remove strong flavors or impurities before cooking. This can be done by soaking the food in cold water (as for salted ham) or by sprinkling sliced vegetables (cucumber, for example) with salt, covering with weighted plate, leaving up to one hour, and pressing out excess liquid with a heavy plate.

Devil To marinate or to apply a seasoned/spiced sauce to meat, fish or poultry pieces before broiling or frying. A devil or barbecue sauce can be served separately.

Dice Meat, fruit or vegetables which have been cut into small squares.

Double boiler Two saucepans, one of which fits into the other. The food in the upper pan is cooked by the simmering water in the lower. The principle difference between a double boiler and a bain-marie is that the food in a double boiler is cooked over, not in, hot water.

Dredge To cover liberally with, or to immerse in, sifted flour or sugar.

Flan ring A fluted or smooth French pastry ring with no bottom, used for making tart shells. The ring is set on a baking sheet, the pastry is molded into it and baked. When done, the ring is removed from the tart shell and the shell is placed on a serving dish and filled. There is also a flan pan which has a removable bottom.

Fines herbes Chopped parsley, or a mixture of herbs: usually, parsley, chervil, tarragon and chives.

Flambe Pouring warmed spirits, brandy or sherry over food in a pan, igniting and continuing to cook the dish. This adds flavor to the food and helps to burn off excess surface fat.

Fondue A Swiss party dish made with Gruyere and Emmenthal cheese, white wine and kirsch, served at the table in a casserole over a burner. Using long handled fondue forks, cubes of bread are dipped in it.

Food Mill A food grinder used to puree soups, sauces, vegetables, fruits, raw fish or mousse mixtures. The best type has three removable discs, one for fine, medium or coarse pureeing.

Fool Fruit puree mixed with thickened or whipped cream.

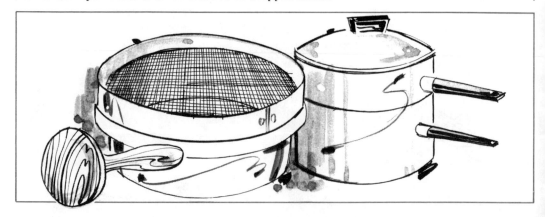

Forcemeat (or farce) A savory meat stuffing mixture used to flavor meat, fish or poultry which is usually stuffed into cavities or between portions. It can be baked or fried separately and served with the main dish.

Fricassee Reheated cooked chicken served in a white sauce or a stew of meat/fish/poultry/and vegetables. The stew is usually served with a white or veloute sauce.

Fritter Cooked meat or raw vegetables or fruit dipped into a thick batter and deep-fat fried.

Fry

    1 *Dry*: to cook steaks or chops over high heat in a minimum of shortening or oil.

    2 *Shallow*: to cook eggs, fish or breaded cutlets briskly without burning in a quarter to three-quarter inch layer of shortening or oil.

    3 *Deep*: to immerse and fry food, which has been dipped in breadcrumbs or flour, in shortening or oil. Deep-fat frying is meant to seal juices in foods. The shortening or oil should be kept very hot.

Fold To blend a fragile mixture, such as beaten egg whites, very delicately into a heavier mixture, such as a souffle base.

Fumet Well reduced fish stock or essence of fish, meat or game.

Garlic press A press or squeezer used to puree whole garlic cloves.

Garnish Decorating foods with bits of fruits or vegetables cut in unusual and attractive shapes before serving. Typical garnishments are carrot or celery curls, radish roses, onion and pepper rings and parsley.

Glace A thin sugar icing for cakes, biscuits and crystallized fruits.

Grater

    1 *Free standing*: shreds raw vegetables, lemon peel, apple, cheese. This type of grater usually has four sides with different sized perforations ranging from fine to extra coarse.

    2 *Hand held*: The best is the French Mouli, a small grater used for cheese and small vegetables and nuts. It has a revolving piece which grates hard cheese. However, soft cheese tends to form long tendrils or ribbons of cheese which are very nice when used as a garnish for salads.

Gratine To brown the top of a sauced dish under a broiler. Bread crumbs, grated cheese and dots of butter help to form a light brown covering (gratin or au gratin) over the sauce.

Infuse To steep in liquid in order to draw flavor into the liquid (as a vanilla pod in milk).

Junket Milk set to a curd with rennet.

Knead To work dough by repeatedly drawing it out and pressing it together with the heel of the hand to the required elasticity. This is especially important in breadmaking.

Lardon Small thin strips of fat used to give extra fat and flavor to lean meats. These strips are larded or sewn into the meat with a larding needle.

Liaison Mixture used as the thickening or binding agent in sauce, gravy or soup. Examples are roux, egg yolks, cream and kneaded butter.

Macerate To soak or infuse, generally fruit in a liqueur or syrup.

Mandoline A French vegetable slicer made of wood with two adjustable blades, plain and fluted.

Marinate To soak raw meat or fish in a spiced liquid (marinade) of wine or herbs, oil and vegetables. Leaving it for several hours or days tenderizes and flavors the meat. The marinade can be used in the final sauce.

Mirepoix Basic preparation for flavoring sauces. Diced vegetables are cooked gently for a few minutes in butter to draw out the flavor.

Morels Delicately flavored mushrooms having a sponge-like surface and elongated caps. They can be found growing in the United States in early spring. Canned or dried morels are sold in specialty shops.

Mortar and Pestle Small wooden porcelain or marble bowl shaped container useful for grinding herbs, pounding nuts and pureeing foods. The pestle is a small clublike implement used to pound the food.

Mousse
> *Sweet*: a smooth, rich confection made from whipped egg whites or cream, sugar and flavorings.
>
> *Savory*: made from pureed meat, fish or poultry, usually in a gelatin base, served chilled.

Noisette 1 Small round slice of meat (especially lamb) as from a fillet or eye of a chop. **2** A nutbrown color (as to cook butter to a noisette).

Offal The culinary term for specialty or variety meats such as heart, tripe or brain.

Papillote (en) Food wrapped and cooked in a casing of oiled heavy paper. This conserves the juices and aromas.

Pate A cooked meat, fish or specialty meat mixture, well seasoned, minced and molded and served cold, usually as an appetizer. Pate en croute is a pate covered and baked in a pastry crust and served either hot or cold. Pate de foie gras is fattened goose liver cooked in a covered dish or in pastry.

Patisserie A small cake, gateau or pastry.

Poach To cook in gently boiling water.

Puree Fruit, vegetables or meat which is usually precooked, then sieved or blended to a thick cream.

Quiche A number of French dishes which consists of a pastry shell filled with a savory egg and cream custard to which meat, seafood or vegetables may be added.

Ragout A highly seasoned dish of stewed vegetables and meat.

Ramekin 1 A casserole dish, usually of cheese, baked in small individual earthenware bowls (also spelled ramequin).

Rasher A thin slice or portion of meat, especially bacon.

Ratatouille A savory Mediterranean vegetable dish served hot or cold.

Reamer A juicer for citrus fruits consisting of a inverted fluted cone surrounded by a bowl-like dish.

Reduce To rapidly boil a liquid (such as gravy) to reduce it in quantity and concentrate the flavor.

Refresh To place blanched and drained vegetables or meat into cold water, thus stopping the cooking process.

Render To melt down solid fat, and strain to remove impurities.

Roux (white, blond or brown) A shortening and flour mixture which is the basis of all flour sauces. The amount of shortening is generally slightly more than that of flour. To prepare, melt shortening, stir in flour (off heat) and pour in water, stock or milk. Stir until roux thickens, season, bring to boil and cook.

Saute To cook very rapidly in an open pan using a small amount of butter.

Savarin A rich, yeast-leavened cake, which is baked in a special savarin ring mold, then soaked in a kirsch, rum or liqueur flavored syrup. It is often glazed and decorated with almonds and fruits; its center filled with soft custard or whipped cream and fruit.

Seasoning An added ingredient which enhances the flavor of food, such as condiments, aromatics, pungent sauces, herbs and spices.

Slake To mix arrowroot or cornflower with a little cold water before adding to a liquid for thickening.

Souffle A sweet or savory fluffy baked dish consisting of a sauce and egg yolk mixture with flavorings and stiffly beaten egg whites. A souffle dramatically puffs very high when baked in a special high-walled souffle dish.

Souse Steeping food in a wine vinegar and spice mixture. The meat or fish is cooked slowly and allowed to cool in the same liquid.

Sugar Clear sweet crystals obtained by processing juice of sugar cane, sugar beet and sugar maple. When fully refined it is white and called granulated sugar. Raw sugar is the yellowish residue which remains after the molasses has been removed. Brown sugar is unrefined sugar which has a molasses-like taste. Super fine or Castor sugar is exceedingly fine granulated sugar. Powdered sugar is granulated sugar which has been ground into a powder. Confectioners' sugar or Icing sugar is finely powdered sugar which has cornstarch as an additive.

Tamis A type of strainer very much like a metal sieve; however, it has a cloth mesh bottom. It is often used to "dust" flour or confectioners' sugar in baking.

Tart A small pastry shell which has a sweet or savory filling and is most often served individually.

Tempura A Japanese dish of seafood or vegetables dipped in batter and fried.

Timbale A small hors d'oeuvre pastry fried in a timble iron (fluted drum- or heart-shaped mold) and filled with a savory filling.

Tournedos A 1½" - 2" thick tenderloin fillet steak which is wrapped with a strip of bacon and broiled or fried.

Truffle Several types of highly regarded underground fungi. Resembling a small gnarled sweet potato, it has a delicate flavor and is most commonly used sparingly as a garnishment.

Truss To prepare fowl for cooking by securely binding the legs and wings close to the body.

Vol-au-vent A tart shell of extremely flaky puff paste, usually filled with a sauce and creamed meat, shellfish or poultry. May also be used with sweet dessert fillings.

Wash A water or milk base mixture applied to pastry to glaze it while baking.

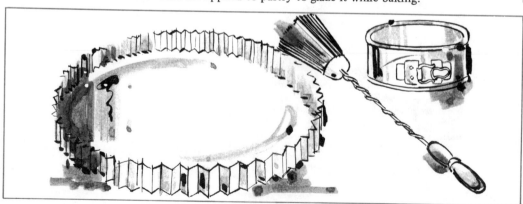

Photograph of these recipes on cover.

CURRIED ROCK LOBSTER

  4 9-oz. packages frozen South
      African rock lobster-tails
  6 tbsp. butter or margarine
  6 tbsp. flour
  1 1/2 tsp. salt
  1/4 tsp. pepper
  1/2 tsp. garlic powder
  1 1/2 tbsp. curry powder
  1 qt. milk
  8 hard-cooked eggs, sliced
  1 1/2 lb. thin spaghetti
  1 1/2 c. sliced ripe pitted olives
  3 tbsp. chopped pimento
  3 c. grated Cheddar cheese

Drop frozen lobster-tails into boiling, salted water. Bring to a boil; cook for 2 to 3 minutes. Drain immediately. Drench with cold water; cut away underside membrane. Pull out lobster meat; dice. Melt butter in large saucepan; stir in flour, salt, pepper, garlic powder and curry powder. Stir in milk gradually; cook over low heat, stirring constantly, until sauce bubbles and thickens. Stir in lobster pieces and eggs. Cook spaghetti according to package directions; drain. Toss while hot with olives, pimento and cheese. Pour spaghetti mixture into serving dish; top with hot curried lobster.

ROCK LOBSTER AMERICAINE

  5 9-oz. packages frozen South
      African rock lobster-tails
  2 tbsp. butter
  2 tbsp. olive oil
  1 clove of garlic, chopped
  2 onions, minced
  2 carrots, minced
  1/4 c. brandy
  1 c. tomato sauce
  1 pt. canned tomatoes, chopped
  1 c. white wine
  1/2 tsp. crumbled basil

Cut frozen lobster in shell into 1-inch crosswise slices with sharp knife. Heat butter and oil. Add garlic, onions and carrots; saute for 5 minutes. Add lobster pieces. Add remaining ingredients; cover tightly. Cook over low heat, stirring occasionally, for about 20 minutes. Season with salt and pepper, if desired.

VICHYSOISSE LOBSTER IN SHELL

  5 9-oz. packages frozen South
      African rock lobster-tails
  2 10 1/4-oz. cans frozen cream of
      potato soup, thawed
  1/2 c. light cream
  2 tbsp. sherry
  1/4 c. frozen chopped chives
  1 1/2 tsp. paprika
  1 1/2 c. grated mozzarella cheese

Drop frozen lobster-tails into boiling, salted water. Bring to a boil; cook for 2 to 3 minutes. Drain immediately; drench with cold water. Cut away underside membrane. Pull out lobster meat; cut in 1/2-inch crosswise slices. Reserve shells. Combine lobster slices, potato soup, cream, sherry, chives and paprika; heat through. Spoon into reserved shells; place on broiler pan. Sprinkle with cheese; broil until bubbly and golden.

COLOR PHOTO EXPLANATION

This edition of the Beta Sigma Phi International Cookbook series contains hundreds of magnificent gourmet recipes from members of Beta Sigma Phi. Beautiful full-color photographs, chosen by the editors of Favorite Recipes Press, feature a variety of menu ideas. Located throughout the volume, the photographs — along with their accompanying recipes — will add to your cooking enjoyment.

An Acadian Creole Dinner With Recipes

by Mrs. Gerald Domingue (Hazel)
Preceptor Gamma   New Orleans, Louisiana

MENU

Cold hors-d'oeuvre
chicken liver pate

Soup
crayfish bisque

Intermediate course
Supreme de crabe

Entree
Filet de Boeuf a l'ail (garlic)
with wine and mushroom sauce
Louisiana rice dressing
Herbed broccoli
Hot French bread

Salad
Endive with onion and Mandarin oranges

Dessert
Pot de creme au chocolat
demi-tasse (coffee)
liqueur: Grand Marnier

Wine: Saint Germain Champagne
Wine: Valpolicella

HERBED BROCCOLI

2 bunches broccoli
Herbs, Olive oil, Red wine
Fresh lemon juice
Salt and pepper to taste

Cook broccoli in boiling, salted water until just tender; cool. Prepare salad dressing from favorite recipe, using desired herbs, olive oil, wine and lemon juice. Pour over broccoli; marinate for 2 hours. Place on flat dish; sprinkle with salt and pepper. Garnish with lemon and boiled eggs.

ENDIVE WITH ONION AND MANDARIN ORANGES

Endive
3 sm. onions
1 can mandarin orange slices
Olive oil
Wine vinegar
Salt and pepper

Wash and clean endive; break into crystal salad bowl. Slice onions thin; separate into rings. Drain orange slices. Place onions and orange slices in bowl with endive. Prepare dressing from favorite recipe, using olive oil, vinegar, salt and pepper. Add to salad; toss gently.

CRAYFISH BISQUE

3 qt. crayfish tails, cleaned
2 1/2 lg. onions, chopped
1/4 bell pepper, chopped
1/2 c. cooking oil
1 stick butter
1/2 c. crayfish fat
1 c. fresh bread crumbs
1/2 c. heavy cream
Salt and pepper to taste
Chopped green shallots or onion tops to taste
Chopped parsley to taste
2 garlic cloves, chopped
50 cleaned crayfish head shells

Grind crayfish tails; add onions, bell pepper, oil, butter and crayfish fat. Simmer in large pot until onions and bell pepper are tender. Add bread crumbs and cream; season with salt and pepper. Add shallots, parsley and garlic; cook over low heat for 10 minutes. Remove from heat. Skim off excess fat; stuff in crayfish shells. Roll shells in flour; place in shallow pan. Bake at 350 degrees until brown.

Bisque

2/3 c. flour
3/4 c. salad oil
2 garlic cloves, chopped
1 lg. onion, chopped
1/2 bell pepper, chopped
2 celery stalks, chopped
2 bay leaves
1 med. sliced lemon
1/4 c. tomato paste
1 qt. whole crayfish tails
Salt and pepper to taste
Chopped green shallots to taste
Chopped fresh parsley to taste

Mix flour and oil in a heavy iron pot until smooth. Place pot over low heat; cook, stirring constantly, until dark brown. Remove from heat. Stir in 1 cup warm water. Add vegetables, bay leaves, lemon and tomato paste, then add crayfish tails and 7 cups water. Cook until crayfish tails are done. Add baked crayfish; bring to a simmer. Add salt and pepper; cook until thick. Add shallots and parsley. Serve in soup bowls with 1 heaping tablespoon rice.

POT DE CREME AU CHOCOLAT

1 1/2 lb. sweet cooking chocolate
2 c. heavy cream
8 egg yolks
Dash of salt

Grate chocolate. Place cream in pot; bring to a boil over low heat. Add chocolate. Stir gently; remove from heat. Beat egg yolks briskly until smooth. Mix egg yolks and chocolate mixture, stirring constantly. Add salt; cook, stirring, for about 3 minutes. Pour into pot de creme cups; cover. Refrigerate overnight. Remove from refrigerator 30 minutes before serving; serve with generous helpings of whipped cream.

CHICKEN LIVER PATE

1 lb. chicken livers
1 c. dry white wine
1 8-oz. package cream cheese, softened
1 lg. onion, minced
1 tsp. garlic powder
Salt and pepper to taste
3 tbsp. cocktail sherry
Rye or sesame wafers

Remove all fibrous tissue from chicken livers. Cook livers in wine over medium heat until done. Remove from heat; cool for several minutes. Drain; reserve liquid. Mash livers with potato masher. Blend in cream cheese; beat until smooth. Add onion, garlic powder, salt, pepper and sherry; blend. Add reserved liquid if additional moisture is needed. Place in crystal dish; cover. Refrigerate for 1 hour. Garnish with lemon slices and fresh parsley. Spread on wafers at serving time.

SUPREME DE CRABE

1 stick butter
4 green shallots, chopped
4 sprigs of parsley
1 6-oz. can sliced mushrooms, drained
1/4 tsp. curry powder
1/4 tsp. garlic powder
1/2 pt. heavy cream
1 lg. box fresh back fin crab meat
Fresh bread crumbs
8 tbsp. sherry
Salt and pepper to taste
1 c. grated Gruyere cheese
1/2 c. grated Parmesan cheese

Melt butter in large skillet over medium heat. Cook shallots and parsley in butter for about 3 minutes or until tender. Add mushrooms, curry powder and garlic powder. Reduce heat to low; cook for 3 minutes longer. Add cream slowly, stirring constantly. Fold in crab meat gently. Thicken with bread crumbs; heat for 5 minutes, without stirring, over low heat. Remove from heat; stir in sherry gently. Season with salt and pepper. Spoon into scallop shells. Mix Gruyere and Parmesan cheeses; spread over crab mixture. Bake at 450 degrees until cheese melts; garnish with lemon ring and parsley sprigs.

FILET DE BOEUF A L'AIL WITH WINE AND MUSHROOM SAUCE

Garlic cloves, sliced
Salt to taste
Paprika to taste
1 12-lb. tenderloin

Mix garlic, salt and paprika. Cut small slits in tenderloin with a pointed, very sharp knife; insert garlic in slits. Place in baking pan. Roast in 400-degree oven until medium done. Let stand for 10 minutes.

Sauce

1 c. sliced mushrooms
4 tbsp. butter
1 1/2 c. hot beef broth
1/2 c. thinly sliced onions
2 tbsp. flour
1/2 c. Madeira
Salt and pepper to taste
Paprika to taste

Saute mushrooms in 2 tablespoons butter until tender. Add 1/2 cup beef broth; cover. Simmer for 10 minutes. Saute onions in remaining butter in separate pan. Sprinkle flour over onions; stir well. Add remaining beef broth and Madeira; cover. Simmer for 15 minutes or until thickened. Add mushroom mixture; place over low heat. Season with salt, pepper and paprika; heat through.

LOUISIANA RICE DRESSING

1 lb. chicken gizzards
1/2 lb. ground lean pork
1/4 c. salad oil
2 garlic cloves, finely chopped
2 lg. onions, chopped
2 celery stalks, chopped
1/2 lb. chicken livers
Chopped green shallots to taste
Chopped fresh parsley to taste
4 lobster-tails, cooked
4 c. cooked rice
Salt and pepper to taste

Grind gizzards; mix with pork. Cook pork mixture in oil until done. Add garlic, onions and celery; cook over low heat for 10 minutes. Chop livers; add to onion mixture. Add small amount of water; cook until liver is done. Add shallots and parsley. Add lobster just before serving; toss with rice. Season with salt and pepper; serve warm.

Hors d'Oeuvres and Canapes

Beta Sigma Phis have traditionally been involved in social, civic
and cultural activities and the need for new and varied hors d'oeuvre
and canape recipes for these functions can, at times, be staggering.
Teas, showers, inititations, luncheons and pre-dinner appetizers
call for a variety of different types of hors d'oeuvres. Even
the season of the year and the time of day determine
the aptness of an appetizer.

In this section, Beta Sigma Phis share with you an intriguing
selection of hors d'oeuvres and canapes. There are fondues such
as Shrimp Tarragon, Chocolate, and Swiss Beer in addition to several
marvelous pate recipes. One of these pate recipes that is as
interesting as it is delicious is Pate Atlantis.

And what hors d'oeuvres section would be complete without
recipes for such exotics as caviar, artichokes and mushrooms?
Beta Sigma Phis Gourmet selection of appetizers
is truly an outstanding one.

BACON AND CHESTNUT ROLL-UPS

1 lb. lean bacon
1 jar pickled watermelon rind
1 can chestnuts, drained

Cut bacon slices in half. Slice watermelon rind into thin slices; cut chestnuts in half. Wrap a bacon slice around chestnut half and watermelon rind slice; secure with wooden picks. Place on baking sheets. Bake at 350 degrees for 30 minutes or until bacon is crisp and golden.

Arlene Johnson, Prog. Chm.
Alpha Rho No. 8671
Temple City, California

HOT BACON SURPRISES

1 lb. sliced bacon
1 1-lb. package pitted dates

Slice each piece of bacon into thirds. Wrap each date with bacon; secure with toothpick. Place on broiler pan rack. Bake at 350 degrees for 10 minutes or until bacon is browned. Drain on paper towels. Serve in chafing dish over hot water. May be prepared ahead and refrigerated until ready to bake.

Beverly Parrott, Rec. Sec.
Zeta Chi No. 5650
Bradenton, Florida

RUMAKI BACON BOBS

1 c. sauterne
1/4 c. soy sauce
1 lb. thin bacon strips
1/2 lb. chicken livers, halved
1 pkg. frozen potato bites

Combine sauterne and soy sauce; pour over bacon strips and chicken livers. Marinate for 1 hour. Preheat oven to 400 degrees. Cut bacon slices in half; wrap bacon around livers and potato bites. Thread on skewers or secure with wooden picks; place on rack in shallow pan. Bake for 10 minutes or until bacon is crisp and golden. Yield: 8-10 kabobs.

Elizabeth Brennan, Pres.
Epsilon No. 6261
Mayaguez, Puerto Rico

BEIGNETS

1/4 c. butter
1 c. flour
1/2 tsp. salt
Dash of cayenne pepper
3 eggs
2 c. shredded Cheddar cheese

Melt butter in saucepan in 1 cup boiling water; add flour, salt, and cayenne. Stir vigorously over low heat until mixture forms a ball. Remove from heat; add eggs, one at a time, beating well after each addition. Stir in cheese. Drop from teaspoon into hot oil at 350 degrees; fry until golden brown.

Sondra Weaser, VP
Chi Xi No. 5478
Fullerton, California

CHEESE PUFFS

1 lg. loaf unsliced bread
1/4 lb. sharp Cheddar cheese, grated
1 3-oz. package cream cheese
6 tbsp. butter
Juice of 1 sm. onion
1 tsp. hot sauce
3 egg whites, beaten
Paprika

Remove crust from bread; slice 1 inch thick. Cut into 1-inch cubes; refrigerate. Melt cheeses and butter in top of double boiler over hot water; add onion juice and hot sauce. Cool slightly; fold egg whites into cheese mixture. Keep sauce warm. Dip bread cubes in sauce; place on waxed paper. Refrigerate or freeze until ready to serve. Dust with paprika; arrange on greased baking sheets. Bake at 375 degrees for 10 minutes. Bake frozen puffs for 15 minutes.

Gladis Nickelson, W and M Chm.
Preceptor Alpha Beta XP380
Palos Verdes Estates, California

CUCUMBER PARTY SANDWICHES

2 cucumbers
1 tsp. garlic salt
Pepper to taste
1/2 c. tarragon vinegar
2 tbsp. red wine
1/4 c. olive oil
Bread rounds
Softened cream cheese

Peel cucumbers; slice thinly. Place cucumbers in shallow glass bowl. Combine garlic salt, pepper, vinegar, wine and olive oil; blend thoroughly. Pour vinegar mixture over cucumbers. Marinate, covered, for at least 4 hours; drain well. Spread bread rounds with cream cheese. Top half the bread rounds with cucumber slices; cover with remaining rounds. Wrap sandwiches in damp paper towels; cover with waxed paper. Refrigerate until ready to serve. Yield: 24 party-sized sandwiches.

Josie Kirsch, Treas.
Xi Psi X1738
High Point, North Carolina

GUACAMOLE

1 c. mashed avocado
1 tbsp. lime juice
1 tsp. salt
1 1/2 tsp. grated onion
1 tsp. Worcestershire sauce
1/4 c. Roquefort or bleu cheese,
*   mashed*

Beat all ingredients together until smooth; chill. Serve with potato chips, melba toast or crackers.

Mrs. Earnest Tilghman, Pres.
Epsilon Phi No. 7842
Ashland City, Tennessee

SHRIMP DIP

1 7 1/2-oz. can shrimp, drained
*   and minced*
1 8-oz. package cream cheese,
*   softened*
1 tbsp. Worcestershire sauce
1 tbsp. (or more) horseradish
1 tbsp. lemon juice
Catsup

Combine shrimp, cream cheese, Worcestershire sauce, horseradish, lemon juice and enough catsup to give desired consistency; chill. Serve with assorted crackers and chips.

Dorothy Zientarski, Pres.
Xi Lambda X1984
New Britain, Connecticut

MEXICAN CHEESE DIP

4 tbsp. margarine
4 tbsp. flour
1 tsp. paprika
3/4 tsp. cumin
1/2 tsp. dry mustard
Garlic powder to taste
1 tsp. chili powder
1 1/2 c. milk
2 diced jalapeno peppers
2 tbsp. jalapeno sauce
16 oz. grated Velveeta

Melt margarine in saucepan over low heat; stir in flour. Cook, stirring constantly, for 1 minute. Stir in paprika, cumin, mustard, garlic powder, chili powder, milk, jalapeno peppers and sauce; blend thoroughly. Add cheese gradually, stirring until mixture is smooth.

Linda Mahnker, Parliamentarian, Lib.
Alpha Chi No. 3434
North Little Rock, Arkansas

PARTY CHEESE DIP

1/4 to 1/2 tsp. hot sauce
1 3-oz. package cream cheese,
*   softened*
1 pt. sour cream
1 env. dry onion soup mix
1 2 1/4-oz. can deviled ham

Blend hot sauce with cream cheese. Blend in sour cream gradually. Add onion soup mix and deviled ham; mix well. Turn into serving dish. Serve with halved artichoke hearts, fresh mushroom halves, fresh cauliflowerets, scallions and cherry tomatoes.

Photograph for this recipe on page 16.

19

APPETIZER CHICKEN CURRY MOLD

1 c. milk
2 env. unflavored gelatin
2 chicken bouillon cubes
2 eggs, separated
1/4 tsp. salt
2 tsp. curry powder
3 c. mild creamed cottage cheese
2 tbsp. lemon juice
2 c. minced cooked chicken
1/4 c. minced chutney
1/4 c. diced pimento
2 tbsp. minced onion
1 c. heavy cream, whipped

Pour milk into saucepan; sprinkle with gelatin. Add bouillon cubes and slightly beaten egg yolks; mix well. Cook over low heat, stirring constantly, for 5 minutes or until gelatin and bouillon cubes dissolve and mixture thickens slightly. Remove from heat; stir in salt and curry powder. Beat cottage cheese at high speed with electric mixer until smooth; stir into gelatin mixture. Stir in lemon juice, chicken, chutney, pimento and onion. Chill until gelatin mixture mounds slightly when dropped from a spoon. Beat egg whites until stiff but not dry; fold into gelatin mixture. Fold in whipped cream. Turn into 8-inch springform pan; chill until firm. Loosen side of pan with tip of knife; release springform. Remove side of pan. Garnish with ring of toasted slivered almonds and white grapes on lemon leaves.

SWISS BEER FONDUE

1/2 lb. Gruyere
1/2 lb. Emmenthaler
1 1/2 tbsp. cornstarch
1 tsp. dry mustard
1/2 tsp. garlic salt
Dash of pepper
1   12-oz. can beer

1 tbsp. lemon juice
French bread

Shred Gruyere and Emmenthaler coarsely; mix with cornstarch, mustard, garlic salt and pepper. Heat beer and lemon juice in a fondue pot over moderate heat. When bubbles start to rise to the surface, add cheese mixture, a spoonful at a time, stirring slowly in a figure 8 with a wooden spoon until cheese mixture is smooth and blended. Serve with French bread cut into 1-inch cubes, having crust on one side of each cube.

Mrs. Ralph Yetka, Publ. Chm.
Beta Psi No. 5298
Mobile, Alabama

GINGER PANCAKES WITH CRAB MEAT

1/2 c. minced onion
2 tbsp. butter
1 can cream of mushroom soup
1/3 c. milk
1/2 tsp. curry powder
1 6-oz. package King crab meat, drained
1 c. packaged pancake mix
1 tsp. powdered ginger

Saute onion in butter in large skillet; stir in soup, milk, curry powder and crab meat. Heat through. Combine pancake mix with ginger; prepare mix according to package directions. Cook 8 pancakes in small skillet; keep warm on platter, layered between paper towels, in 140-degree oven. Place 1 tablespoonful crab mixture on each pancake; fold pancake over mixture. Arrange on heated platter. Spoon remaining crab mixture over pancakes. Serve immediately.

Gale Easterly, Hist.
Epsilon Psi No. 2465
Litchfield, Illinois

SAVORY HAM BALLS

1/3 c. fine dry bread crumbs
1/4 c. milk
Catsup
1/4 c. minced onion

1 slightly beaten egg
1/4 tsp. salt
Dash of pepper
1 lb. ground ham
1 lb. ground pork
1 c. apricot preserves
1 tbsp. Worcestershire sauce
1 tbsp. prepared mustard
2 tbsp. vinegar

Combine crumbs, milk, 1/4 cup catsup, onion, egg, salt and pepper in large bowl. Add ham and pork; mix thoroughly. Shape into 5 dozen balls. Place in 13 x 9 x 2-inch baking pan. Bake in 350-degree oven for 25 to 30 minutes; cool. Refrigerate. Combine preserves, Worcestershire sauce, mustard, 2 tablespoons catsup and vinegar with 1/4 cup water in large skillet; blend thoroughly. Add meatballs; simmer, stirring occasionally, until heated through. Turn into chafing dish over hot water. Meatballs may be frozen, if desired.

Jacqueline Coughlan, Pres.
Xi Beta Nu X2589
Joseph, Oregon

STEAK TARTARE

2 lb. ground steak
1/2 c. chopped onions
1/2 c. drained capers
8 anchovy fillets, chopped
4 egg yolks
1 tsp. salt
1/8 tsp. pepper
1/4 c. finely chopped watercress
Crackers or party rye bread

Combine ground steak, onions, capers, anchovy fillets, egg yolks, salt, pepper and watercress; toss lightly with 2 forks just to blend. Mound on serving platter; chill for at least 3 hours. Serve surrounded by crackers or rye bread. May be packed into a mold before chilling and unmolded on platter just before serving. Garnish with additional anchovies and capers, if desired.

Virginia Warrick, VP
Preceptor Alpha Nu XP1037
Tampa, Florida

TUNA PATE

1 8-oz. package cream cheese,
 softened
2 tbsp. chili sauce
1 tsp. instant minced onion
2 tbsp. snipped parsley
1 tsp. hot sauce
2 6 1/2-oz. cans of tuna, drained

Blend cream cheese, chili sauce, onion, parsley, hot sauce and drained tuna. Blend thoroughly. Pack in 4-cup mold; chill thoroughly for at least 3 hours. Unmold on serving plate; garnish with sliced stuffed green olives, if desired. Serve with assorted crackers.

Cora Seib, Scrapbook Chm.
Alpha Epsilon Beta No. 7469
Friendswood, Texas

CURRIED SHRIMP BALLS

1 1/3 c. shredded coconut
1 1/2 tsp. curry powder
2 8-oz. packages cream cheese,
 softened
1 4 1/2-oz. can shrimp, drained
 and chopped
2 tbsp. minced onion
Dash of monosodium glutamate

Toss coconut with curry powder; spread mixture on baking sheet. Bake at 350 degrees for 5 to 8 minutes or until lightly browned; cool. Combine cream cheese, shrimp, onion and monosodium glutamate; blend well. Form 50 to 55 small balls; roll in curried coconut mixture. Chill until ready to serve.

Leona Sayer, Pres.
Beta Alpha No. 6175
Salmon, Idaho

TOASTED CRAB CANAPES

1 can crab meat, drained
1/2 c. mayonnaise
2 3-oz. packages cream cheese
1 egg yolk
1 tbsp. minced onion

1 tsp. prepared mustard
Bread slices
Butter

Combine crab meat and mayonnaise; blend well. Blend the cream cheese, egg yolk, onion and mustard. Remove crusts from bread; toast. Cut into small squares; butter lightly. Top squares with crab mixture; cover with cheese mixture. Broil 4 to 5 inches from source of heat until lightly browned. Serve immediately.

Pam Buchanan, Corr. Sec., Soc. Chm.
Delta Iota No. 8763
Prescott, Arizona

SALMON PARTY LOG

1 1-lb. can salmon
1 8-oz. package cream cheese
1 tbsp. lemon juice
2 tsp. grated onion
1 tsp. prepared horseradish
1/4 tsp. salt
1/4 tsp. liquid smoke
1/2 c. chopped pecans
3 tbsp. snipped parsley

Drain and flake salmon; remove skin and bones. Combine salmon, cream cheese, lemon juice, onion, horseradish, salt and liquid smoke in bowl; blend thoroughly. Chill, covered, for several hours. Shape mixture into 8 x 2-inch log. Combine pecans and parsley; roll log in nut mixture, coating well. Chill thoroughly. Serve with assorted crackers.

Barbara E. Walton, Pres.
Zeta Theta No. 8730
Thomson, Georgia

OYSTERS ON THE HALF SHELL

4 to 6 oysters in shell per person
Crushed ice
Avery Cocktail Sauce
Crackers

Wash oysters; chill thoroughly. Open and serve on cracked ice with Avery Cocktail Sauce and crackers.

Avery Cocktail Sauce

1/4 tsp. hot sauce
1 c. chili sauce
2 tbsp. lemon juice
1/2 tsp. salt
1 tbsp. horseradish
1 tsp. grated onion (opt.)

Add hot sauce to chili sauce; mix well. Stir in remaining ingredients. Chill.

STUFFED CHERRY TOMATOES

3 boxes cherry tomatoes
2 tsp. horseradish
1 can deviled ham
2 c. sour cream

Cut tops from tomatoes; scoop out centers. Drain, inverted. Combine horseradish, ham and sour cream; mix well. Stuff tomatoes with ham mixture. Chill for 24 hours.

Bonnie Smith
Northern California Coun. Roster Dir.
Mu Chi No. 4282
Oakland, California

FANTASTIC ARTICHOKE HEARTS

5 hard-cooked eggs
1 can shrimp, drained
3 tbsp. mayonnaise
1 tsp. mustard
1 tsp. lemon juice
1 tsp. grated onion
1 tsp. Worcestershire sauce
Seasoned salt and pepper to taste
Dash of hot sauce
1 tsp. chopped pimento
2 jars marinated artichoke hearts
1 sm. can ripe olives, drained

Shred eggs; chop shrimp finely. Combine eggs, shrimp, mayonnaise, mustard, lemon juice, onion, Worcestershire sauce, seasoned salt, pepper, hot sauce and pimento; blend well. Chill, covered, for several hours. Drain artichoke hearts well on paper toweling. Fill each heart with 1 teaspoon shrimp mixture. Slice olives; place 1 olive slice on each artichoke heart. Chill well before serving. Yield: 18 canapes.

Joanie Halverson, Pres.
Xi Gamma Nu X1191
Chico, California

23

Pottages and Ragouts

Pottages and Ragouts are those delicious ethnic casseroles, soups and stews that are as savory as they are hearty. From California, a member of Beta Sigma Phi shares with us a recipe for an Italian dish called Sopa de Albondiagas and from the Talahi Island off the coast of Savannah, Georgia comes a ragout recipe called Carbonade Flamade.

There are soups of every description and every taste included in this section. Vichyssoise, a potato and leek soup which can be served hot or cold, winter or summer, appears in the following pages. Spanish Gazapcho and Tiffany's Bean Pot Soup are two other pottage and ragout recipes that were sent in by a Beta Sigma Phi who enjoys the satisfaction in creating and recreating gourmet dishes.

The French, who are famous for their pottages, keep the pot-au-fea (stock pot) simmering all day, every day, but many of those recipes which called for day long cooking have been successfully duplicated in less than an hour in this section. Consommes, Dove Gumbo or Artichoke-Crab Bisque make excellent first course or main dish pottages. All of these special recipes are yours in the following section on Pottages and Ragouts.

CREAMY MUSHROOM BISQUE

2 4-oz. cans sliced button
    mushrooms
1/4 c. butter
1 qt. milk
1 c. light cream
1/4 c. flour
1 tsp. salt
1/8 tsp. pepper
1/4 tsp. angostura bitters

Drain mushrooms. Slice 1 mushroom; chop remaining. Melt butter in skillet; add chopped mushrooms. Saute mushrooms until golden brown. Pour milk and cream into saucepan; sprinkle flour, salt, pepper and bitters on surface of milk mixture. Beat with rotary beater until blended. Add mushrooms. Cook, stirring occasionally, until bisque is hot. Do not boil. Pour into tureen or individual serving dishes. Garnish with mushroom slices. Serve immediately. Yield: 6 servings.

Photograph for this recipe on page 24.

ARTICHOKE-CRAB BISQUE

2 artichokes
1 13 3/4-oz. can chicken broth
1/2 c. whipping cream
1 egg yolk
2 tbsp. flour
1/4 tsp. salt
1/2 c. finely chopped carrots
2 tbsp. sliced green onions
1 7 1/2-oz. can crab meat, drained
2 tsp. lemon juice

Remove outer layers of artichoke leaves; cut stems to 1/2-inch thickness. Quarter artichokes. Cook, covered, in boiling salted water for 15 to 20 minutes or until tender. Drain; remove and discard choke. Remove pulp from each leaf by scraping firmly across base of each with knife; discard leaves. Place pulp heart in blender container; add chicken broth, cream, egg yolk, flour and salt. Blend to smooth puree. Place carrots and green on-ions in small amount of water in saucepan; cook, covered, for 5 minutes or until tender. Add artichoke puree; cook, stirring constantly, until mixture is thickened and bubbly. Stir in crab meat and lemon juice; heat through. Canned artichokes and frozen crab meat may be substituted, if desired. Yield: 8 servings.

Carolyn Dykhuizen
Gamma Theta No. 1899
Ft. Wayne, Indiana

CANADIAN CHEESE SOUP

1/4 c. butter
1/2 c. finely diced onion
1/2 c. finely diced celery
1/2 c. finely diced carrots
1/4 c. flour
1 1/2 tbsp. cornstarch
1 qt. chicken stock
1 qt. milk
1/8 tsp. soda
1 c. grated Cheddar cheese
Salt and pepper to taste
2 tbsp. finely chopped parsley

Melt butter in Dutch oven or soup pot. Add onion, celery and carrots; saute over low heat until soft. Add flour and cornstarch; cook, stirring, until bubbly. Add stock and milk slowly, stirring, to make a smooth sauce. Add soda and cheese. Season with salt and pepper. Sprinkle with parsley just before serving.

Mary Berryman, Memshp. Com.
Xi Kappa Theta X3031
Ballinger, Texas

VEGETABLE CHEESE SOUP

2 c. cubed potatoes
2/3 c. minced onions
1/2 c. diced celery
1/2 c. carrots, cut in 1/2 in.
    slices
1/2 med. green pepper, diced
2 1/2 c. boiling water

2 1/2 tsp. salt
2 c. Rich Cheese Sauce
1 c. tomatoes

Combine potatoes, onions, celery, carrots, green pepper, water and salt in 3-quart saucepan. Bring to a boil; simmer, covered, for about 20 minutes or until vegetables are tender. Stir in cheese sauce. Add tomatoes; heat thoroughly. Yield: 6-8 servings.

Rich Cheese Sauce

2 c. medium white sauce
2 c. grated nippy Cheddar cheese
2 tsp. dry mustard
1 tsp. Worcestershire sauce
1 tbsp. sherry

Combine all ingredients in heavy saucepan; heat until cheese is melted, stirring constantly.

Dorothy Hahn
Phi No. 542
Grand Junction, Colorado

CHEESEBURGER CHOWDER

1 lb. ground beef
1/2 c. finely chopped celery
1/4 c. chopped onion
2 tbsp. chopped green pepper
3 tbsp. flour
1/2 tsp. salt
4 c. milk
1 tbsp. beef-flavored gravy base
4 oz. shredded sharp natural
    Cheddar cheese

Brown ground beef in large saucepan; add celery, onion and green pepper. Cook, stirring frequently, until tender. Blend in flour and salt, stirring until smooth and bubbly; stir in milk and gravy base. Simmer, stirring constantly, until smooth and thickened. Add cheese; simmer, stirring constantly, just until cheese melts. Yield: 4-6 servings.

Jean-Marie Longmore, Pres.
Xi Alpha Xi X2183
Las Cruces, New Mexico

CLAM CHOWDER

1 onion, chopped
1 green pepper, chopped
1/2 c. chopped bacon
2 sm. cans minced clams
2 sm. cans tomatoes
1/2 tsp. garlic
1/4 tsp. salt
1/4 tsp. pepper
2 c. chopped potatoes

Brown onion, green pepper and bacon in skillet. Place clams and 3 cups water in 3-quart saucepan; add onion mixture, tomatoes, garlic, salt and pepper. Cook, covered, over medium heat for 1 hour and 30 minutes. Stir in potatoes. Cook, covered, for 30 minutes longer.

Mrs. Eddie M. Teeter, Pres.
Gamma Omega No. 5527
Mooresville, North Carolina

PARMESAN CORN CHOWDER

2 c. diced potatoes
1/2 c. sliced carrots
1/2 c. sliced celery
1/4 c. chopped onion
1 1/2 tsp. salt
1/4 tsp. pepper
1/4 c. margarine
1/4 c. flour
2 c. milk
1 c. grated Parmesan cheese
1 1-lb. can cream-style corn

Combine potatoes, carrots, celery and onion with salt and pepper in saucepan; add 2 cups boiling water. Simmer, covered, for 10 minutes. Melt margarine in large saucepan over medium heat; stir in flour until smooth and bubbly. Add milk gradually; cook, stirring constantly until mixture is smooth and thickened. Stir in cheese until melted. Add corn and potato mixture; cook, stirring, until just heated through. Yield: 6-8 servings.

Madge Isbell, Pres.
Preceptor Alpha Lambda XP834
Springfield, Missouri

BELGIAN HERB SOUP

4 10-oz. packages frozen
   California Brussels sprouts
1 c. sliced scallions or green
   onions
1/4 c. butter or margarine
2 tbsp. flour
1 tsp. salt
1 tsp. crushed chervil
Dash of white pepper
5 c. chicken stock or bouillon
2 tbsp. chopped parsley
1 pt. light cream

Cook Brussels sprouts according to package directions; drain. Cook scallions in butter in saucepan over low heat until just tender. Mix in flour, salt, chervil and pepper; stir in stock gradually. Cook, stirring, until mixture boils for 1 minute. Remove from heat; add parsley and cream. Combine cream mixture and Brussels sprouts in blender container; blend by portions until smooth. Return to saucepan; heat, stirring, to serving temperature. Garnish with chervil or parsley, if desired.

AVOCADO SOUP

2 1/2 tbsp. butter
1 tbsp. flour
4 c. jellied chicken stock
1 shallot, finely chopped
1 stalk celery, chopped
Salt and pepper to taste
Pinch of nutmeg
2 avocados
2 egg yolks, beaten
2 to 2 1/2 tbsp. heavy cream

Melt butter in a heavy saucepan; stir in flour until smooth. Cook over low heat, stirring, until golden. Pour in stock; add shallot, celery and seasonings. Cook, stirring constantly, until mixture comes to a boil. Cover; simmer for 10 to 15 minutes. Strain. Peel avocados and remove seeds. Mash avocados with fork, then puree in blender or work through strainer with a small amount of the soup. Stir small amount of hot soup into avocado puree, then pour puree gradually into remaining soup, stirring constantly. Mix until smooth; bring to a boil. Mix yolks and cream in bowl with a wooden spoon. Stir in small amount of hot soup, then add gradually to remaining soup. Simmer, stirring constantly, until thickened.

Peg McElhinney, Soc. Chm.
Xi Sigma X673
Dodge City, Kansas

CHILLED APRICOT SOUP

1 lb. dried apricots
1/3 c. sugar
1 c. dry white wine
1 c. whipping cream
Lemon juice to taste
Apricot nectar, light cream or water

Place apricots and sugar in saucepan. Add wine and enough water to cover. Bring to a boil; cover and simmer for 3 minutes. Remove from heat; let stand, covered, for 45 minutes. Puree apricots in blender or food mill. Stir in cream and lemon juice to taste. Thin to desired consistency with apricot nectar. Chill. Garnish with fresh fruit to serve.

Irma Edwards
Xi Alpha Eta X 2390
Asheville, North Carolina

JUMBO GUMBO

1 lb. medium shrimp
1 pt. oysters
1 No. 2 1/2 can tomatoes
1 1/2 c. chopped onions
1/4 c. bacon drippings
2 tbsp. flour
1 8-oz. can tomato sauce
1 10-oz. package frozen okra
3 c. cubed ham
2 bay leaves
Pinch of thyme
1/4 tsp. crushed red pepper
Hot sauce to taste
3 c. chicken broth
1 lb. crab meat
2 tbsp. file powder

Shell and devein shrimp; drain oysters, reserving liquid. Drain tomatoes, reserving 1 cup liquid; chop coarsely. Brown onions in bacon drippings in large Dutch oven; stir in flour until smooth and bubbly. Stir in reserved oyster liquid, tomatoes, tomato sauce, okra, ham, bay leaves, thyme, red pepper and hot sauce. Simmer, stirring frequently, for 45 minutes. Add reserved tomato liquid and chicken broth; bring to a boil. Reduce heat; add shrimp, oysters and crab meat. Simmer, covered, for 10 minutes. Remove 1/2 cup gumbo liquid; combine with file powder. Stir file mixture into gumbo. Serve immediately over rice.

Chris Prescott
Preceptor Chi No. 725
Tallahassee, Florida

BEEF RAGOUT

1/4 c. flour
2 tsp. salt
1/4 tsp. pepper
2 to 2 1/2 lb. boneless beef chuck,
*   cut into 1 1/2-in. cubes*
1/4 c. butter or margarine
1 c. chopped onion
1 clove of garlic, minced
1/2 c. dry red wine or tomato juice
1 beef bouillon cube

1 sm. bay leaf
1/4 tsp. ground marjoram
8 sm. pared potatoes
1 c. 3/4-inch carrot chunks
1/2 lb. mushrooms, sliced
1 c. peas

Combine flour, 1 teaspoon salt and pepper in bowl; coat beef with flour mixture. Saute beef in butter in ovenproof Dutch oven over medium heat; stir to brown well on all sides. Add onion and garlic; sprinkle remaining flour mixture over all. Stir in 1/2 cup water, wine, bouillon cube, bay leaf and marjoram; blend well. Bake, covered, at 300 degrees for 2 hours. Add potatoes, carrots, mushrooms and remaining salt; stir carefully. Bake, covered, for 50 minutes longer. Add peas; stir carefully. Bake, covered, for 10 minutes longer. Yield: 6-8 servings.

Carol Elias, Pres.
Theta Iota No. 6253
Indianapolis, Indiana

BLACK WALNUT STEW

6 lb. beef chuck rib, cut in
*   bite-sized pieces*
1 can beef broth
1 lg. onion, halved
Salt and pepper to taste
1 lb. beef round, ground twice
3 jars pickled black walnuts
Flour

Place beef chuck, broth and 1 broth can water in kettle; add onion, salt and pepper. Cover; cook slowly for 3 hours, skimming off fat. Form ground beef into small balls; add to stew. Mash 1 jar walnuts; add walnuts and juice to stew. Cover; cook for 1 hour longer. Brown flour; stir in enough water to make a smooth paste. Stir into stew; cook until thickened. Add remaining walnuts; cook until heated through. Serve with rice or noodles. Yield: 8 servings.

Mrs. Barry Goldwater, Honorary Member
Beta Sigma Phi International
Scottsdale, Arizona

GOURMET STEW

1 1/2 lb. stew beef
2 tbsp. oil
2 c. red wine
1 can bouillon
1 can sm. onions
1 tsp. basil
1/2 tsp. salt
1 bay leaf
3 to 4 garlic cloves, chopped
1 tbsp. tomato paste
1/2 lb. mushrooms
5 tbsp. butter
3 tbsp. flour

Brown beef in oil in large skillet over medium heat. Stir in wine, bouillon, onions, basil, salt, bay leaf, garlic and tomato paste; blend well. Reduce heat; simmer, covered, until beef is tender. Simmer mushrooms in 2 tablespoons butter; stir into beef mixture. Combine remaining butter with flour; mix until smooth. Add small amount of beef liquid to flour mixture, stirring until smooth. Stir flour mixture into beef mixture; cook until smooth and thickened.

Pam Wedekind, Pres.
Beta Omega No. 4897
Yachats, Oregon

POLYNESIAN-STYLE SWEET AND SOUR PORK STEW

3 lb. pork
2 med. onions
2 med. bell peppers
1 sm. can tomato sauce
1 med. can pineapple tidbits
1/3 c. vinegar
1/3 c. (packed) brown sugar
3 tbsp. cornstarch
Garlic salt to taste
Salt to taste

Cut pork into bite-sized pieces; saute until brown in Dutch oven. Drain off fat. Slice onions and bell peppers into 1/2-inch round slices. Add onions, bell peppers, tomato sauce and pineapple tidbits with juice to pork; stir in enough water to cover. Stir in vinegar and brown sugar. Combine corn-starch with enough water to moisten; stir into stew. Mix well. Add garlic salt and salt to taste. Bring to a boil; simmer, covered, for 1 hour.

Mrs. Robert R. Jones, Pres.
Mexico Area City Council
Centralia, Missouri

ROMAN-STYLE LAMB STEW

2 lb. stewing lamb
1/4 c. olive oil
1 clove of garlic, minced
1/2 tsp. salt
1/2 tsp. pepper
1/2 tsp. dried rosemary
1/2 tsp. sage
1 tbsp. flour
1/2 c. white wine
1/2 c. white wine vinegar
3 anchovy fillets, chopped

Trim fat from lamb; cut lamb into cubes. Brown lamb in olive oil in large skillet over high heat, stirring frequently to brown on all sides. Add garlic, salt, pepper, rosemary, sage and flour; stir to blend well. Brown for 1 minute longer; stir in wine and vinegar. Simmer, covered, for 45 minutes or until lamb is tender; stir occasionally. Add anchovy fillets just before serving; stir just to blend. Serve immediately over rice. May be baked at 225 degrees for 1 hour and 30 minutes, if desired. Yield: 4 servings.

Marlene Kelley
Xi Upsilon X566
Colorado Springs, Colorado

VENISON STEW

2 lb. venison
1 tsp. salt
1/2 tsp. garlic salt
1/2 tsp. pepper
1/2 tsp. paprika
1 tsp. chili powder
1/4 c. dry red wine (opt.)
2 lg. onions
4 med. potatoes
4 carrots
3 stalks celery
1 1-lb. can stewed tomatoes

Cut venison into 2-inch cubes. Combine salt, garlic salt, pepper, paprika and chili powder; mix well. Coat venison with salt mixture. Pour wine over venison; marinate for 1 hour. Brown venison on all sides in fat in Dutch oven over medium heat; drain off excess fat. Add hot water just to cover venison. Simmer, covered, for 1 hour and 30 minutes or until venison is almost tender; stir occasionally. Peel and quarter onions and potatoes; scrape and halve carrots. Trim celery; cut into large pieces. Add onions, carrots, celery and tomatoes to venison. Simmer, covered, for 45 minutes longer; add potatoes. Simmer, covered, for 30 minutes longer. Yield: 6 servings.

Norma Jeanne Long, Pres.
Xi Beta Iota X2307
Cortez, Colorado

IRISH-AMERICAN LAMB STEW

4 1/2-lb. lamb neck slices
2 tbsp. butter
2 tsp. salt
1/4 tsp. pepper
1/4 tsp. thyme leaves
3 med. potatoes, halved
6 sm. white onions
1 1/2 lb. fresh green peas
1/4 lb. mushrooms, sliced
1 c. light cream or milk
1/4 c. flour

Brown lamb in butter in large Dutch oven or kettle; add 2 1/2 cups water and seasonings. Cover; simmer for 45 minutes. Skim off excess fat. Add potatoes and onions; cover. Simmer for 15 minutes. Add peas and mushrooms; simmer, covered, for 15 minutes or until lamb and vegetables are tender. Blend cream into flour; stir into stew. Boil for 1 minute, stirring. Correct seasonings; serve. May simmer lamb ahead of time and chill to remove fat, if desired. Yield: 6 servings.

BORSCHT

3 c. shredded beets
2 carrots, shredded
1 onion, diced
1 can beef consomme
3 c. shredded red cabbage
1 can pork and beans
1 tbsp. lemon juice
Sour cream

Place beets, carrots and onion in saucepan in 2 cups boiling salted water and consomme; cook for 20 minutes or until tender. Add cabbage and beans; simmer, covered, for 15 minutes longer. Stir in lemon juice. Serve hot or chilled, topped with sour cream. Yield: 6-8 servings.

Jana L. Howell, Corr. Sec.
Xi Beta Upsilon X2070
Madison, Indiana

CREAM OF MUSHROOM SOUP

1 lb. fresh mushrooms
9 tbsp. margarine
1 med. onion, finely chopped
6 tbsp. flour
6 c. chicken stock
1 lg. egg
3/4 c. cream
Salt and white pepper to taste

Separate mushroom caps and stems. Slice caps and chop stems. Saute lightly in 2 tablespoons melted margarine; remove from pan. Melt 2 tablespoons margarine in pan; saute onion until transparent. Remove from pan. Add remaining margarine and flour to pan; cook, stirring, until smooth. Do not brown. Add chicken stock; cook, stirring, until thickened. Add mushrooms and onion. Simmer for 15 minutes. Beat egg and cream together. Add soup gradually to the egg mixture until mixture is warm, then add mixture to soup slowly, stirring constantly. Simmer for about 5 minutes longer. Season with salt and pepper. Yield: 4-6 servings.

Janet C. Smith, Pres.
Gamma Xi No. 3904
Grand Junction, Colorado

CAULIFLOWER SOUP

1 med. head cauliflower
3 tbsp. butter
3 tbsp. flour
1 qt. chicken stock
Salt and pepper to taste
3 tbsp. cream
3 egg yolks, well beaten

Discard leaves from cauliflower; separate into flowerets. Cook for 10 minutes in boiling water. Drain; set aside to cool. Reserve several flowerets for garnish. Melt butter in saucepan; add flour. Cook, stirring, until lightly browned. Add chicken stock gradually; cook, stirring constantly, until mixture is thick and smooth. Add cauliflower; simmer until soft enough to mash. Puree in blender or press through sieve. Season with salt and pepper; return to saucepan. Bring to a boil. Combine cream and 3 egg yolks; blend slowly, stirring constantly, into hot mixture. Serve in soup bowls. Garnish with reserved flowerets and butter-fried croutons.

Mrs. Edward Amey
Preceptor Kappa XP 362
Columbus, Ohio

VICHYSSOISE

4 green onions, finely sliced
1 med. onion, finely sliced
1/4 c. butter
5 med. potatoes, thinly sliced
1 qt. chicken broth
Salt and pepper to taste
3 c. milk
2 c. heavy cream
Nutmeg
Chives

Cook onions in butter until soft but not brown. Add potatoes and broth; cook at a slow boil for 30 minutes. Pour into blender container; blend until smooth. Pour into saucepan. Season with salt and pepper; add milk. Bring to a boil. Stir in cream and a dash of nutmeg. Chill thoroughly. Sprinkle with chives to serve.

Bernice Cogburn, Corr. Sec.
Xi Zeta Nu X3563
Plantation, Florida

FRENCH ONION SOUP

5 c. thinly sliced onions
3 tbsp. butter
2 tbsp. oil
Salt to taste
1 tsp. sugar
3 tbsp. flour
3 cans consomme
Pepper to taste
1/2 c. dry vermouth or
   dry white wine
2 c. grated Gouda cheese
Thin-sliced hard-toasted French
   bread

Saute onions in butter and oil, covered, in heavy 4-quart saucepan. Stir in 2 teaspoons salt and sugar. Cook over medium heat for 20 minutes or until onions are golden; stir frequently. Blend in flour; cook, stirring constantly, for 3 minutes. Bring consomme to a boil in saucepan; stir into onion mixture. Season with pepper and additional salt, if desired. Add vermouth; bring just to a boil. Remove from heat. Pour soup into ovenproof soup bowls; sprinkle with 1/3 of the cheese. Add small amount of grated onion, if desired. Place French bread over cheese; sprinkle with remaining cheese. Bake at 325 degrees for 20 minutes or until cheese is melted and lightly browned. May be broiled, if desired.

Gwynette Carley, Serv. Chm.
Beta Beta No. 6339
Charleston, South Carolina

SAVORY APPETIZER TOMATO SOUP

1/2 c. chopped celery
4 tbsp. chopped green onion
2 tbsp. butter
4 tsp. all-purpose flour
2   8-oz. can stewed tomatoes
2 c. water
1/2 c. dry white wine
2 chicken bouillon cubes
4 slices crisp-cooked bacon,
   crumbled

Cook celery and onion in butter until tender but not brown. Blend in flour until smooth.

Add remaining ingredients except bacon; cook, stirring, until slightly thickened. Reduce heat; simmer for 15 minutes, stirring occasionally. Pour into individual bowls; garnish with crumbled bacon just before serving. Yield: 4 servings.

Kay Frost, W and M Chm.
Gamma Psi No. 6157
Falls Church, Virginia

SPANISH GAZPACHO

1 c. finely chopped peeled tomato
1/2 c. finely chopped green pepper
1/2 c. finely chopped celery
1/2 c. finely chopped cucumber
1/4 c. finely chopped onion
2 tsp. snipped parsley
1 tsp. snipped chives
1 sm. clove of garlic, minced
2 to 3 tbsp. wine vinegar
2 tbsp. olive oil
1 tsp. salt
1/4 tsp. freshly ground pepper
1/2 tsp. Worcestershire sauce
2 c. tomato juice

Combine all ingredients in a stainless steel or glass bowl. Cover; chill for at least 4 hours. Serve in chilled cups. Serve with croutons.

Mary Lou Biagiotti
Gamma Eta No. 3356
Lighthouse Point, Florida

WINE SOUP

5 c. beef consomme
2 lg. ripe tomatoes, skinned and
   diced
Salt and pepper to taste
1/2 c. dry sherry
1/2 c. Burgundy

Pour the consomme into 4-quart saucepan. Add tomatoes; simmer for 15 minutes. Season with salt and pepper. Add the sherry and Burgundy just before serving; bring almost to a boil. Serve hot with Holland rusk or melba toast. Yield: 8 servings.

Lorene Harrison, Honorary Member
Beta Sigma Phi International
Anchorage, Alaska

Accompaniments

Creativity in the kitchen is demonstrated in this chapter on
Accompaniments. A supply of homemade jams, jellies, pickles and
relishes shimmering in a rainbow of tints offers a homemaker a great
deal of creative material with which to work. Variety in color,
texture and taste are at your fingertips, enabling you to
perk up any dish . . . and "sign your name" to it.

Preserving accompaniments is a skill well worth learning, and
on the following pages Beta Sigma Phis share their knowledge of
this art. Undoubtedly, there is no feeling of accomplishment like the
one you will have when your family praises the beauty, taste
and aroma of freshly preserved chow chow, chutney,
conserves and relish.

WINE-CHEESE FONDUE

1 c. Rhine wine
1 8-oz. package Cheddar cheese
  slices, cubed
1 tbsp. flour
Hard crust bread or rolls

Pour wine into fondue pot; add cheese. Place over medium heat until cheese is melted and mixture is smooth, stirring constantly. Combine flour and 2 tablespoons water. Add flour mixture to cheese mixture; cook, stirring, until thickened. Reduce heat, allowing mixture to bubble gently. Cut bread into bite-sized pieces. Dip bread cubes into cheese mixture with fondue forks.

Photograph for this recipe on page 34.

FROZEN STRAWBERRY JAM

5 c. sugar
3 c. mashed strawberries
1 pkg. pectin

Combine sugar and strawberries in large bowl. Let stand for 20 minutes. Bring pectin and 1 cup water to a boil; boil for 1 minute. Pour pectin mixture over strawberries, stirring constantly for 2 minutes; let stand for 24 hours. Place in freezer containers; freeze until ready to use.

Nelda Grasmick, VP
Xi Gamma Sigma X3885
Rocky Ford, Colorado

BAKED BANANAS

4 bananas
1/4 tsp. nutmeg
1/4 tsp. cinnamon
1/4 c. (packed) brown sugar
1/2 c. orange juice
1/2 to 3/4 c. rum
1 tbsp. butter

Peel bananas and cut in half lengthwise; place in baking dish. Combine nutmeg, cinnamon, brown sugar, orange juice and rum in saucepan. Cook, stirring, until sugar is dissolved; pour over bananas. Dot with butter. Bake at 450 degrees for 10 minutes or until tender. Baste frequently with juice. Sprinkle additional rum over top before serving. Yield: 4 servings.

Norma Montgomery, Pres.
Epsilon Lambda, No. 6692
Markham, Ontario, Canada

CINNAMON APPLES

2 c. sugar
1 c. water
1/2 c. red cinnamon candies
Few drops of red food coloring
8 med. Winesap apples

Mix first 4 ingredients; bring to a boil. Peel and quarter apples; place in syrup. Cover. Reduce heat; simmer, turning apples occasionally, until tender and transparent.

Mary Carolyn McDaniel, Pres.
Delta Kappa No. 8606
Fairhope, Alabama

PEARS GERTRUDE

12 ripe pears
1 tbsp. lemon juice
4 c. (packed) brown sugar
1 c. sherry
1/3 c. orange powdered drink mix
Heavy cream

Peel pears, leaving whole with stems on; place in bowl of cold water with lemon juice. Bring brown sugar and 6 cups water to a boil; boil for 5 minutes. Add pears. Simmer until tender and transparent. Do not overcook. Remove pears carefully from syrup; dip into sherry. Place in shallow dish. Boil syrup until thickened; add sherry and powdered drink mix. Pour over pears; chill. Serve with cream. If desired, freeze cream for 1 hour and 30 minutes or until just crystallized.

Jane Rotay, Soc. Chm.
Kappa Kappa No. 7970
Norristown, Pennsylvania

CRANBERRY-ORANGE SAUCE

4 c. cranberries
1 orange
2 c. sugar

Wash and drain cranberries; cut orange into small pieces, removing seeds. Force cranberries and orange through food chopper; place in saucepan; bring to a boil. Boil briskly for 10 minutes, stirring occasionally. Add 1 cup boiling water and sugar; cook, stirring, until sugar is dissolved. Reduce heat; simmer for 5 minutes. May be poured into 4-cup mold or serving bowl. Mixture will jell when cool.

Zona B. Mummert, Pres.
Gamma Chi No. 6479
Slidell, Louisiana

SPICED PINEAPPLE

1   20-oz. can pineapple chunks
2/3 c. cider vinegar
1 c. sugar
Dash of salt
8 to 10 whole cloves
1 cinnamon stick

Drain pineapple; reserve syrup. Bring 2/3 cup reserved syrup, vinegar, sugar, salt, cloves and cinnamon to a boil. Reduce heat; simmer for 10 minutes. Add pineapple chunks; bring to a boil. Cool; chill until ready to serve.

Beverly Conner, Sec.
Xi Gamma Phi X2768
Gary, Indiana

HOT PEPPER JELLY

1/2 c. ground hot peppers
3/4 c. ground green peppers
1 1/2 c. cider vinegar
1 c. white vinegar
6 1/2 c. sugar
1 bottle fruit pectin
Green food coloring

Combine hot peppers, green peppers, cider vinegar, white vinegar and sugar in large saucepan; bring to a boil. Boil for several minutes; stir in pectin and desired amount of food coloring. Bring to a boil; remove from heat. Place in hot sterilized jars; seal.

Kay Conway, Rec. Sec.
Rho No. 8910
Pine Bluff, Arkansas

CRAZY CRANBERRY JELLY

3 c. cranberry juice cocktail
1/4 c. lemon juice
5 c. sugar
1/2 bottle fruit pectin

Combine cranberry juice cocktail, lemon juice and sugar in large saucepan; mix well. Bring to a boil, stirring constantly. Stir in pectin; bring to a rolling boil. Boil, stirring constantly, for 1 minute. Remove from heat; skim carefully. Place in sterilized jars; seal.

Beverly Tudor, Pres.
Preceptor Gamma Alpha XP1133
Port Neches, Texas

PARADISE JELLY

1 qt. whole cranberries
10 med. quinces, peeled
20 med. unpeeled apples, sliced
1 box powdered fruit pectin
9 c. sugar
Paraffin

Combine cranberries, quinces and apples in large saucepan or kettle; cover with water. Cook until soft. Sterilize ten 8-ounce jelly glasses; leave in hot water until ready to fill. Ladle fruit into jelly bag; strain juice. Combine 7 cups juice with pectin in large kettle. Bring mixture to a hard boil over high heat, stirring occasionally. Add sugar all at once. Bring to a full rolling boil; boil hard for 1 minute, stirring constantly. Remove from heat; skim off foam with metal spoon. Pour at once into glasses, leaving 1/2-inch space at top. Cover immediately with 1/8 inch hot paraffin.

Sandy McCleary, Pres.
Xi Beta Lambda X1326
Chambersburg, Pennsylvania

BLUEBIRD MARMALADE

1 med. orange
1 med. lemon
3 c. crushed blueberries
5 c. sugar
1/2 6-oz. bottle pectin

Remove peel from orange and lemon carefully; scrape excess white from peel. Cut peel into fine shreds; place in large saucepan. Add 3/4 cup water; bring to a boil. Reduce heat; simmer, covered, for 10 minutes, stirring occasionally. Remove white membrane from orange and lemon; chop pulp finely, discarding seeds. Add orange and lemon pulp and blueberries to cooked peel. Simmer, covered, for 12 minutes; add sugar. Bring to a rolling boil; boil for 1 minute, stirring constantly. Remove from heat; stir in pectin immediately. Skim off foam; stir and skim for 7 minutes. Ladle into hot jars. Seal immediately. Yield: 6 cups.

Bernice Cruickshank, Publ., Scrapbook Chm.
Beta No. 735
New Westminster, British Columbia, Canada

ARTICHOKES VINAIGRETTE

2 9-oz. packages frozen artichoke hearts
1 4-oz. can pimento, drained and chopped
1/2 c. olive oil
1/2 c. white wine vinegar
2 tbsp. chopped sweet pickle
1 tbsp. sweet pickle liquid
1/2 tsp. crumbled oregano
1/2 tsp. crumbled basil

Cook artichoke hearts in boiling salted water according to package directions. Drain; place in earthenware or glass bowl. Add pimento. Combine remaining ingredients in jar or bowl; shake or beat until blended. Pour marinade over artichoke hearts, tossing lightly to coat evenly. Let stand at room temperature for at least 30 minutes, stirring occasionally. Serve immediately or refrigerate until ready to serve. Yield: 8 servings.

Photograph for this recipe on next page.

MARINATED CAULIFLOWER AND GREEN BEANS

1 10-oz. package frozen cauliflowerets
1 9-oz. package frozen cut green beans
2 tbsp. frozen chopped chives
2 tbsp. frozen chopped parsley
1 hard-boiled egg, chopped
1/3 c. cider vinegar
1/2 c. olive oil
1 tsp. sugar
1 tsp. salt
1/4 tsp. freshly ground pepper

Cook cauliflowerets and beans in boiling salted water according to package directions. Drain; place in earthenware or glass bowl. Add chives, parsley and egg. Combine remaining ingredients; mix well. Pour marinade over vegetables. Let stand at room temperature for at least 30 minutes, stirring occasionally. Serve immediately or refrigerate until ready to serve. Yield: 8 servings.

Photograph for this recipe on next page.

DILLED CARROTS

1 1-lb. package frozen whole baby carrots
2 tbsp. chopped fresh dill
1 clove of garlic, quartered
1/3 c. olive oil
1/3 c. frozen lemon juice
1 tsp. sugar
1 tsp. salt
1/4 tsp. freshly ground pepper

Cook carrots in boiling salted water according to package directions. Drain carrots; place in earthenware or glass bowl. Add dill and garlic. Combine remaining ingredients; mix well. Pour over carrots, tossing lightly to coat evenly. Let stand at room temperature for at least 30 minutes, stirring occasionally. Remove garlic. Serve immediately or refrigerate until ready to serve. May substitute 1/4 cup dill sprigs for fresh dill, if desired. Yield: 6 servings.

Photograph for this recipe on next page.

MUSHROOMS A LA GRECQUE

2 10-oz. packages frozen whole
   mushrooms
1/2 c. olive oil
1/2 c. cider vinegar
1 tsp. salt
1/4 tsp. freshly ground pepper
1/4 tsp. crumbled chervil
1 bay leaf
1 clove of garlic, quartered
1 hard-boiled egg yolk, sieved
2 tbsp. drained capers

Thaw mushrooms; place in earthenware or glass bowl. Combine remaining ingredients except egg yolk and capers in saucepan; bring to a boil. Pour hot mixture over mushrooms. Let stand at room temperature for at least 30 minutes, stirring occasionally. Remove garlic and bay leaf. Refrigerate until ready to serve. Stir in sieved egg yolk and capers just before serving. Yield: 6 servings.

NECTARINE CHUTNEY

2 c. cider vinegar
1 1-lb. box brown sugar
1 1/2 tsp. salt
1 tsp. ground ginger
1/4 tsp. cayenne pepper
2 c. pared diced apples
1 c. thinly sliced onions
1 c. raisins
1/2 lemon, thinly sliced
3 c. chopped fresh nectarines

Combine first 5 ingredients in large saucepan; cook over low heat until reduced to about half. Add apples, onions, raisins and lemon; cook for about 10 minutes. Add nectarines; bring just to boiling point. Chill well. Serve with poultry, pork or ham. May be blended in a blender and poured over block of cream cheese to spread on crackers as appetizer.

Suzy Wilkes, City Coun. Pres.
Xi Beta Delta X2824
Oklahoma City, Oklahoma

PICKLED MUSHROOMS AND ONIONS

1/3 c. red wine vinegar
1/3 c. salad oil
1 sm. onion
1 tsp. salt
2 tsp. dried parsley flakes
1 tsp. prepared mustard
1 tbsp. brown sugar
2 6-oz. cans mushroom caps,
   drained

Combine vinegar and oil in saucepan. Slice onion thin; separate into rings. Drop into vinegar mixture; add salt, parsley, mustard and brown sugar. Bring mixture to boiling point. Add mushrooms. Reduce heat; simmer, covered, for about 6 minutes. Pour into bowl. Refrigerate, covered, for several hours or overnight. Stir occasionally. Drain mushrooms. Serve on cocktail picks as hors d'oeuvres or on a relish plate.

Edna Corner
Zeta Pi No. 7422
Bayfield, Colorado

PEACH PICKLE

4 lb. peaches
1 tbsp. whole cloves
Vinegar
4 c. sugar
1 tsp. whole ginger
2 3-in. sticks cinnamon

Place peaches in large container; cover with boiling water. Let stand for several minutes; dip in cold water. Skins should slip off easily; peel. Stick 1 clove in each peach. Combine 2 quarts water and 2 tablespoons vinegar. Pour over peaches. Combine sugar, 1 1/2 cups vinegar and 3/4 cups water in large kettle. Combine ginger, remaining cloves and cinnamon in cheesecloth; tie with string. Drop spice bag into sugar mixture; bring to a boil. Drain peaches, then add to sugar mixture. Cover; boil for about 10 minutes or until tender. Let stand overnight. Drain, reserving liquid. Remove spice bag. Pack peaches into hot sterilized pint jars. Bring syrup to a boil; pour over peaches, leaving 1/2 inch from top of jars. Place lids on jars. Process in boiling water bath for 30 minutes. Remove jars from canner; tighten tops, if necessary. Yield: 4 to 5 pints.

Gayle Davidson, City Coun. Rep., Serv. Chm.
Zeta Upsilon No. 4590
Independence, Missouri

ZUCCHINI RELISH

10 c. unpeeled chopped zucchini
4 c. chopped onions
3 or 4 bell peppers, chopped
5 tbsp. salt
4 1/2 c. sugar
2 1/2 c. white vinegar
1 tbsp. dry mustard
1 tsp. turmeric
2 tbsp. cornstarch
2 tbsp. celery seed
1 tsp. nutmeg
1/2 tsp. pepper

Place zucchini, onions, peppers and salt in large kettle. Cover with water; let soak overnight. Rinse in cold water and drain. Set aside. Combine sugar, vinegar, mustard, turmeric, cornstarch, celery seed, nutmeg and pepper; mix well. Pour sugar mixture over vegetables; cook over low heat for about 30 minutes. Place in pint jars; seal. Yield: 8 pints.

Donna Sparks, Rec. Sec.
Xi Beta Iota X2307
Cortez, Colorado

SPICED PICKLED PRUNES

1 lb. prunes
1/2 c. sugar
1/2 c. vinegar
1 c. water
2 tsp. whole cloves
3 3-in. sticks cinnamon, broken
1 tsp. allspice

Place prunes in large pan. Combine sugar, vinegar, water, cloves, cinnamon and allspice. Add sugar mixture to prunes; bring to a boil. Cover; cook over low heat for about 20 minutes. Stir several times so prunes will be thoroughly covered with syrup.

Mary Jones
Xi Delta Alpha X1321
Los Molines, California

GOLDEN GLOW

6 lb. cucumbers
6 lg. onions
3 sweet red peppers
3 green peppers
1/4 c. salt
2 c. sugar
2 c. (packed) light brown sugar
2 c. vinegar
1 tsp. turmeric
1 tsp. celery seed
1 tsp. mustard

Peel cucumbers; discard seeds. Peel onions; cut peppers, removing seeds and pulp. Dice vegetables;combine in large bowl. Stir in salt; mix well. Let stand overnight. Drain well; rinse in water. Drain thoroughly. Combine sugar, brown sugar, vinegar, turmeric, celery seed and mustard in large kettle; add vegetables. Simmer, stirring constantly, for 20 minutes or until cucumbers are transparent. Place in hot sterilized jars; seal. Yield: 6 pints.

Mrs. James E. Ferrell, Pres.
Xi Theta X-798
Staunton, Virginia

CORN RELISH

3 med. ears of corn
1 tbsp. chopped green onion
1 tbsp. chopped green pepper
1 tbsp. chopped pimento
1/2 c. vegetable oil
1/4 c. vinegar
1 tbsp. sugar
2 tsp. salt
1/4 tsp. pepper

Cook corn in boiling, salted water in saucepan; drain, reserving 1 cup corn liquid. Cut corn crosswise into 1/2-inch rounds. Combine corn, green onion, green pepper and pimento. Blend oil, vinegar, reserved liquid, sugar, salt and pepper; pour over corn mixture. Marinate in refrigerator for 3 hours. Yield: 4-6 servings.

Elaine M. Sulhan
Xi Eta Omega X3745
Chesterland, Ohio

GOURMET CHOWCHOW

1 peck green tomatoes, chopped
4 c. chopped onions
4 c. chopped cabbage
4 c. chopped celery
1 c. grated carrots
5 1/2 c. chopped green peppers
2 3/4 c. chopped red peppers
1/2 c. salt
6 c. sugar
4 c. vinegar
2 tbsp. mustard seed
1/2 tsp. turmeric

Combine vegetables; cover with salt. Let stand overnight. Rinse; drain thoroughly. Combine sugar, vinegar, 2 cups water, mustard seed and turmeric; blend well. Pour over vegetables in large kettle. Bring to a boil;

reduce heat. Simmer for 3 minutes, stirring occasionally. Place in hot sterilized jars; seal. Yield: 15 pints.

Mary Eileen Schulte, Prog. Chm.
Xi Chi X783
Jefferson City, Missouri

GREEN AND RED PEPPER RELISH

7 1/2 c. chopped sweet red peppers
2 1/2 c. chopped green peppers
5 c. chopped onions
3 tbsp. salt
2 c. sugar
2 c. cider vinegar

Wash peppers; remove seeds. Peel onions; grind peppers and onions in food chopper using medium blade. Combine all ingredients in large kettle; bring to a boil. Cook for 10 minutes. Pour immediately into hot jars; seal.

Mary Humphrey
Gamma Iota No. 4701
Wilson, North Carolina

TOMATO BUTTER

5 lb. ripe tomatoes
1 1/4 c. cider vinegar
3 c. sugar
1 1/2 tsp. salt
1/8 tsp. pepper
1 1/2 tsp. allspice
1   1 1/2-in. cinnamon stick

Peel tomatoes; chop finely. Place tomatoes in bowl; add vinegar. Let stand, covered, overnight. Drain well, reserve liquid. Place sugar and 3/4 cup reserved liquid in kettle; stir in salt and pepper. Tie allspice and cinnamon in cheesecloth bag; add to sugar mixture. Bring to a boil; boil for 5 minutes. Add tomatoes. Simmer for 3 hours or until sauce is thickened. Remove spice bag; ladle into hot sterilized jars. Seal immediately.

Ruth Van Tassel, W and M Chm.
Preceptor Alpha Lambda XP1089
Ottawa, Ontario, Canada

Salads

In this section on Salads, Beta Sigma Phis can turn their culinary
talents toward creating unforgettable dishes featuring crisp garden
vegetables. Many of these recipes can do double duty as either
the first course at a dinner or buffet, or as a very light
but filling entree.

For flavor and eye-appeal, a tossed Tropical Lobster Salad
is unbeatable. A salad plate with slightly tart uncooked spinach,
crisp lettuce, carrot curls and a creamy dressing is outstanding
with a bowl of hot soup or a plate of grilled, open-faced
appetizer-sandwiches.

Salads are marvelous, and appropriate for any time, place or
occasion. There are dozens of tantalizing recipes in this section.
These dishes offer you a chance to serve your favorite foods,
and to earn compliments in the process.

Beta Sigma Phis from all over the world have sent in their
favorite congealed, fruit, seafood, meat, cheese and
egg salad recipes for all of us to share.

CHERRIES IN PORT

3/4 c. sugar
2 c. water
6 whole cloves
1 2-in. piece stick cinnamon
1 4-in. strip orange or lemon peel
1 c. port
3 c. sweet Bing cherries, pitted
2 env. unflavored gelatin
1/2 c. orange juice

Combine sugar, water, spices and peel in medium saucepan. Bring to a boil; simmer for 5 minutes. Add port and cherries with several cherry pits for flavor. Simmer for 5 minutes longer. Sprinkle gelatin over orange juice; stir into hot mixture. Cover; cool for 30 minutes. Remove spices and cherry pits with slotted spoon. Pour gelatin mixture into 5-cup mold or glass bowl; chill for several hours or until set. Unmold on chilled plate. Yield: 6 servings.

Teri Renfro, Pres., White Mountain Area Coun.
Gamma Rho No. 8151
Pinetop, Arizona

COLORFUL RIBBON SALAD

2 3-oz. packages lime gelatin
5 c. hot water
4 c. cold water
1 3-oz. package lemon gelatin
1/2 c. miniature marshmallows
1 1-lb. 4-oz. can crushed pineapple
1 8-oz. package cream cheese
1 c. heavy cream, whipped
1 c. mayonnaise
2 3-oz. packages cherry gelatin

Dissolve lime gelatin in 2 cups hot water; add 2 cups cold water. Pour into 14 x 10 x 2-inch pan; chill until partially set. Dissolve lemon gelatin in 1 cup hot water. Add marshmallows; stir until melted. Drain pineapple; reserve syrup. Add 1 cup reserved syrup to marshmallow mixture. Add cream cheese; beat until blended. Stir in pineapple; cool slightly. Fold in whipped cream and mayonnaise; chill until thickened. Pour over

lime gelatin layer; chill until almost firm. Dissolve cherry gelatin in remaining hot water; add remaining cold water. Chill until syrupy. Pour over pineapple layer; chill until firm. Yield: 24 servings.

El Dene Skodack, Pres.
Preceptor Xi XP1021
Boise, Idaho

FROSTED CRANBERRY SQUARES

1 c. pineapple juice
2 3-oz. package strawberry gelatin
1 sm. lemon-lime carbonated drink
1 2/3 c. crushed pineapple
1 can jellied cranberry sauce
1 pkg. dessert topping mix
1 8-oz. package cream cheese
1/2 c. chopped pecans

Bring pineapple juice to a boil. Add gelatin; stir until dissolved. Add carbonated drink. Blend pineapple with cranberry sauce; add to gelatin mixture. Pour into 9 x 13-inch pan; chill until firm. Prepare dessert topping mix according to package directions; mix with cream cheese. Spread over gelatin mixture; sprinkle with pecans. Cut into squares; serve on lettuce.

Martha L. Royalty, Pres.
Xi Delta Kappa X3510
Evansville, Indiana

PERSIAN PEACH SALAD

1 No. 2 can peach halves
1/4 c. vinegar
1/4 tsp. salt
6 1-in. cinnamon sticks
12 whole cloves
1 pkg. orange gelatin
1 1/2 pt. chive cottage cheese
1 bunch watercress

Drain peaches; reserve 1 cup juice. Combine reserved juice, vinegar, salt, cinnamon and cloves. Simmer for 10 minutes; strain. Combine peach juice with gelatin; stir until gelatin is dissolved. Arrange peach halves, cut side up, in oiled ring mold; pour gelatin mixture over peach halves. Chill until firm. Turn out on platter; fill center with chive cottage cheese. Garnish with watercress. Yield: 6 servings.

Happy Hankins, Pres.
Preceptor Beta XP142
Portland, Oregon

APRICOT MOUSSE

1   30-oz. can apricot halves,
*   drained*
2 env. unflavored gelatin
3/4 c. sugar
1/8 tsp. salt
3 eggs, separated
1 1/4 c. milk
1 tsp. grated lemon peel
2 tbsp. lemon juice
1 c. heavy cream, whipped

Puree enough apricots in electric blender or food mill to make 1 cup puree; reserve remaining apricots for garnish. Mix gelatin, 1/2 cup sugar and salt thoroughly in top of double boiler. Beat egg yolks and milk together. Add to gelatin mixture. Cook over boiling water, stirring constantly, for about 5 minutes or until gelatin is dissolved. Remove from heat; stir in lemon peel, juice and apricot puree. Chill mixture to consistency of egg white. Beat egg whites until stiff in large bowl, beating in remaining sugar. Fold gelatin mixture into beaten egg whites. Fold whipped cream into gelatin mixture. Turn into greased 6-cup mold; chill for 6 or more hours or until set. Loosen edge of mold with point of small knife; shake mold gently. Invert onto serving plate; garnish with remaining apricots.

ORANGE DELIGHT SALAD

1 6-oz. package orange gelatin
1 pt. orange sherbet
2 cans mandarin oranges
1 c. whipped cream

Dissolve gelatin in 1 cup boiling water; add orange sherbet. Stir until sherbet melts; blend thoroughly. Add oranges. Chill until partially set; add whipped cream. Pour into mold; chill until firm.

Beverly Connolly, Pres.
Beta Nu No. 4292
Enterprise, Oregon

SWEET-TART SALAD

2 pkg. cranberries
4 lg. oranges
6 lg. apples
2 c. shelled pecans
6 stalks celery
2 10-oz. cans crushed pineapple
2 c. sugar
2 pkg. strawberry gelatin

Grind cranberries, oranges and 1 apple; mix well. Cube remaining apples; chop pecans and celery. Combine with cranberry mixture. Drain pineapple, reserving juice. Add pineapple and sugar to cranberry mixture; blend well. Prepare gelatin according to package directions, substituting 1 cup reserved juice for water. Chill until slightly thickened. Stir in cranberry mixture. Pour into mold; chill until firm. Unmold; serve on bed of lettuce. Yield: 10 servings.

Rayneal B. Calfee, VP
Zeta Zeta, No. 8734
Belhaven, North Carolina

TROPICAL SEAS SALAD

1 3-oz. package orange gelatin
1/3 c. sugar
1 tsp. vanilla
1 c. sour cream
1 7-oz. can crushed pineapple
1 can mandarin oranges, drained

1/3 c. sliced almonds
1/2 c. flaked coconut

Dissolve gelatin in 1 cup boiling water; add sugar, stirring until dissolved. Add vanilla and sour cream; blend until smooth; Add crushed pineapple, oranges, almonds and coconut. Pour into oiled mold. Chill until set. Yield: 8-12 servings.

Lois Ellison, VP
Preceptor Nu XP1038
Phoenix, Arizona

MEXICAN CHEF'S SALAD

1 lb. ground beef
1 15-oz. can kidney beans, drained
1/4 tsp. salt
1 onion
4 tomatoes
1 head lettuce
4 oz. grated Cheddar cheese
8 oz. Thousand Island or French
    dressing
Hot sauce to taste
1 sm. bag corn chips
1 lg. avocado

Brown ground beef in large skillet; stir in beans and salt. Simmer for 10 minutes; keep warm. Chop onion, tomatoes and lettuce; toss with cheese and dressing. Season with hot sauce. Crush corn chips; add to tomato mixture. Peel and slice avocado; add to tomato mixture. Combine tomato mixture with beef mixture. Serve immediately.

Margarette Karakas, Pres.
Preceptor Beta Nu, XP711
Whittier, California

ORIENTAL HAM SALAD

2 c. diced cooked ham
1/4 c. French dressing
1 tsp. soy sauce
1 1-lb. can bean sprouts
1/4 c. chopped onion
1/2 c. chopped sweet pickle
1 tsp. salt
Dash of pepper

1/4 tsp. monosodium glutamate
3/4 c. mayonnaise

Marinate ham in mixture of French dressing and soy sauce for 30 minutes in refrigerator. Add remaining ingredients; toss lightly. Serve on crisp salad greens. Veal may be substituted for ham, if desired.

Carolyn Cunanan, Pres.
Xi Theta X1683
Moose Jaw, Saskatchewan, Canada

ROAST BEEF SALAD

2 lb. cooked roast beef
2 Spanish onions
1 lb. green beans
1/4 c. vinegar
2 tbsp. Dijon mustard
1 tsp. salt
1 tsp. pepper
1 c. olive oil
2 lb. potatoes
1/4 c. minced shallots
3 tbsp. beef broth

Cut beef into 2 x 1/4-inch squares. Slice onions; separate slices into rings. Cook beans in salted boiling water for 7 minutes or until just tender; drain. Cool under water; dry on paper toweling. Trim beans; cut into 1-inch lengths. Combine vinegar, mustard, salt, pepper and olive oil; blend thoroughly. Toss beans in bowl with 1/2 cup mustard mixture. Boil potatoes; peel and slice thinly while warm. Combine potatoes, shallots and beef broth in bowl; toss gently until broth is absorbed. Pour remaining dressing over potatoes; toss gently to coat well. Arrange in large shallow bowl, from outside in, layers of onion rings, green beans, potato slices and beef. Decorate center with rosette of onion rings. Sprinkle salad with chopped chives and parsley,if desired. Serve at room temperature. Lemon juice may be substituted for vinegar.

Joanne Schmidt, Pres.
Beta Tau No. 3892
Windsor, Ontario, Canada

HAWAIIAN CHICKEN SALAD

1 8-oz. can pineapple tidbits
3 c. diced cooked chicken
1 c. diced celery
1/2 c. sliced almonds
1 c. seedless grapes
1 tbsp. olive oil
1 tsp. vinegar
1/2 c. mayonnaise
1 tsp. salt

Drain pineapple, reserving 1 tablespoon syrup. Combine chicken, celery, pineapple, almonds and grapes in large bowl. Combine reserved syrup, oil, vinegar, mayonnaise and salt in small bowl; mix well. Pour over chicken mixture; toss to mix well. Arrange on lettuce leaves. Garnish with olives, pickles and parsley.

Peggy Baker, Pres.
Gamma Xi No. 5328
Blountville, Tennessee

OVEN CHICKEN SALAD

1 8-oz. can water chestnuts
2 c. diced cooked chicken
3/4 c. diced celery
1 tbsp. chopped pimento
1 3 1/2-oz. can French fried
  onions
2 tbsp. mayonnaise or salad dressing
1 tsp. salad seasoning
1 1 1/4-oz. package chicken gravy
  mix
1 c. milk

Drain and slice water chestnuts. Combine chicken, celery, pimento, water chestnuts, half the onions and mayonnaise in a large mixing bowl. Prepare chicken gravy according to package directions, using 1 cup milk in place of water. Pour hot gravy over chicken mixture; blend thoroughly. Pour into a 1-quart baking dish; top with remaining onions. Bake in 400-degree oven for 10 minutes or until heated through. Cover with foil if onions brown too quickly. Yield: 4 servings.

Indulis Liepins
Xi Gamma Psi X3441
Birmingham, Michigan

Salads

TURKEY-CRANBERRY MOLD

1 c. boiling water
2 3-oz. packages red gelatin
1 1-lb. can jellied cranberry
   sauce
1 1/2 c. cold water
1 tbsp. lemon juice
1/4 tsp. salt
1/2 c. mayonnaise
1 c. chopped cooked turkey
1 apple, pared and diced

Pour boiling water over gelatin in bowl; stir until gelatin is completely dissolved. Mash cranberry sauce with fork; stir into gelatin. Add cold water, lemon juice and salt. Chill until thick enough to mound slightly when dropped from spoon. Stir well; reserve 2 cups. Pour remaining thickened gelatin into 2-quart mold; refrigerate. Add mayonnaise to reserved gelatin; beat with rotary beater until light and fluffy. Fold in turkey and apple. Spoon over gelatin in mold. Chill until firm. Yield: 10 servings.

Mary E. Miller, Pres.
Gamma Omega No. 1433
Quincy, Illinois

TUNA SALAD MOLD

2 tbsp. unflavored gelatin
1/2 c. cold water
1 1/2 c. hot water
4 tbsp. lemon juice
2 tsp. prepared mustard
1/2 tsp. salt
1/2 tsp. paprika
2 7-oz. cans tuna, flaked
2 c. chopped celery
1 c. mayonnaise

Soften gelatin in cold water; dissolve in hot water. Add lemon juice and seasonings; chill until partially set. Add tuna and celery; fold in mayonnaise. Chill until firm. Yield: 12 servings.

Mabel H. Best, Pres.
Xi Pi Pi X3850
Forestville, California

SWEDISH HERRING SALAD

1 1/2 c. finely diced cooked
   potatoes
1 1/2 c. finely diced pickled beets
1 med. apple, cored and diced
1/4 c. minced dill pickle
1/4 c. minced onion
1/2 c. minced herring in wine sauce
1 1/2 tsp. salt
1/4 tsp. pepper
1 c. heavy cream, whipped
2 hard-cooked eggs, cut in wedges
Parsley

Toss potatoes with beets, apple, pickle, onion, and herring in large bowl; sprinkle with salt and pepper. Fold in cream. Pack tightly into medium bowl; refrigerate, covered, for at least 12 hours. Unmold salad on platter; garnish with eggs and parsley. Yield: 8 servings.

Marilyn Hartke, Treas.
Epsilon Psi No. 2465
Litchfield, Illinois

SALMON MOUSSE

1 lg. can salmon
1/2 c. chopped celery
1/4 c. minced onion
2 pkg. unflavored gelatin
1/2 c. catsup
1/4 c. vinegar
1/2 c. mayonnaise

Drain salmon; reserve liquid. Flake salmon; mix with celery and onion. Soften gelatin in 1/2 cup water. Combine salmon liquid, catsup and vinegar; bring to a boil. Stir in gelatin until dissolved. Blend gelatin mixture into salmon mixture carefully. Stir in mayonnaise. Grease large fish mold with additional mayonnaise. Pour salmon mixture into mold. Chill until set. Unmold on salad greens; garnish with slice of ripe olive for eye, if desired.

Amy C. Movic, Pres.
Xi Gamma Delta X2091
McKeesport, Pennsylvania

FLORIDA GRAPEFRUIT BASKETS

3 Florida grapefruit

Cut grapefruit in half. Insert 2 wooden picks 1/2 inch apart on each side of grapefruit. Cut through the peel 1/4 inch below the top of the half to make handle; do not cut between the picks. Cut around each section of fruit loosening from membrane. Cut around entire edge of grapefruit. Remove picks. Lift handles and tie together. Attach flower to handle.

Photograph for this recipe on page 49.

ROAST TURKEY WITH ORANGE-RICE STUFFING

1   12 to 14-lb. turkey
Salt and pepper to taste
Orange-Rice Stuffing

Wash turkey in cold running water. Pat inside dry with paper toweling, leaving outside moist. Sprinkle turkey cavities with salt and pepper. Stuff turkey with Orange Rice Stuffing. Fasten neck skin to body with skewer. Push legs under band of skin at tail or tie to tail. Place turkey, breast side up, on rack in shallow open roasting pan. Cover with a loose covering or tent of aluminum foil, if desired. Bake in a preheated 325-degree oven for 4 hours and 30 minutes to 5 hours or until tender.

Orange-Rice Stuffing

1 c. butter or margarine
1 c. chopped onion
4 c. water
2 c. Florida orange juice
3 tbsp. grated orange rind
4 c. chopped celery
2 tbsp. salt
1 tsp. poultry seasoning
5 1/3 c. packaged precooked rice
1/2 c. chopped parsley

Melt butter in a large saucepan; add onion and cook until tender but not brown. Add water, orange juice, orange rind, celery, salt and poultry seasoning. Bring to a boil; stir in rice. Cover; remove from heat and let stand for 5 minutes. Add parsley and fluff with fork. Any leftover stuffing may be wrapped in foil and placed in oven last 30 minutes of baking time.

Photograph for this recipe on page 49.

BAKED TANGERINES WITH ORANGE-CRANBERRY RELISH

6 Florida tangerines or Temple oranges
2 tbsp. sugar
2 tbsp. butter or margarine
2/3 c. Florida orange juice
Orange-Cranberry Relish

Make 8 vertical cuts in the tangerine skin from the blossom end to about 1 inch from the bottom. Pull peel down and turn pointed ends in. Remove white membrane. Loosen sections at the center and pull apart slightly. Fill each center with 1 teaspoon sugar and dot with 1 teaspoon butter. Pour orange juice over tangerines. Bake in preheated 325-degree oven for 30 minutes. Garnish center with a small amount of Orange-Cranberry Relish. Serve with turkey.

Orange-Cranberry Relish

2 Florida oranges, quartered and seeded
4 c. fresh cranberries
2 c. sugar

Force orange quarters with peel and cranberries through food chopper. Add sugar and mix well. Chill in refrigerator for several hours before serving. This relish will keep well in refrigerator for several weeks.

Photograph for this recipe on page 49.

ORANGE CREPES
WITH ORANGE SAUCE

3 eggs
2 egg yolks
1/2 c. milk
1/2 c. Florida orange juice
2 tbsp. salad oil
1 c. all-purpose flour
3/4 tsp. salt
1 tbsp. sugar
1 tsp. grated orange rind

Beat eggs and egg yolks together. Add remaining ingredients and beat until smooth. Let stand at room temperature for at least 1 hour. Brush hot 7 or 8-inch skillet lightly with additional salad oil. Add 2 tablespoons batter to skillet; turn and tip skillet so mixture covers bottom evenly. Batter will set immediately into thin lacey pancake. Loosen with spatula and flip over in about 15 to 20 seconds or when browned. Brown other side and turn crepe out onto foil or waxed paper. Repeat with remaining batter.

Orange Sauce

1/2 c. soft butter
1/2 c. confectioners' sugar
1 tbsp. grated orange rind
3 tbsp. orange liqueur
1/3 c. Florida orange juice
1 c. Florida orange sections

Cream butter with confectioners' sugar and orange rind. Blend in orange liqueur gradually. Spread about 1/2 teaspoon mixture over side of crepe that was browned second. Roll up crepes. Place remaining mixture with orange juice in large skillet or chafing dish; heat until bubbly. Add rolled crepes and heat, spooning sauce over tops. Add orange sections; heat for just 2 to 3 minutes longer. Yield: 6 servings.

Photograph for this recipe on page 49.

LAMB CHOP AND TOMATO BROIL
WITH HORSERADISH SAUCE

6 1-in. thick loin lamb chops
3 med. tomatoes, halved
1/4 c. butter, melted
1/2 tsp. salt
1/8 tsp. pepper
12 sm. boiled potatoes
Chopped parsley
3 tbsp. drained horseradish
1 c. sour cream

Place lamb chops and tomato halves on rack in shallow pan. Broil 4 to 6 inches from source of heat for 8 to 12 minutes or to desired degree of doneness, turning once. Combine butter, salt and pepper; brush chops and tomatoes frequently with butter mixture. Peel potatoes; brown lightly in additional butter in skillet. Arrange chops, tomatoes and potatoes on heated platter; sprinkle tomatoes with parsley. Blend horseradish with sour cream. Season to taste with additional salt. Serve sauce with lamb chop dish. Yield: 6 servings.

Photograph for this recipe on page 50.

CRAB MEAT MOUSSE

1 tbsp. unflavored gelatin
3 tbsp. cold water
1/4 c. mayonnaise
2 tbsp. lime juice
2 tbsp. lemon juice
1 tbsp. chopped parsley
1 tbsp. chopped chives
3 tbsp. chopped celery
1 tbsp. prepared mustard
Salt and pepper to taste
2 c. flaked cooked crab meat
3/4 c. heavy cream, whipped
1 avocado

Soften gelatin in cold water; dissolve over hot water. Combine gelatin with mayonnaise, lime and lemon juice, parsley, chives, celery, mustard, salt and pepper. Fold in crab meat and whipped cream. Pour mixture into a buttered ring mold; chill until set. Unmold mousse on chilled platter; garnish with thin slices of lime. Peel and mash avocado; add additional lime and lemon juice to taste. Spoon into center of mousse; sprinkle additional chopped chives over avocado mixture.

Genevieve Phillips, VP
Preceptor Beta Chi XP0749
Orinda, California

ELEGANT OLIVE-CRAB MOUSSE

1 c. canned pitted California
ripe olives
1 10-oz. package frozen
asparagus spears
2 env. unflavored gelatin
1/2 c. mayonnaise
2 tbsp. lemon juice
1/2 tsp. salt
1/2 tsp. Worcestershire sauce
Hot pepper sauce to taste
1/4 c. catsup
1 7 1/2-oz. can crab meat
2 c. sour cream

Slice olives. Cook asparagus according to package directions until just tender; drain. Sprinkle gelatin on 3/4 cup cold water to soften. Place gelatin over low heat, stirring constantly until dissolved. Remove from heat. Add gelatin mixture to mayonnaise gradually, beating briskly. Blend in lemon juice, salt, Worcestershire sauce, hot sauce and catsup. Drain and flake crab meat. Reserve desired amount of ripe olive slices and asparagus spears for garnish. Chop remaining asparagus; fold into gelatin mixture. Add remaining ripe olives, sour cream and crab meat. Chill until slightly thickened. Place reserved ripe olives in bottom of 6-cup mold. Cover with small amount of thickened gelatin. Arrange reserved asparagus spears, tips down, against side of mold. Chill until firm. Spoon remaining gelatin mixture into mold. Chill until firm. Unmold; decorate with salad greens and whole pitted ripe olives. Yield: 8-10 servings.

Photograph for this recipe on page 42.

THE FISHERMAN'S FIND

2 c. cooked lobster
1 c. cooked crab meat
2 c. cooked shrimp
1 c. cooked whitefish
3 tomatoes, diced
1/3 c. sliced ripe olives
1/2 c. diced celery
3 green onions, chopped
1 sm. cucumber, diced
1 sm. head lettuce, torn
2 c. small shell macaroni
1/4 tsp. pepper
1/2 tsp. salt
2 tbsp. sugar
3 tbsp. grated onion
1/8 tbsp. cayenne pepper
3/4 c. heavy cream
1/4 c. dry sherry
1 1/2 c. mayonnaise

Combine lobster, crab meat, shrimp and whitefish in large bowl; add tomatoes, olives, celery, onions, cucumber and lettuce. Cook macaroni according to package directions; cool. Combine pepper, salt, sugar, grated onion, cayenne pepper, cream, sherry and mayonnaise; mix well. Add macaroni to seafood mixture; pour on dressing. Toss to coat.

Phyllis Gorze, Committees
Xi Kappa X1565
Minot, North Dakota

TROPICAL LOBSTER SALAD

8 sm. lobster-tails
4 tbsp. butter
1/4 c. lemon juice
1/4 c. (firmly packed) light brown
  sugar
1 pineapple
1 1/2 c. cottage cheese
1/2 c. chopped celery
1/3 c. green grapes, halved and
  seeded
1/2 tsp. salt
Salad greens

Remove meat from lobster-tails and cut into bite-sized pieces; reserve and chill shells. In small saucepan, melt butter; add lemon juice and sugar. Bring to a boil; add lobster. Saute for 3 to 5 minutes or until lobster is tender. Remove from heat; chill thoroughly. Peel, core and cut pineapple into spears. Drain lobster; add cottage cheese, celery, grapes and salt. Place 2 lobster shells on bed of salad greens for each serving; fill with lobster mixture. Serve with pineapple spears and additional grapes. Yield: 4 servings.

Trudy England
Xi Beta Xi, X1978
Ocala, Florida

ROCK LOBSTER-STUFFED TOMATOES

4 9-oz. packages frozen South
  African rock lobster-tails
12 lg. ripe tomatoes
Salt and pepper to taste
Shredded lettuce
1 1/2 pt. cooked pastina
1 c. chopped celery
1/2 c. chopped stuffed olives
1/4 c. chopped onion
1 c. mayonnaise

Drop frozen lobster-tails into boiling, salted water. Bring to a boil; cook for 2 to 3 minutes. Drain immediately; drench with cold water. Cut away underside membrane. Pull out lobster meat; dice. Core tomatoes; turn upside down. Cut each tomato into 8 sections, cutting not quite all the way through. Open out tomato; sprinkle with salt and pepper. Place tomatoes on bed of shredded lettuce. Combine remaining ingredients with lobster pieces; blend well. Stuff tomatoes with lobster mixture; chill until ready to serve. Yield: 12 servings.

Photograph for this recipe on cover.

ROCK LOBSTER JELLIED IN SHELL

3 9-oz. packages frozen South
  African rock lobster-tails
4 env. unflavored gelatin
1/2 c. cold water
1 1/2 pt. tomato juice
2 3-oz. packages cream cheese,
  softened
1 c. mayonnaise
1/4 c. lemon juice
1 pt. chicken broth
Strips of pimento

Drop frozen lobster-tails into boiling, salted water. Bring to a boil; cook for 2 to 3 minutes. Drain immediately; drench with cold water. Cut away underside membrane. Pull out lobster meat; dice. Reserve shells. Soak gelatin in cold water for 5 minutes. Place over low heat; stir until dissolved. Beat tomato juice into cream cheese gradually; beat in mayonnaise and lemon juice. Beat in chicken broth gradually; stir in gelatin and lobster pieces. Chill until slightly thickened. Stir to blend; spoon into reserved lobster shells. Chill until firm. Garnish with pimento strips. Any remaining gelatin mixture may be chilled in small decorative mold and used to decorate platter. Yield: 12 servings.

Photograph for this recipe on cover.

SHRIMP MOLD

1 can tomato soup
1 env. unflavored gelatin
1 8-oz. package cream cheese
1 c. finely chopped celery
1 c. finely chopped onion

1 c. mayonnaise
1 lb. cooked shrimp, chopped

Pour soup in saucepan; do not dilute. Bring to a boil. Soften gelatin in 1/2 cup cold water; add to hot soup, stirring until dissolved. Soften cream cheese with mixer; add to soup mixture. Add celery, onion, mayonnaise and shrimp to cream cheese mixture. Spoon into fish mold; chill overnight. Serve on bed of lettuce.

Pat Brook, Rec. Sec.
Kappa Psi No. 4863
Mansfield, Ohio

TOMATO ASPIC SALAD

1 1/2 c. tomato juice
1 pkg. lemon gelatin
1/2 c. chili saice
1 tsp. Worcestershire sauce
1 c. finely chopped celery
1/2 c. finely chopped onion
1 can shrimp, cut up

Bring tomato juice to a boil; add gelatin, stirring to dissolve. Add chili sauce, Worcestershire sauce, celery, onion and shrimp; mix well. Pour into 1 1/2-quart mold; chill until firm. Yield: 6 to 8 servings.

Virginia Trapnell, Pres.
Preceptor Epsilon XP457
Statesboro, Georgia

WALNUT SALAD ATHENA WITH LEMON HERB DRESSING

2 tbsp. butter
1/2 tsp. dried rosemary, crushed
1 c. California walnut halves
Lemon Herb Dressing
2 c. cooked cleaned prawns or
   lg. shrimp
1 tbsp. minced parsley
2 tbsp. minced chives or green
   onion
Crisp salad greens
6 radishes, whole or sliced
6 pitted ripe olives, whole or
   sliced
6 stuffed green olives, whole
   or sliced

1/2 c. small pickled onions
3 med. firm ripe tomatoes,
   cut in wedges
3/4 c. crumbled cheese

Melt butter with rosemary in heavy skillet; add walnuts. Saute, stirring occasionally, over low heat for about 10 minutes or until walnuts are lightly toasted. Remove and cool. Pour Lemon Herb Dressing over prawns. Add parsley and chives; mix gently. Cover; marinate in refrigerator for 1 hour or longer. Line chilled serving dish with salad greens. Toss radishes, ripe olives, green olives, onions, tomatoes and cheese with prawns. Arrange prawn mixture on greens.

Lemon Herb Dressing

1/2 c. olive oil
1/2 c. lemon juice
1 tbsp. sugar
1 tsp. seasoned salt
1/4 tsp. seasoned pepper
1/8 tsp. garlic powder
1/2 tsp. dried oregano
1/2 tsp. dried marjoram

Combine all ingredients in jar; cover. Shake until well blended.

ARGENTINA SALAD

1 med. head lettuce
1 can marinated artichoke hearts
1 c. pitted green olives
2 tbsp. white vinegar
3 tbsp. Italian olive oil
1 tsp. salt
1/2 tsp. paprika
2 tbsp. mayonnaise
2 chives, chopped
1/2 c. Parmesan cheese

Tear lettuce into small pieces. Drain artichoke hearts, reserving 1/4 cup liquid. Combine lettuce, artichokes and olives in large bowl. Combine reserved liquid, vinegar, olive oil, salt, paprika, mayonnaise, chives and Parmesan cheese; pour over lettuce mixture. Toss until well mixed.

Linda Burks, W and M Com.
Alpha Nu No. 787
Stillwater, Oklahoma

ASPARAGUS SALAD

1 can asparagus soup
1 8-oz. package cream cheese,
softened
1 3-oz. package lime gelatin
2 tbsp. mayonnaise
Juice of 1 lime or lemon
1/4 tsp. salt
1/2 c. chopped celery
1/2 c. chopped pecans
1/2 sm. green pepper, chopped

Heat soup in saucepan; blend in cream cheese. Dissolve gelatin in 1/2 cup hot water. Blend gelatin mixture and mayonnaise into soup mixture; cool. Blend in lime juice, salt, celery, pecans and green pepper. Turn into mold; chill until set. Yield: 8 servings.

Grace E. Maley, Corr. Sec.
Xi Theta Alpha X2080
Glendora, California

CAESAR SALAD

1 clove of garlic, quartered
3/4 c. salad oil
2 c. 1/4-inch bread cubes

1 lg. head romaine
1 lg. head iceberg lettuce
1/4 c. grated Parmesan cheese
1/4 c. crumbled bleu cheese
1 tbsp. Worcestershire sauce
1/2 tsp. salt
1/4 tsp. pepper
1 egg
2 lemons, halved

Place garlic in 1/4 cup oil; let stand overnight. Place bread cubes in shallow pan. Bake at 300 degrees for 20 minutes. Tear romaine and lettuce into small pieces; place in bowl. Sprinkle cheeses on top. Combine remaining oil with Worcestershire sauce, salt and pepper. Add to lettuce mixture; toss gently. Break egg into lettuce mixture. Ream juice from lemons over salad with fork; toss well. Remove garlic from oil; pour over bread cubes. Toss well. Sprinkle on salad; toss to mix.

Judith Mersereau, Pres.
Xi Mu Gamma X2887
Sonora, California

BROCCOLI SALAD

3 hard-cooked eggs
1 pkg. frozen chopped broccoli
1 env. unflavored gelatin
1 can beef consomme
1/4 tsp. salt
1/4 c. lemon juice
1 c. mayonnaise
1/4 c. sour cream

Chop eggs; set aside. Prepare broccoli according to package directions; drain thoroughly. Cool. Combine gelatin with 1/4 cup water; let stand for 5 minutes. Bring half the consomme and salt to a boil; stir into gelatin mixture until gelatin is dissolved. Add remaining consomme; chill until thickened. Blend lemon juice with 3/4 cup mayonnaise; add to gelatin mixture. Stir in eggs and broccoli. Pour into oiled mold; chill until set. Combine remaining mayonnaise with sour cream, blending well; serve with salad. Yield: 4-6 servings.

Hertha Smith, Sec. Elect
Iowa Preceptor Lambda XP0739
Cedar Rapids, Iowa

CREAMY TOMATO ASPIC

2 1/2 c. tomato juice
1 bay leaf
1/4 tsp. celery salt
1/4 tsp. onion salt
1/4 tsp. salt
2 env. unflavored gelatin
1/2 c. strained dill pickle vinegar
1 c. cottage cheese
1 tbsp. salad dressing

Mix 2 cups tomato juice, bay leaf, celery salt, onion salt and salt; bring to a boil. Soften gelatin according to package directions. Add to tomato juice mixture; stir until gelatin is dissolved. Mix remaining tomato juice, vinegar, cottage cheese and salad dressing; stir in gelatin mixture. Pour into 1-quart mold or individual molds. Chill until firm.

Linda Jean Prichard, Pres.
Phi Nu P732
Denver, Colorado

GOURMET SALAD

1 9-oz. package frozen artichokes
1 6-oz. package Italian salad
   dressing mix
1 c. thinly sliced mushrooms
1 3-oz. package lemon gelatin
1 tbsp. diced pimento
1 c. mayonnaise

Prepare artichokes according to package directions; drain and cool slightly. Cut artichokes in half; set aside. Prepare salad dressing according to package directions. Combine salad dressing, artichokes and mushrooms in large bowl. Refrigerate for 1 hour; drain, reserving liquid. Chill reserved liquid. Prepare gelatin according to package directions, using 3/4 cup water. Refrigerate until of consistency of unbeaten egg white. Fold in artichoke mixture and pimento. Pour into a greased 4-cup mold; chill, covered, until set. Mix mayonnaise with reserved liquid; serve as dressing.

Vera E. Lofton, Pres.
Gamma Phi No. 6196
Eugene, Oregon

CUCUMBER-HORSERADISH MOLD

1 3-oz. package lime gelatin
1 c. mayonnaise
2 3-oz. packages cream cheese
1 tsp. horseradish
1/4 tsp. salt
2 tbsp. lemon juice
3/4 c. shredded unpeeled
   cucumbers
1/4 c. shredded green onions

Dissolve gelatin in 3/4 cup hot water in mixer bowl; add mayonnaise, softened cream cheese, horseradish and salt. Beat until smooth; add lemon juice. Chill until slightly thickened. Drain cucumbers and onions well on paper toweling. Add cucumbers and onion to gelatin mixture. Chill until set.

Jan Ryan, Corr. Sec.
Xi Rho X2629
Lead, South Dakota

JELLIED BEET SALAD

1 No. 2 1/2 can diced beets
1/2 c. sugar
1/2 c. vinegar
2 tbsp. unflavored gelatin
2 tsp. salt
1 1/2 c. diced celery
1 tbsp. finely diced onion
3 tbsp. horseradish

Drain beets; reserve liquid. Combine sugar and vinegar; place beets in bowl. Pour vinegar mixture over beets; marinate, chilled, for 2 hours. Soften gelatin in 1/2 cup water. Add enough water to reserved liquid to measure 1 1/2 cups liquid; pour into saucepan. Add salt. Bring to a boil; remove from heat. Stir in gelatin; chill until thickened. Fold in celery, onion, horseradish and beet mixture. Pour into greased 2-quart mold; chill until set. Unmold on platter; garnish with greens and deviled eggs, if desired. May be served with cream horseradish sauce.

Elizabeth B. Murray, Pres.
Omicron Delta No. 8808
Bradenton, Florida

DELUXE SALAD

6 c. bite-sized pieces of lettuce
6 to 8 tbsp. lemon mayonnaise
1 med. onion, thinly sliced
4 1/2 tsp. sugar
Salt and pepper to taste
1 1/2 c. cooked peas
1 c. Swiss cheese strips
1/2 lb. crisp bacon, chopped

Place 1/3 of the lettuce in a large bowl; dot with 1/3 of the mayonnaise. Top with 1/3 of the onion slices; sprinkle with 1/3 of the sugar, salt and pepper. Add 1/3 of the peas and 1/3 of the cheese. Repeat layers twice; chill, covered for at least 2 hours. Sprinkle with bacon; toss lightly just before serving.

Louise Cardey
Xi Xi X1461
Victoria, British Columbia, Canada

ELEGANT BEAN SALAD

1 1-lb. can whole Blue Lake green
*   beans*
6 lg. onion slices
1/2 c. oil
1/4 c. wine vinegar
1/4 tsp. garlic powder
1 tsp. brown sugar
1/4 tsp. ginger
2 drops of hot sauce
1 tsp. prepared horseradish
Salad greens
Pimento strips

Drain beans; place in small bowl. Top with onion slices. Combine remaining ingredients except greens and pimento. Pour over onion; chill for 4 to 6 hours, basting once. Drain beans; arrange over salad greens. Top each serving with onion rings; garnish with pimento strips. Yield: 6 servings.

KOREAN SALAD

1/2 c. oil
1/3 c. sugar
1/3 c. catsup
1/4 c. vinegar
1 tsp. paprika
1 tsp. steak sauce
1 sm. onion, grated
1 lb. fresh spinach
4 c. fresh bean sprouts
8 slices bacon, crisply fried
2 hard-boiled eggs
1 can water chestnuts, drained

Mix first 7 ingredients; chill. Tear spinach off stems; place in large bowl. Chop bean sprouts; add to spinach. Crumble bacon; sprinkle over bean sprouts. Chop eggs; add to spinach mixture. Slice water chestnuts; add to bowl. Toss well; serve with chilled dressing. Two cans bean sprouts, chilled and drained, may be substituted for fresh bean sprouts.

Carolyn D. Chirrey, VP
Alpha Alpha No. 2385
Decatur, Alabama

FESTIVE POTATO SALAD

3 to 4 c. diced potatoes
2 tbsp. vinegar
1 tbsp. salad oil
1/4 c. chopped dill pickle
Salt and pepper to taste
1/2 c. grated carrot
1 c. mayonnaise
1 tbsp. mustard
1/2 c. chopped ripe olives
1 sm. jar diced pimento
2 tbsp. grated onion
1/3 c. chopped bell pepper
1 tbsp. Worcestershire sauce
1 1/2 c. grated cabbage

Cook potatoes in jackets in boiling water until tender. Remove jackets from potatoes while hot. Cool potatoes partially; dice. Add remaining ingredients except cabbage; mix well. Stir in cabbage; refrigerate for 3 to 4 hours before serving.

Bonnie Jo Husband, Pres.
Psi Phi No. 6150
Midland, Texas

SHEPHERD'S SALAD

3 lb. ripe tomatoes, chopped
2/3 c. chopped onions
1 c. chopped green peppers
1 c. chopped cucumber
1/8 tsp. garlic powder
3 tsp. fresh lime juice
3 tbsp. vinegar
Salt and pepper to taste
3 tbsp. oil
3 c. tomato juice

Combine tomatoes, onions, green peppers and cucumber in large bowl. Combine garlic powder, lime juice, vinegar, salt, pepper, oil and tomato juice; pour over tomato mixture. Chill thoroughly. Tomato juice may be increased to 4 1/2 cups for cold soup.

Joan Young, VP
Xi Alpha Rho X3484
Scottsdale, Arizona

FREEZER SLAW

1 med. cabbage, shredded
1 tsp. salt
1 carrot, grated
1 green pepper, chopped
1 c. vinegar
1/4 c. water
1 tsp. mustard seed
1 tsp. celery seed
2 c. sugar

Combine cabbage and salt in bowl; let stand for 1 hour. Squeeze out excess moisture; add carrot and green pepper. Combine vinegar, water, seeds and sugar in saucepan; bring to a boil. Boil for 1 minute. Cool to lukewarm; pour over slaw mixture. Pack into containers. Cover and freeze. Thaw for several minutes before serving.

Diane Formby
Delta Phi No. 8028
Walnut Ridge, Arkansas

TWENTY-FOUR HOUR COLESLAW

1 head cabbage
1 sm. onion
1 green pepper
12 stuffed olives, sliced
3/4 c. sugar
1 c. white vinegar
1 tsp. salt
1 tsp. celery seed
1 tsp. prepared mustard
1/2 c. salad oil
1/8 tsp. pepper

Shred cabbage thinly. Slice onion and pepper thinly. Combine cabbage, onion, pepper and olives in bowl. Combine remaining ingredients in saucepan. Bring to boil; boil for 3 minutes. Remove from heat; pour over vegetables. Blend thoroughly. Let stand, covered, for 24 hours in refrigerator. Yield: 6-8 servings.

Norita D. Goodwin, Pres.
Xi Psi X2129
Sweet, Idaho

SPINACH SALAD

2 pkg. fresh spinach
1/2 lb. bacon
8 hard-boiled eggs
1 pkg. herb dressing mix
Mexican Dressing
Paprika

Tear spinach into pieces in salad bowl. Fry bacon until crisp; drain. Break bacon into pieces over spinach; dice 6 eggs. Add eggs and dry dressing mix to salad bowl. Add desired amount of Mexican Dressing; toss well. Slice remaining eggs; place over salad. Sprinkle with paprika.

Mexican Dressing

1 med. onion, finely chopped
2/3 c. sugar
1 tsp. salt
1/2 tsp. pepper
1 tsp. (heaping) celery seed
3 tbsp. prepared mustard
1/2 c. vinegar
1/2 c. salad oil

Combine onion, sugar, salt, pepper, celery seed and mustard; blend well. Add vinegar and oil; mix with rotary beater. Refrigerate overnight. Dressing will keep indefinitely.

Aileene C. Hatton, Honorary Member
Beta Sigma Phi International
Chillicothe, Ohio

SWEET-SOUR VEGETABLE SALAD

1 can French-style green beans, drained
1 can green peas, drained
1 can pimentos, chopped
1 lg. bell pepper, chopped
1 med. onion, chopped
4 stalks celery, chopped
1 c. sugar
1 c. vinegar
1/2 c. salad oil
1/2 tsp. salt
1 tsp. paprika

Combine vegetables in large bowl; toss lightly. Combine remaining ingredients for dressing; pour over vegetables. Cover bowl; refrigerate overnight or longer. Yield: About 15 servings.

Anna Barron, Pres.
Xi Beta Zeta X3779
Telford, Tennessee

CELERY SEED SALAD DRESSING

1 c. salad oil
1 c. sugar
1/4 c. finely chopped onion
1/3 c. vinegar
1 tsp. (scant) celery seed
1/3 c. catsup

Combine all ingredients; beat with electric mixer until mixed. May be mixed in blender.

Barbara Priest, Pres.
Mu Mu No. 8013
Sarasota, Florida

ROQUEFORT DRESSING

1 1 1/4-oz. wedge Roquefort cheese
2 c. mayonnaise
1 tsp. coarsely ground pepper
1 tsp. garlic powder
1/2 tsp. Worcestershire sauce
1 c. sour cream
1/2 c. buttermilk

Crumble Roquefort cheese. Add remaining ingredients in order listed, mixing well after each addition. Chill. Excellent served on baked potatoes. Yield: 1 quart.

Mrs. Darrell P. Klopp, Civil Def. Chm.
Xi Rho Omicron X 4105
Huntington Beach, California

EVERGREEN KNOLL DRESSING

1 c. tomato soup
2/3 c. salad oil
1 c. (packed) brown sugar
1/2 c. catsup

1/2 c. salad dressing
1/4 c. vinegar
1 tsp. garlic salt
1 tsp. salt
1 tsp. pepper
1 sm. onion, diced
1 tsp. mustard
Juice of 1 lemon

Combine all ingredients in blender container in order listed; blend until smooth. Yield: About 1 quart.

Joycette Christianson, Corr. Sec.
Beta Gamma No. 7534
Huron, South Dakota

SWEET AND SOUR DRESSING

1 c. mayonnaise
1/2 c. sugar
1 tbsp. mustard
1/4 c. white vinegar

Combine all ingredients; beat with electric mixer at medium speed until well blended.

Sally A. Mann
Gamma Omicron No. 1798
Palmyra, Pennsylvania

THOUSAND ISLAND DRESSING

1/4 tsp. horseradish
1 c. mayonnaise
1 tbsp. chopped bell pepper
3 tbsp. chopped stuffed olives
1/3 c. chili sauce
2 hard-boiled eggs, chopped
1/4 tsp. paprika

Mix horseradish and mayonnaise. Add remaining ingredients; mix well. May be served on lettuce wedges.

Virginia Docking, Honorary Member
Beta Sigma Phi International
Topeka, Kansas

COLESLAW DRESSING

3/4 c. vinegar
1 c. salad oil

1 1/4 c. sugar
1/2 tsp. pepper
1 tsp. salt
1 tbsp. celery seed
1 c. salad dressing

Blend vinegar, oil, sugar, pepper, salt and celery seed with a wire whip; add salad dressing gradually. Blend thoroughly. Pour into quart jar; seal. Refrigerate until ready to serve.

Yvonne Snodgrass, Pres.
Xi Gamma Sigma X1591
Columbus, Ohio

CREAMY ITALIAN DRESSING

3/4 c. mayonnaise
1 tbsp. vinegar
1 tbsp. lemon juice
1 tbsp. salad oil
1 tsp. Worcestershire sauce
1/2 tsp. dried oregano leaves
1 tsp. sugar
1 sm. garlic clove, minced

Combine all ingredients; blend thoroughly. Chill for at least 1 hour.

Ellen C. Moore, Pres.
Alpha Tau No. 3072
Dublin, Virginia

WAIOLI GUAVA SALAD DRESSING

1 c. mayonnaise
1 c. tomato catsup
1/4 c. vinegar
1/2 c. salad oil
1 tsp. dry mustard
2 tsp. lemon juice
1/2 tsp. garlic salt
1/2 c. guava jelly

Combine all ingredients; beat with mixer until well blended. Chill; serve over salad greens.

Margaret Langley, Sponsor
Iota No. 3122
Eleele, Hawaii

Meats

From the simplicity of Ham with Pineapple and Raisin Sauce to the elegance of a Jamaican Roast Suckling Pig with Flaming Rum-Mango Sauce, different cuts of meat offer the gourmet a chance to vary her cuisine with a multitude of delicious dishes.

On those occasions when you want to serve the very best and show your family just how much you think of them, turn your culinary talents towards roasting a tempting standing rib roast of beef, basted with its own juices. Or explore the epicurean world of seldom served lamb, veal or specialty cuts.

On the following pages, sisters of Beta Sigma Phi share with you their best epicurean meat dishes. All of these recipes were lavishly and lovingly prepared and contributed by a Beta Sigma Phi, especially for you, the creative cook. Bon appetit!

BEEF BURGUNDY

1/2 lb. mushrooms, sliced
1/4 c. butter or margarine
6 slices bacon
3 lb. stew beef, cut in 1 1/2-in.
  pieces
1/4 c. sliced green onions
1/2 tsp. minced garlic
1/4 c. finely chopped carrots
2 c. Burgundy
3 tbsp. tomato paste
2 beef bouillon cubes
1/2 tsp. salt
2 peppercorns
1 bay leaf
1/2 tsp. thyme
1/4 c. flour
1/2 c. water

Saute mushrooms in butter in 6 or 8-quart pressure cooker until tender. Remove from cooker; set aside. Fry bacon in cooker until crisp. Remove from cooker; crumble. Set aside. Brown beef in fat in cooker; add remaining ingredients except flour and water. Cover. Set control at 10; cook for 25 minutes after control jiggles. Cool cooker normally for 5 minutes, then place under faucet. Remove cover after pressure returns to normal. Mix flour and water; stir into stock. Cook until thickened, stirring constantly. Add mushrooms and bacon; serve with buttered noodles, rice or small boiled potatoes. Cook beef mixture for 3 hours if no pressure cooker is used. Recipe may be halved and cooked in 4-quart pressure cooker.

Janis Ruth Hunter, Ext. Off.
Sigma Chi No. 5100
Sunnyvale, California

BEEF CURRY

4 lb. boneless stew beef
2 onions, chopped
2 tbsp. butter
2 bouillon cubes
2 c. hot water
1 tsp. salt
1/2 tsp. Worcestershire sauce
1/2 tsp. dry mustard

1 bay leaf
4 peppercorns
1 tsp. garlic powder
3 tbsp. catsup
2 tsp. curry

Brown stew beef. Brown onions in butter; add to stew beef. Dissolve bouillon cubes in hot water; pour over beef mixture. Combine remaining ingredients; add to beef mixture. Bring to a boil; reduce heat. Simmer for about 2 hours; serve over rice. May be frozen.

Loette K. Johnson, Pres.
Xi Xi X1941
Alexander City, Alabama

BEEF KIDNEYS A LA CARTE

2 lb. beef kidneys
1 can beef broth
1/2 c. chopped onion
1 clove of garlic, minced
1/2 tsp. salt
1 c. chopped carrots
1 c. chopped celery
2 tbsp. red wine
2 tbsp. flour

Cut kidneys into 1-inch squares. Combine kidneys, broth, onion, garlic and salt in 2-quart saucepan. Simmer, covered tightly, for 1 hour and 30 minutes. Add carrots and celery; simmer, covered, for 30 minutes longer. Blend wine, 2 tablespoons water and flour until smooth; stir into kidney mixture until smooth and thickened. Serve over rice.

Madelyn Forbis
Alpha Pi No. 925
Lawton, Oklahoma

DAUBE OF BEEF

1 2-lb. beef arm roast
1/4 lb. sliced bacon
1 tbsp. cooking oil
4 carrots, sliced
2 lg. onions, thinly sliced
1 lg. can tomatoes
2 cloves of garlic, minced
1 tsp. salt

3 sprigs of parsley
1/2 c. dry red wine
3 slices orange rind
12 lg. pitted ripe olives, cut in
half

Trim fat from roast; slice beef very thin. Dip bacon in boiling water for 2 minutes; drain. Place 1/2 of the bacon in bottom of 2-quart casserole; add oil. Place 1/2 of the carrots, onions and tomatoes in layers on bacon; place 1/2 of the beef on tomatoes. Repeat layers. Mix garlic, salt, parsley and wine; pour over beef. Place orange rind over top; refrigerate for at least 2 hours or overnight. Bake at 300 degrees for 3 hours. Remove orange rind; garnish with olives. One half teaspoon thyme and 1 bay leaf may be added before baking, if desired. One small can ripe olives may be substituted for large olives.

Mary Foreman, Corr. Sec.
Xi Iota X287
Durango, Colorado

OSSO BUCO

1/2 c. cooking oil
1 1/2 c. finely chopped onions
1/2 c. finely chopped carrots
1/2 c. finely chopped celery
1 tsp. finely chopped garlic
6 meaty beef shanks
Salt and pepper to taste
Flour
1 c. dry Burgundy
1/2 tsp. powdered basil
3/4 c. chicken broth
1/2 tsp. powdered thyme
2 bay leaves
3 c. canned tomatoes, coarsely
chopped

Heat 1/4 cup oil in heavy, shallow casserole or Dutch oven, until foam subsides. Add onions, carrots, celery and garlic; cook, stirring occasionally, for about 15 minutes or until vegetables are light brown. Remove from heat. Season beef shanks with salt and pepper; roll in flour. Heat remaining oil in heavy skillet; brown beef in oil, adding more oil, if needed. Place beef on vegetables in

casserole. Pour oil from skillet, leaving just a film. Add Burgundy to skillet; boil down to 1/2 cup. Add remaining ingredients; bring to a boil. Pour over beef mixture. Bake in preheated 350-degree oven until beef is tender. Arrange beef on platter; pour sauce over and around beef. Serve with cooked noodles.

Creamolata

1 tbsp. grated lemon peel
1 tsp. finely chopped garlic
Lemon juice to taste
Salt to taste

Mix all ingredients; sprinkle over beef mixture.

Esther Kellner, Honorary Member
Beta Sigma Phi International
Richmond, Indiana

BEEF TIPS NAPOLI

3 lb. boneless chuck, rump or lean
stew beef
1 tsp. salt
1/4 tsp. pepper
2 tbsp. salad oil
2 6-oz. cans tomato paste
1 1/2 c. water
2 tbsp. lemon juice
1/2 tsp. sugar
1 tsp. marjoram or oregano
1 sm. carrot, thinly sliced
1 clove of garlic, minced
1 lb. seashell macaroni
1/4 c. grated Parmesan cheese
2 tbsp. chopped parsley

Cut beef into 2-inch cubes; sprinkle with salt and pepper. Brown in oil in large skillet. Mix tomato paste with water, lemon juice, sugar, marjoram, carrot and garlic; pour over beef. Cover. Simmer for 1 hour and 30 minutes to 2 hours or until beef is tender, adding water and salt, if needed. Cook macaroni according to package directions; drain well. Mix with cheese and parsley. Serve beef mixture over macaroni mixture. Yield: 6 servings.

Duane Case, VP
Iota No. 497
Hixson, Tennessee

OYSTER-BEEF CUBES

1 lb. beef sirloin
1/2 lb. fresh mushrooms
1/4 c. bottled oyster sauce
2 tbsp. salad oil
2 tbsp. soy sauce
1 clove of garlic, mashed
2 green onions, chopped
1/4 tsp. sugar
3 green onions
1   6 1/2-oz. can water chestnuts,
    drained

Cut beef into bite-sized cubes. Wash and drain mushrooms. Combine oyster sauce, salad oil, soy sauce, garlic, chopped onions and sugar in bowl. Add beef and mushrooms; marinate in refrigerator for 1 to 2 hours. Cut green onions into bite-sized pieces. Alternate beef, mushrooms, water chestnuts and green onion pieces on skewers. Broil 5 inches from heat for 5 to 7 minutes, turning once; serve hot.

Pat Siems, Soc. Co-Chm.
Tau Eta No. 5166
Hemet, California

ADELLE DAVIS' SLOW ROAST

1 beef roast
Oil
Salt
Pepper

Brush beef with oil; place on roasting rack. Bake at 300 degrees for 1 hour. Reduce heat to internal temperature desired when meat is done, 145 degrees for medium-rare prime rib. Bake for 20 to 24 hours or a minimum of approximately 3 times the standard moderate-temperature baking time plus the hour of preheating. Season when desired. A meat thermometer insures success. Beef will be juicy and tender. Shrinkage is minimal and food value retained. The longer the meat cooks, the tenderer it will be.

Judy Kalich, W and M Chm.
Washington Gamma Pi No. 4236
Chehalis, Washington

BOURBON POT ROAST

1   2 to 4-lb. boneless pot roast
Meat tenderizer
1/4 c. (packed) brown sugar
1/4 c. bourbon
1 tbsp. Worcestershire sauce
1 tbsp. lemon juice
1   5-oz. bottle soy sauce

Treat roast with meat tenderizer according to directions on label. Combine remaining ingredients with 1 1/2 cups water; mix well. Place roast in large glass baking dish; pour sauce over roast. Marinate for 4 to 5 hours in refrigerator, turning roast occasionally. Place roast on outdoor grill, turning and basting with sauce. Grill to desired degree of doneness; serve immediately.

Virginia Arps
Phi Alpha Lambda P2622
Wauwatosa, Wisconsin

FRENCH WINE ROAST

1   4-lb. round roast
1 c. red wine
1 tsp. basil
1/2 tsp. thyme
1 c. chopped onion
4 lemon slices
Olive oil
1 doz. stuffed olives
2 bunches green onions
4 carrots
1 c. beef bouillon
1 lg. can sm. potatoes

Marinate roast overnight in red wine, basil, thyme, chopped onion and lemon. Brown roast in small amount of olive oil; place in casserole. Add olives, green onions, carrots, bouillon and marinade. Bake, covered, at 325 degrees for 2 hours and 40 minutes; add potatoes. Bake, covered, for 20 minutes longer. Wine may be added, if needed. Yield: 6-8 servings.

Mrs. Robert Opsahl
Xi Alpha Nu X3725
Merrill, Wisconsin

SAUERBRATEN

1 3 to 3 1/2-lb. beef round rump,
*   cut thick*
1 tsp. salt
1/2 tsp. pepper
4 bay leaves
8 tsp. peppercorns
8 whole cloves
2 med. onions, sliced
1 sm. carrot, minced
1 stalk celery, chopped
1 1/2 c. red wine vinegar
2 1/2 c. water
1/4 c. butter

Rub beef with salt and pepper; place in deep earthenware crock or ovenproof glass bowl. Add spices and vegetables. Mix vinegar and water; heat to boiling point. Pour over beef; cool. Cover crock well; refrigerate. Marinate for at least 48 hours, turning beef twice a day. Remove beef from marinade; dry with paper towels. Melt butter in Dutch oven or kettle; brown beef in butter on all sides. Strain marinade; pour over beef. Cover tightly. Simmer for 2 1/2 to 3 hours or until fork-tender. Remove beef to warmed serving platter; slice. Keep warm.

Gingersnap Gravy

2 tbsp. sugar
2/3 c. gingersnap crumbs
1/2 c. sour cream (opt.)
Salt to taste

Melt sugar in skillet, stirring constantly until golden brown. Stir in 1 1/2 cups hot marinade and 1/2 cup water gradually. Add gingersnap crumbs; cook, stirring, until mixture thickens. Add sour cream and salt; heat through. Ladle some of the gravy over Sauerbraten; serve remaining gravy in bowl.

Elender H. Barrett
Eta Psi Chap.
Albany, Missouri

PAMPERED FILLETS WITH ROYAL MUSHROOM SAUCE

2 tbsp. margarine
4 6-oz. beef fillets

1/2 c. chopped mushroom
1/4 c. finely chopped green onion
4 tsp. cornstarch
1 c. Burgundy
1/2 c. water
2 tbsp. snipped parsley
1 tsp. salt
Dash of pepper

Heat margarine in heavy skillet till golden brown and bubbling. Brown fillets in butter on both sides over moderately high heat; place on squares of heavy-duty foil on baking sheet. Add mushrooms and onion to margarine remaining in skillet; cook till tender. Blend in cornstarch. Add remaining ingredients; cook, stirring, till mixture thickens. Spoon over fillets. Bring corners of foil together; twist gently, leaving slightly open. Bake in 500-degree oven for 15 minutes. Cubed venison or birds, cut in half, may be substituted for fillets. Mushrooms may be marinated in jalapeno pepper juice for 2 hours before cooking, if desired.

Lillie Gilligan, City Coun. Pres.
Xi Kappa Phi X3185
Laredo, Texas

FLANK STEAK WITH BLUE CHEESE BUTTER

1 2 1/2 to 3-lb. flank steak
2/3 c. Italian dressing
1/4 c. blue cheese
2 tbsp. butter or margarine
2 tsp. freeze-dried chives

Trim steak; score each side in diamond pattern with point of knife about 1/8 inch deep. Place steak in baking dish; pour dressing over steak. Cover; refrigerate, turning once, for about 4 hours. Preheat broiler for 10 minutes. Blend blue cheese, butter and chives until smooth; set aside. Place steak on broiler rack in broiler pan; broil for about 5 minutes on each side for medium rare. Spread immediately with blue cheese mixture; cut diagonally into thin slices to serve.

Patricia Hydock,
Xi Gamma Xi X2487
Johnstown, Pennsylvania

KAREWAI STEAK

2 tbsp. clarified butter
1 garlic clove
4 1/2-lb. rib eye steaks
Salt and pepper to taste
1/4 c. butter
1/4 lb. mushrooms, sliced
3/4 c. catsup
3/4 c. dry white wine
1 tbsp. parsley flakes
4 slices bread, cut into rounds
1/4 lb. liverwurst

Heat clarified butter in frypan; rub frypan with garlic. Season steaks with salt and pepper; sear on both sides in butter to desired doneness. Remove from frypan; keep warm. Crush garlic clove in saucepan. Add half the butter; cook for several minutes. Add mushrooms and catsup; cook for 2 minutes. Add wine and parsley; simmer for 5 minutes. Add remaining butter to frypan; fry bread rounds until brown. Spread bread with liverwurst; place on serving dish. Place steaks on bread; spoon sauce over steaks. Garnish with fresh parsley, if desired.

Mrs. Diane Parrette, Coun. Pres.
Beta Phi No. 7207
Ledyard, Connecticut

CHINESE PEPPER STEAK

1 lb. round steak, 1 in. thick
1/4 c. butter
1 clove of garlic, minced
1/2 tsp. salt
1/4 tsp. pepper
4 tbsp. soy sauce
1/2 tsp. sugar
1 c. bean sprouts
2 tomatoes, quartered
2 green peppers, cut into 1-in.
pieces
1/2 tbsp. cornstarch
2 tbsp. cold water
4 green onions, chopped

Slice steak as thin as possible in short, crosswise pieces. Heat butter in skillet. Add garlic, salt, pepper and steak; cook until brown. Add soy sauce and sugar; cover. Cook over high heat for 5 minutes. Add bean sprouts, tomatoes and green peppers; cover. Cook for 5 minutes. Mix cornstarch with cold water; stir into steak mixture. Cook, stirring, until sauce is thickened. Sprinkle with green onions; serve.

Cecilia Klimer
Xi Eta Nu X3543
Parma, Ohio

AUSTRALIAN CARPETBAG STEAK

12 to 18 oysters
1 lb. mushrooms, chopped
3/4 c. butter
1 c. bread crumbs
1 tbsp. parsley flakes
Grated rind of 1/2 lemon
Salt and paprika to taste
1 egg, beaten
1 boned sirloin steak, 2 in. thick,
with pocket

Place oysters and mushrooms in heated butter; cook for 5 minutes. Transfer to bowl; stir in bread crumbs, parsley, lemon rind, salt and paprika. Add egg; mix well. Press into pocket in steak; sew or skewer edges together. Place in baking pan. Roast at 325 degrees for 1 hour; cut steak crosswise into 6 servings.

Toni Olff, VP
Xi Epsilon Beta
Marietta, Ohio

STEAK DIANE

4 6-oz. sirloin steaks
8 tbsp. butter
4 tbsp. finely chopped shallots
2 tbsp. Worcestershire sauce
Salt and freshly ground pepper
Chopped parsley

Place sirloin steaks between pieces of waxed paper or foil; pound to 1/3-inch thickness. Heat 2 tablespoons butter in small saucepan. Add shallots; cook until lightly browned. Add Worcestershire sauce; heat until bubbling. Keep hot. Heat remaining butter in

12-inch skillet or chafing dish until butter begins to brown. Add steaks; cook for 3 minutes. Turn; cook for 2 to 3 minutes longer. Transfer to serving dish and sprinkle with salt to taste and generous amount of pepper. Spread shallot sauce over steaks; sprinkle with parsley.

Gloria Fenter, Pres.
Chi Psi No. 5545
Newhall, California

BOEUF VIGNERONNE

1   3 1/2-lb. sirloin steak
1/2 c. butter
2 tsp. Beau Monde seasoning
1/2 c. brandy
2 tbsp. beef stock base
2 tsp. Bouquet Garni for Beef
1 tsp. garlic powder
2 c. red dinner wine
1 lb. small white onions
8 tender carrots
2 tbsp. arrowroot

Trim excess fat from steak; cut into 1 x 2-inch strips. Saute steak in butter in large heavy skillet, stirring to brown well on all sides. Sprinkle with Beau Monde seasoning. Pour brandy over steak; ignite brandy. Spoon pan juices over steak. Combine beef stock base, Bouquet Garni, garlic powder, wine and 2 cups water; pour over steak when flames cease. Simmer, covered, for 1 hour and 30 minutes or until steak is tender. Pare onions and carrots; cut carrots into small strips. Cook onions and carrots in boiling salted water for 20 minutes or until tender; drain well. Combine arrowroot with 1/2 cup water; stir into steak mixture until smooth and thickened. Stir in carrots and onions carefully. Serve immediately.

Shirley Castro, Past Pres.
Xi Alpha Iota X559
Hayward, California

STEAK COLBERT WITH RICE

1 1/2 lb. sirloin steak
3 tbsp. butter

1 tsp. salt
1/4 tsp. pepper
1/2 c. Burgundy
1 can beef bouillon
1   4-oz. can mushroom stems and pieces
1   5-oz. can water chestnuts
3 c. hot cooked rice

Cut steak into 1/8-inch thick strips; saute in butter in heavy pan until brown. Season with salt and pepper. Add Burgundy, bouillon and mushrooms and liquid. Drain water chestnuts; slice. Add to steak mixture; cover. Simmer for about 20 minutes or until liquid is reduced to half and steak is tender; serve over rice.

Karen M. Krause
Gamma Theta No. 6120
Racine, Wisconsin

AVOCADO SIRLOIN

1 sirloin steak
1 recipe mild horseradish sauce
1 avocado, sliced

Place steak on broiler pan. Broil about 6 inches from source of heat almost to desired doneness. Spread both sides of steak with horseradish sauce. Arrange avocado slices on steak. Broil for about 2 minutes longer.

STEAK IN A BAG

1 boned porterhouse steak,
* 3 in. thick*
1 tbsp. seasoned salt
1 tbsp. seasoned pepper
3 tbsp. garlic spread
3 tbsp. salad oil
1/2 loaf dried cheese bread

Cut steak into 2 pieces. Mix salt, pepper, garlic spread and oil. Grate bread in blender. Spread oil mixture on all sides of steak; press bread crumbs onto steak. Place each piece of steak in a brown lunch bag; place bags on cookie sheet. Bake at 375 degrees for 50 minutes for medium rare; slice to serve.

Mrs. Gerre Rehbein
Xi Theta Psi X2315
Orange, California

UCELLI SCAPATE

1 hard-cooked egg, chopped
1 med. onion, chopped
1 stalk celery, chopped
Salt and pepper to taste
12 diagonally-cut slices salami
12 1/4-in. breakfast steaks
Butter
Flour
1/4 c. red wine
1/2 c. mushrooms

Mix chopped egg, onion and celery; season to taste with salt and pepper. Place one slice salami on each slice beef; top with egg mixture. Roll up; secure with wooden picks. Brown well in skillet in small amount of butter. Place in baking dish. Bake at 375 degrees for 20 minutes or until tender. Combine pan drippings with small amount of flour and desired amount of water; add wine and mushrooms, stirring until smooth and thickened. Serve roll-ups and gravy over hot cooked rice or noodles. Yield: 4 servings.

Julie Imo, Pres.
Kappa Beta No. 7019
St. Louis, Missouri

SWISS BLISS

1/2 tbsp. butter
2 lb. chuck steak
1 env. onion soup mix
1/2 lb. mushrooms, sliced
1 green pepper, cut in pieces
1 1-lb. can tomatoes
1/4 tsp. salt
Pepper to taste
1 tbsp. A-1 sauce
1 tbsp. cornstarch

Tear off 20-inch square of aluminum foil; spread center of foil with butter. Cut steak into serving portions; arrange on foil. Sprinkle with soup mix; add mushrooms and green pepper. Drain tomatoes; reserve 1/2 cup juice. Add tomatoes to steak mixture; season with salt and pepper. Mix reserved juice, A-1 sauce and cornstarch; pour over beef mixture. Bring foil up; double-fold edges to seal tightly. Bake in 375-degree oven for 2 hours; serve with rice. Yield: 4 servings.

Doris Murphy, Pres.
Preceptor Theta X1020
Torrington, Connecticut

BEEF TYROLEAN

1 beef fillet
Salt and pepper
Mashed garlic
2 tbsp. butter or margarine
1 lg. onion, chopped
1 carrot, chopped
1/2 c. chopped celery
2 6-oz. packages Swiss cheese
* slices*

Remove all fat and sinews from beef fillet. Slash fillet lengthwise on one side; open out. Sprinkle on all sides with salt and pepper; rub with garlic. Heat butter in small skillet. Add onion, carrot and celery; saute until soft and lightly browned. Spoon onto cut surface of fillet. Dice 1 package Swiss cheese fine; sprinkle over onion mixture. Fold fillet over; fasten opening with toothpicks and string. Place in shallow pan. Bake in preheated 400-degree oven for 40 minutes.

Remove from oven; remove string and tooth-picks. Place remaining cheese slices over roast; bake for 5 minutes longer or until cheese is melted. Cut into thick slices; gar-nish with whole baby carrots and asparagus spears.

Cathy Lucich, VP
Xi Beta Lambda X 828
Whittier, California

FILET DE BOEUF WELLINGTON

4 c. all-purpose flour
Salt
1/2 c. butter
1/2 c. shortening
2 eggs, lightly beaten
1/2 c. (about) ice water
1   2 1/2 to 3 lb. fillet of beef
2 tbsp. cognac
Freshly ground pepper to taste
6 slices bacon
8 oz. pate de foie gras
3 or 4 truffles (opt.)

Place flour, 1 teaspoon salt, butter and shortening in bowl; blend with tips of fingers or with pastry blender. Add 1 egg and just enough ice water to hold ingredients to-gether. Wrap in waxed paper; chill. Rub fillet all over with cognac; season with salt and pepper. Place bacon over top, securing with string, if necessary. Place fillet on rack in roasting pan. Roast in preheated 450-degree oven for 15 minutes for rare or for 20 to 25 minutes for medium. Remove from oven; remove bacon. Cool to room temperature. Spread pate over top and sides of beef. Cut truffles into halves; sink in pate in line along top of beef. Roll out pastry into 18 x 12 x 1/4-inch rectangle. Place fillet, top down, in middle of rectangle; draw long sides up to overlap on bottom of fillet. Brush with re-maining egg; seal. Trim ends of pastry; make an envelope fold, brushing again with egg to seal closure. Place on baking sheet, seam side down; brush all over with egg. Cut out decorative shapes from pastry trimmings; arrange pieces down center of pastry. Brush shapes with remaining egg. Bake in pre-heated 425-degree oven for about 30 min-utes or until pastry is brown. Serve hot or cold. Puff pastry may be used to wrap beef; care should be taken to roll very thin. Bri-oche dough may also be used. Chicken liver pate may be substituted for pate de foie gras.

Mary Ernsberger, Pres.
Beta Kappa No. 2989
Lantana, Florida

BAKED MACARONI AND MEAT IN CREAM SAUCE

2 med. onions, chopped
Butter
2 lb. ground beef
1   8-oz. can tomato sauce
1/2 c. water
Dash of cinnamon
Dash of nutmeg
Salt
1/2 tsp. pepper
1   1-lb. package macaroni
1 qt. milk
6 tbsp. flour
Grated Parmesan cheese
9 eggs

Brown onions in 1 tablespoon butter in skil-let. Add beef; cook, stirring, until brown. Add tomato sauce, water, cinnamon, nut-meg, 1 tablespoon salt and pepper; cook for 15 minutes. Cook macaroni in 2 quarts salted boiling water until tender. Pour milk into saucepan; bring to a boil. Remove from heat. Melt 2 tablespoons butter in a sauce-pan; blend in flour, stirring until smooth. Add hot milk and salt to taste. Cook, stirring constantly, over medium heat until thick. Add 1 cup cheese; cook, stirring, until cheese is melted. Set aside. Drain macaroni; place in large pan. Add small amount of but-ter, 8 beaten eggs and 1 cup cheese; mix well. Pour half the macaroni mixture into buttered 15 x 10-inch pan. Cover with beef sauce, spreading evenly. Cover with remain-ing macaroni mixture; spread cream sauce on top. Beat remaining egg; spread over cream sauce. Sprinkle with cheese. Bake at 350 degrees for 30 minutes. Cut in squares.

Paulene Butcher, Soc. Com. Co-Chm.
Gamma Psi No. 6157
Arlington, Virginia

LASAGNA

2 lb. hamburger
1/2 c. chopped onions
2 to 3 tsp. oregano
2 to 3 tsp. Italian seasoning
1 to 2 tsp. garlic salt
2 tsp. salt
1 tsp. pepper
3/4 c. parsley
2 6-oz. cans tomato paste
4 cans water
1 ball mozzarella cheese
1 pt. small curd cottage cheese
1 box lasagna noodles

Place hamburger, onions, seasonings and 1/2 cup parsley in skillet; cook until hamburger is brown, stirring frequently. Add tomato paste and water; simmer for 3 to 4 hours or until thickened. Shred cheese; combine with cottage cheese and remaining parsley. Cook noodles according to package directions; rinse well. Make layer of tomato sauce in 10 or 12-inch square baking dish; add thin layer of cheese mixture. Top with layer of noodles. Continue layers, ending with cheese on top. Bake at 350 degrees for 30 minutes to 1 hour or until heated through. Recipe may be divided to make 2 dishes; one may be frozen.

Valerie J. LePont, Rec. Sec.
Phi Kappa P1516
Tucson, Arizona

MEATBALL AND MUSHROOM KABOBS

1/4 c. soy sauce
2 tbsp. salad oil
2 tbsp. water
1/8 tsp. ground ginger
1/8 tsp. ground pepper
1/8 tsp. garlic powder
1 1/2 lb. ground lean beef
1/2 lb. fresh mushrooms
2 sm. green peppers

Combine soy sauce, oil, water, ginger, ground pepper and garlic powder. Shape beef into 1 1/2-inch balls; place in small bowl. Pour soy sauce mixture over meat. Cover; marinate for 1 hour. Rinse mushrooms; pat dry. Trim stem ends. Cut peppers in 1-inch squares. Arrange mushrooms, meatballs and green peppers alternately on skewers. Place skewers over hot charcoal fire or under preheated hot broiler for 8 to 12 minutes or until done, turning and brushing with marinade frequently. Yield: 6 portions.

Esther H. Krueger, Soc. Chm.
Delaware Preceptor Gamma XP 1083
Dover, Delaware

BARBECUED MEAT LOAVES

1/2 c. catsup
1/2 c. water
1/2 tsp. chili powder
1/4 c. sugar
2 tbsp. vinegar
1 tbsp. A-1 sauce
1 1/2 lb. lean ground beef
2 eggs
1 sm. onion, minced
2/3 c. rolled oats
1/2 tsp. salt
8 slices bacon

Combine catsup, water, chili powder, sugar, vinegar and A-1 sauce in small bowl; set aside. Mix ground beef, eggs, onion, oats and salt. Separate into 8 equal portions. Form, but do not pack, each portion into long loaves. Wrap bacon strip around the long edge as for wrapping a filet mignon. Pin securely with toothpick. Place loaves in baking dish; top with prepared barbecue sauce. Bake at 350 degrees for 1 hour. Drain fat before serving.

Billie Burke, Pres.
Preceptor Alpha Upsilon XP1082
Canal Winchester, Ohio

WHITE HOUSE MEAT LOAF

1 1/2 lb. lean ground beef
3 tbsp. bread crumbs
2 tbsp. whipping cream
2 tbsp. tomato sauce
1 egg
1 tbsp. chopped parsley

2 tsp. salt
1/4 tsp. freshly ground pepper
1 tsp. seasoned salt

Mix all ingredients well; form into loaf. Place in loaf pan; cover top with additional tomato sauce. Bake at 375 degrees for 30 minutes. Reduce temperature to 350 degrees; bake for 20 minutes longer. Yield: 6 servings.

Mrs. Richard M. Nixon
The White House
Washington, D. C.

SPICY GLAZED MEAT LOAF

1 1/2 lb. ground beef
3/4 c. gingersnap cookie crumbs
1/2 c. chopped onion
2 eggs
2/3 c. evaporated milk
1 1/2 tsp. salt
1/2 tsp. cinnamon
1/2 c. peach preserves

Combine ground beef, cookie crumbs, onion, eggs, milk and seasonings; mix well. Turn into 1 1/2-quart loaf pan. Bake at 350 degrees for 1 hour. Drain off drippings; cool for 5 minutes in pan. Combine peach preserves and 1/4 cup water in saucepan. Cook, stirring, over low heat until thick. Unmold meat loaf; spread glaze over top and sides. Garnish with peach slices, red maraschino cherries and parsley, if desired. Yield: 6 servings.

WESTERN BEEF AND RICE CASSEROLE

1 c. pitted ripe olives
1 lb. ground lean beef
2 tbsp. cooking oil
1/2 c. chopped onion
1 c. sliced celery
1/4 c. chopped green pepper
1 c. rice
2 1/2 c. canned tomatoes
1 c. water
2 tsp. salt
2 to 3 tsp. chili powder
1/2 tsp. pepper
1/2 tsp. Worcestershire sauce

Cut olives into large pieces. Brown beef in oil. Remove beef from pan; add onion, celery, green pepper and rice. Cook, stirring until brown. Add tomatoes, water, seasonings, beef and olives; bring to a boil. Pour into 2-quart casserole; cover. Bake at 325 degrees for 45 minutes to 1 hour.

Theresa Spelsberg, Treas.
Gamma Pi No. 6060
Charleston, West Virginia

SARMA

1 lb. ground chuck
1 lg. onion, chopped
1/4 c. chopped parsley
1/4 c. chopped green pepper
2 tsp. salt
1/2 tsp. pepper
1/2 c. uncooked rice
1 8-oz. can tomato sauce
Juice of 1/2 lemon
1 jar grape leaves

Combine chuck, onion, parsley, green pepper, salt, pepper, rice, 3/4 can tomato sauce and lemon juice in large bowl; mix well. Place grape leaf on flat surface with wrong side up and stem end toward edge. Place portion of the chuck mixture near stem end; roll leaf, tucking in sides. Repeat, placing leaves closely together in pan making 2 or 3 layers. Pour boiling water to within 1/2 inch of top of leaves; add remaining tomato sauce. Place a plate over top of sarmas to prevent floating. Bring to a boil, then simmer for 45 minutes. Serve with Rice Pilaf. Grape leaves can be purchased in most delicatessens. Cabbage leaves may be substituted. Ground lamb may be used.

Keran Lang, Pres.
Alpha No. 173
Sacramento, California

STUFFED CABBAGE CROWN

1 lb. ground beef
Flour
1 1/2 tsp. salt
1/4 tsp. pepper
1 egg
1 c. milk
2 tbsp. grated onion
1 lg. cabbage
2 tbsp. butter or margarine

Combine ground beef, 1/3 cup flour, salt, pepper and egg in large bowl of electric mixer; beat until blended. Beat in milk, a tablespoon at a time, until smooth and pastelike. Stir in onion. Trim off outside leaves of cabbage. Cut slice about 1 inch thick from core end; set aside. Cut core from cabbage with sharp knife, then hollow out cabbage to make a shell about 1/2 inch thick. Spoon beef mixture into shell; fit cut slice back into place. Tie tightly with string. Place stuffed cabbage, core end down, in kettle; pour in boiling water to cover about 3/4 of the way. Cover. Simmer for 1 hour and 30 minutes or until tender. Pour 1 1/2 cups pan liquid into 2-cup measure; reserve. Heat butter until foamy in small saucepan; blend in 2 tablespoons flour. Cook, stirring constantly, just until bubbly. Stir in reserved liquid; cook and stir until gravy thickens and boils for 1 minute. Season to taste. Place stuffed cabbage on heated serving platter; remove string. Pour gravy into separate bowl; garnish with parsley, if desired. Cut cabbage into wedges; spoon gravy over.

Jo Anne Miller, Sec.
Xi Eta X724
Ogden, Utah

FLAMING POLYNESIAN HAM

1/4 c. sugar
1/4 c. cornstarch
1/4 tsp. salt
1 c. pineapple juice
1/3 c. orange marmalade
1/3 c. vinegar
1 lb. cooked ham, cut in 1-in. cubes
1 can mandarin oranges, drained
1 13 1/2-oz. can pineapple tidbits
3/4 c. green grapes
1/2 c. Cointreau

Combine sugar, cornstarch and salt in blazer pan of chafing dish; mix well. Stir in pineapple juice, marmalade and vinegar. Cook, stirring constantly, over high heat until smooth and thickened. Reduce heat; fold in ham. Add oranges, pineapple and grapes; stir in 1/4 cup Cointreau. Simmer for 20 minutes; add remaining Cointreau, heating through. Serve over rice. Sprinkle with toasted slivered almonds, if desired. Yield: 6 servings.

Donna Lee Smith, 2nd VP
Mu Omega No. 6391
Mattoon, Illinois

HAM LOAF

1 lb. ground ham
1 lb. ground beef
1 c. ground bread crumbs
1/4 tsp. pepper
2 beaten eggs
1 c. milk
1/4 c. vinegar
1/4 c. (packed) brown sugar
1 tbsp. prepared mustard
1/2 c. whipped cream
1 tbsp. horseradish
1 tbsp. salad dressing

Combine ham, beef, bread crumbs, pepper, eggs and milk; mix well. Shape into loaf in rectangular baking pan. Combine vinegar, brown sugar and mustard; spoon over loaf. Bake at 350 degrees for 1 hour and 30 minutes. Blend whipped cream, horseradish and salad dressing together. Serve as sauce for loaf.

Donna J. Moore, Pres.
Xi Kappa Pi X2657
Vacaville, California

BURGUNDY HAM WITH GRAPES

1 tbsp. butter
2 tbsp. sugar
Dash of ginger
1 2 1/4-lb. cooked ham slice
3/4 c. Burgundy
1 tbsp. cornstarch
1 c. seedless green grapes

Melt butter in large skillet; sprinkle sugar and ginger over butter. Brown ham in butter mixture; remove ham. Blend wine into butter mixture; bring to a boil, stirring constantly. Combine cornstarch with 1/4 cup water; add to wine mixture. Cook, stirring constantly, until smooth and thickened; return ham to skillet. Simmer, covered, for 15 minutes; add grapes. Simmer for 2 minutes longer. Yield: 6 servings.

June Boswell, Pres.
Xi Delta X495
Montgomery, Alabama

HAM WITH PINEAPPLE-RAISIN SAUCE

1 1 1/2-in. thick center ham slice
Brown sugar
1 3/4 c. pineapple juice
1 tbsp. flour
1/4 tsp. salt
3 tbsp. lemon juice
1/2 c. raisins
1 c. pineapple chunks
1/2 c. chopped nuts
1/2 c. cherries
1 tbsp. butter

Place ham slice in shallow dish. Combine 2 tablespoons brown sugar and 3/4 cup pineapple juice; pour over ham. Bake at 350 degrees for 20 to 25 minutes, turning once. Blend 1/4 cup firmly packed brown sugar and flour; add remaining pineapple juice. Bring to a boil. Add salt, lemon juice, raisins and pineapple chunks. Simmer for 5 minutes. Add nuts, cherries and butter. Cook until butter melts. Pour sauce over ham to serve.

Mrs. David Halbert, Rec. Sec.
Beta Theta No. 4264
Arkadelphia, Arkansas

BAKED HAM IN BEER

1 boiled or tenderized ham with bone
Whole cloves to taste
1/2 c. dry mustard
1 c. (packed) brown sugar
12 bay leaves
1 qt. beer

Remove most of the fat from ham; score entire surface. Stud ham surface generously with cloves. Combine mustard, brown sugar and enough water to make paste the consistency of prepared mustard. Smear mustard paste over outside of ham; secure bay leaves to ham with wooden picks. Place ham in roaster; add beer. Cover. Bake at 450 degrees for about 20 minutes per pound.

Ada Jones
Preceptor Pi XP-513
Battle Creek, Michigan

HOLIDAY BUFFET HAM

1   12 to 14-lb. fully cooked ham
4 env. unflavored gelatin
1 c. dill pickle liquid
1 c. mayonnaise
2 tsp. prepared mustard
Yellow food coloring (opt.)
Pimentos
Sm. sweet gherkins
Scallion tops
Pickle Mayonnaise
Watercress

Place ham in shallow roasting pan. Bake in 325-degree oven for 15 minutes per pound or until meat thermometer registers 130 degrees. Cool; trim rind and fat evenly. Chill ham thoroughly. Place on rack in shallow roasting pan. Sprinkle 3 envelopes gelatin over 1 3/4 cups water in saucepan. Stir over low heat until gelatin dissolves. Blend pickle liquid with mayonnaise and mustard in medium bowl; stir in gelatin mixture. Add desired amount of food coloring. Place bowl in larger bowl with ice; stir until mixture thickens to consistency of unbeaten egg white. Pour chaud-froid glaze over ham slowly. Leaving ham on rack, place on waxed paper in refrigerator. Chill until glaze is set. Pour glaze that has fallen into pan back into bowl. Reheat glaze and chill again to thickened consistency. Repeat glazing and chilling ham until all glaze is used. Soften remaining gelatin in 1 cup water; stir over low heat until dissolved. Cool thoroughly. Arrange decorations on ham, using pimento and slices of gherkins for flowers and scallion top for leaves and stem. Dip each piece of decoration in clear glaze before applying to ham, using wooden picks when necessary to keep decoration in place. Cut out different shapes of pimento with miniature aspic cutters or sharp knife. Halve gherkins; arrange in border around ham. Chill to set decoration. Pour remaining clear glaze over ham; chill well. Serve with Pickle Mayonnaise; garnish with watercress.

Pickle Mayonnaise

1 c. mayonnaise
1/4 c. chopped dill pickle
4 tsp. prepared mustard

Mix mayonnaise with dill pickle and mustard.

HAM WITH CHERRY SAUCE

1   8 to 10-lb. canned ham
2   10-oz. jars apple or guava jelly
2 tbsp. prepared mustard
2/3 c. unsweetened pineapple juice
1/4 c. dry white wine
2   21-oz. cans cherry pie filling
1 c. white raisins

Place ham, fat side up on rack in shallow pan. Bake according to can directions. Remove ham from oven 30 minutes before baking time is up; score fat in diamond shapes. Combine jelly and mustard in medium saucepan; stir in pineapple juice and wine. Cook, stirring until boiling. Simmer for 2 to 3 minutes. Pour 1/3 of the glaze over ham; return to oven. Spoon on remaining glaze at two 10 minute intervals. Bring cherry pie filling and raisins to boiling point in saucepan, stirring occasionally. Remove ham to serving platter. Add glaze from baking pan to cherry sauce. Bring to a boil; spoon sauce over ham. Pass remaining sauce. Yield: 20-24 servings.

Kathy L. Harmon, Pres.
Phi Omega P2624
Chesnee, South Carolina

ORANGE AND SPICE RACKS OF LAMB

12 1-in. pieces of orange peel
2 racks of lamb, 7 ribs each
1 tsp. salt
1 tsp. ginger
1 tsp. allspice
1/4 c. honey
Baked Pears Piquant

Insert orange peel between the bones of the racks of lamb. Mix salt, ginger and allspice together; sprinkle on all sides of lamb. Place in shallow roasting pan. Bake at 325 degrees for 40 minutes per pound or until meat thermometer registers 175 degrees for medium doneness. Brush lamb with honey during last 45 minutes of baking time. Serve with Baked Pears Piquant.

Baked Pears Piquant

1 1-lb. 13-oz. can Bartlett
*   pear halves*
Whole cloves
2/3 c. dried apricots
1/2 c. golden raisins
1/4 c. white wine vinegar

Drain pears, reserving syrup. Insert whole clove in each pear half. Arrange pears in baking dish. Place 1 apricot in each pear cavity; sprinkle with raisins. Combine reserved syrup and vinegar; pour over pears. Bake at 350 degrees for 30 minutes, basting once or twice.

LAMB AND APRICOT PILAF

1 c. chopped onion
1/2 c. butter
1 lb. lamb, cut in 1-in. cubes
1/2 c. dried apricots, halved
3 tbsp. raisins
1 tsp. salt
1/2 tsp. cinnamon
1/4 tsp. pepper
1 1/2 c. long grain rice

Saute onion in 1/4 cup butter in skillet until golden. Add lamb, stirring to brown well on all sides. Stir in apricots, raisins, salt, cinnamon, pepper and 1 3/4 cups water. Simmer, covered, for 1 hour and 30 minutes or until lamb is tender. Wash rice thoroughly; drain well. Bring 3 cups lightly salted water to a boil. Add rice gradually; boil for 2 minutes. Reduce heat; simmer rice, covered, for 15 minutes. Stir in remaining butter with a fork. Layer rice and lamb mixture in heavy saucepan, beginning and ending with rice. Simmer, covered, for 25 minutes or until rice is tender. Yield: 4 servings.

Helen Voelkerding, VP
Preceptor Mu XP383
Cincinnati, Ohio

LAMB CURRY

1 1/2 lb. boneless lamb shoulder
6 tbsp. butter
2 lg. onions, thinly sliced
2 cloves of garlic, crushed
1 c. finely chopped celery
2 lg. cooking apples
3 lg. tomatoes, cut in wedges
1/4 tsp. ginger
1 1/2 tbsp. curry powder
1 tbsp. sugar
1 1/2 tsp. salt
1/4 tsp. pepper
1/4 c. cornstarch
3 c. cooked rice

Cut lamb into 1-inch cubes. Heat 2 tablespoons butter in electric skillet to 300 degrees; brown lamb in butter, turning to brown well on all sides. Add 2 cups water; reduce heat to 240 degrees. Simmer, covered, for 1 hour or until lamb is tender. Remove lamb from skillet; reserve liquid. Heat remaining butter in electric skillet to 300 degrees. Stir in onions, garlic and celery. Cook, stirring frequently, until onions are lightly browned. Pare and slice apples; add apples, tomatoes, ginger, curry powder, sugar, salt and pepper; blend well. Stir in lamb; add water to reserved liquid to measure 3 cups. Add to lamb mixture; combine cornstarch with small amount of water. Stir cornstarch mixture into lamb mixture; blend thoroughly. Simmer, covered, at 240 degrees for 5 minutes. Serve with rice. Yield: 6-8 servings.

Mrs. Wilber M. Brucker, Honorary Member
Beta Sigma Phi International
Grosse Pointe Farms, Michigan

BARBECUED BUTTERFLY LAMB

1 leg of lamb
1 c. dry red wine
1/2 c. olive oil
2 tbsp. snipped parsley
2 tbsp. chopped chives
2 cloves of garlic, mashed
1/2 tsp. Worcestershire sauce
1/4 tsp. pepper
1/8 tsp. marjoram
1/8 tsp. rosemary
1/8 tsp. thyme
1 tsp. salt

Cut through lamb to bone; remove bone. Place lamb in shallow baking dish. Combine remaining ingredients; blend thoroughly. Pour marinade over lamb. Marinate overnight in refrigerator. Grill over hot coals for 20 minutes; turn. Grill for 20 minutes longer; baste frequently. Yield: 6 servings.

Norma Osborn, Serv. Chm.
Gamma Phi No. 5686
Ontario, Oregon

LAMB SHANKS DELUXE

4 meaty lamb shanks
1/2 lemon

1/4 tsp. garlic powder
1 c. flour
2 tsp. salt
1/2 tsp. pepper
1/2 c. salad oil
1 can beef consomme
1/2 c. dry vermouth
1 med. yellow onion, chopped
4 carrots
4 stalks celery

Rub lamb with lemon; sprinkle with garlic powder. Let stand for 10 minutes. Combine flour, salt and pepper in paper bag. Shake shanks, one at a time, to coat with seasoned flour. Reserve flour mixture. Brown shanks in hot oil in large heavy skillet; remove from pan. Add 4 tablespoons reserved seasoned flour to pan drippings; cook, stirring with wire whip, until brown. Add consomme, 1 cup water, and vermouth gradually; cook, stirring constantly, until slightly thickened. Add onion. Place shanks in large baking pan in single layer; pour consomme mixture over shanks. Refrigerate until baking time. Bake, uncovered, at 350 degrees for 30 minutes. Peel carrots; cut carrots and celery into chunks. Turn shanks over; add carrots and celery. Bake for 1 hour longer.

Barbara Lamb, Pres.
Epsilon Omega No. 5105
Miami, Florida

CHINESE SWEET AND SOUR PORK

Salt
1/2 tbsp. soy sauce
Cornstarch
1 egg yolk
1 lb. pork tenderloin
2 green peppers
4 slices pineapple
Cooking oil
3 tbsp. vinegar
1/4 c. sugar
1/4 c. catsup
1 tbsp. sesame oil

Combine 1/2 tablespoon salt, soy sauce, 1 tablespoon cornstarch, 1 tablespoon cold water and egg yolk for marinade. Cut pork into 1-inch squares; marinate in soy sauce marinade for 30 minutes. Cut green peppers and pineapple into 1-inch squares. Set aside. Heat 2 cups cooking oil in skillet. Coat pork with 1/2 cup cornstarch. Fry pork in hot oil for about 2 minutes or until browned. Remove pork from skillet; drain pan drippings from skillet. Add 2 tablespoons cooking oil; heat. Saute green pepper and pineapple. Combine vinegar, sugar, catsup, 1/2 cup cold water, 3 tablespoons cornstarch, 1 teaspoon salt and sesame oil; stir into sauteed mixture. Cook, stirring constantly, until thickened. Add pork; serve over hot rice.

Mrs. J. Wade Henderson, Rec. Sec.
Misawa Iota, Japan No. 8252
APO, San Francisco

GOURMET PORK CHOPS

2 tbsp. flour
1 tsp. salt
Dash of pepper
6 1/2-inch thick loin pork chops
2 tbsp. shortening
1 10 1/2-oz. can cream of
     mushroom soup
1/2 tsp. ground ginger
1/4 tsp. dried rosemary, crushed
1 3 1/2-oz. can French fried onions
1/2 c. sour cream

Combine flour, salt and pepper; coat chops with seasoned flour. Heat shortening in skillet; brown chops well on each side. Place chops in 11 x 7 x 1 1/2-inch baking dish. Combine soup, 3/4 cup water, ginger and rosemary; pour over chops. Sprinkle with half the onions; cover. Bake at 350 degrees for 50 minutes or until chops are tender. Uncover; sprinkle with remaining onions. Bake for 10 minutes longer. Remove chops to platter. Blend sour cream into soup mixture in skillet; heat. Serve sauce with chops. Yield: 6 servings.

Francie Steiger, Serv. Chm.
Xi Theta Mu XS4015
Hamilton, Ohio

PORK CHOPS WITH CHERRIES

4 1/2-in. pork chops
1 tbsp. shortening
Salt and pepper to taste
1 1-lb. 1-oz. can pitted light
  cherries
1/4 c. slivered almonds
6 whole cloves
1 tbsp. cider vinegar
Few drops of red food coloring (opt.)

Brown pork chops in shortening; season with salt and pepper. Combine cherries with syrup and almonds, cloves, vinegar and food coloring. Drain shortening from pork chops; pour cherry mixture over chops. Simmer for 30 minutes. Yield: 4 servings.

Carol F. McArthur, Rec. Sec., Corr. Sec.
Tau Zeta No. 5164
Palmdale, California

PORK CHOP AND LIMA DINNER

4 pork chops
1/2 tsp. salt
1/4 tsp. pepper
1 med. onion
1 tbsp. shortening
1 10-oz. package frozen lima beans
1/2 c. water
1 can cream of celery soup
2/3 c. evaporated milk
1/4 tsp. poultry seasoning
1/4 tsp. oregano
2 tbsp. flour

Sprinkle both sides of pork chops with salt and pepper. Brown chops and onion in shortening. Remove chops from skillet. Add remaining ingredients. Stir over medium heat until sauce thickens and limas are thawed. Arrange chops in sauce; cover. Simmer for 1 hour, stirring occasionally until chops and limas are tender. Do not boil. Serve over chow mein noodles or cooked rice.

Kathleen Smith, Hist.
Xi Zeta Lambda X-2943
Bowling Green, Ohio

PILAF PORK CHOPS

6 thick loin pork chops
1 1/2 c. rice
1/2 clove of garlic, minced
2 tbsp. salt
2 tbsp. curry powder
1/2 tsp. turmeric
1/4 tsp. hot sauce
1/8 tsp. cumin
1/8 tsp. coriander
1 can chicken consomme
1 1/4 soup cans water
6 slices lime
6 slices onion
6 green pepper rings
6 tbsp. mango chutney

Sear chops on both sides in fat in Dutch oven. Remove chops; pour off all but 3 tablespoons fat. Stir in rice; cook for 5 minutes. Add seasonings. Stir in consomme and water. Cook for 1 minute, stirring. Arrange chops in single layer over rice; cover. Bake at 325 degrees for about 1 hour. Remove cover; bake for 30 minutes longer. Arrange chops and rice on platter. Garnish each chop with 1 lime slice, slice of onion and 1 green pepper ring. Spoon 1 tablespoon chutney into each pepper ring. Yield: 6 servings.

Sharon Strobel, Pres.
Xi Kappa X1051
Coeur D'Alene, Idaho

VIENNESE PORK CHOPS

8 pork chops
1 lg. dill pickle
1/4 lb. boiled ham
1/4 c. finely chopped onions
1 can chicken broth
1/4 tsp. paprika
Salt to taste
Dash of garlic powder
1/2 c. sour cream
2 tbsp. flour
1 egg yolk, beaten

Brown pork chops in Dutch oven in small amount of fat; remove pork chops. Slice dill pickle and ham into thin strips. Place dill pickle, ham, onions and broth in Dutch oven; stir in paprika, salt and garlic powder. Return chops to pan. Bake, covered, at 350 degrees for 1 hour. Combine sour cream, flour and egg yolk; blend well. Stir small amount of broth mixture into sour cream mixture; return to hot mixture, blending well. Simmer for 15 minutes.

Ruby L. Clemens, Treas.
Preceptor Beta Kappa XP691
San Gabriel, California

MARINATED PORK WITH PEANUTS

1 1/2 lb. boneless pork loin
3 tbsp. flour
3 tbsp. (firmly packed) brown sugar
1/4 tsp. salt
Dash of pepper
3 tbsp. soy sauce
1/4 c. peanut oil
1/2 c. coarsely chopped cocktail
   peanuts

Trim excess fat from pork; slice pork thinly. Cut slices into 1/2-inch strips. Combine flour, brown sugar, salt, pepper and soy sauce; mix well. Coat pork strips thoroughly. Cover; chill for 1 hour. Heat peanut oil in skillet; add pork. Cook over moderate heat for about 8 minutes or until pork is done. Stir in cocktail peanuts; cook for 1 minute longer. Yield: 4 servings.

Terine L. Kron, Pres.
Preceptor Alpha XP108
Inglewood, California

ANDY'S IMPROVISED BARBECUED PORK

1 5 to 6-lb. boneless pork roast
Salt and pepper to taste
1 1/2 c. catsup
2 tbsp. lemon juice
2 tbsp. Worcestershire sauce
2 tbsp. prepared mustard
1 sm. grated onion

2 cloves of garlic, crushed
2 cans pineapple chunks, drained

Rub roast lightly with salt and pepper; place in baking pan. Bake at 325 degrees for about 3 hours. Cool for 30 minutes. Slice roast; place slices in large baking dish. Combine all remaining ingredients except pineapple; pour over pork slices, reserving small amount. Bake at 325 degrees for 1 hour. Combine pineapple chunks and reserved sauce. Arrange pineapple over pork slices, pouring sauce over pineapple. Bake for 10 minutes longer.

Andree H. Dugo, Soc. Chm.
Gamma Omicron No. 1554
Hamilton AFB, California

ROAST CROWN OF PORK

1 12 to 14-rib crown pork roast
3 tbsp. chopped onions
3 tbsp. chopped celery
2 tbsp. butter
4 oranges, sectioned
1 lg. grapefruit, sectioned
1 1/2 c. cooked rice
2 c. toasted bread cubes
1 tbsp. crumbled sage
1 tsp. salt
1/4 tsp. pepper
1 tsp. grated orange rind
2 tbsp. honey

Preheat oven to 450 degrees. Cover ribs with foil; insert meat thermometer in roast. Place pork on rack in roasting pan. Place in oven; reduce oven temperature to 350 degrees. Roast for 40 minutes per pound or until thermometer registers 185 degrees. Saute onions and celery in butter in small skillet until tender. Combine onion mixture with orange and grapefruit sections and remaining ingredients. Spoon mixture into center of roast 1 hour before roast is done; baste occasionally. Garnish with additional fruit, if desired. Yield: 6-8 servings.

Joy Ackert
Delta Kappa No. 4059
Fort Myers, Florida

PORK ROAST MARASCHINO

1 tbsp. salad oil
2 cloves of garlic
1 29 1/2-oz. can pineapple chunks
1 c. undrained sweet mixed pickles
1 16-oz. jar maraschino cherries
5 tsp. cornstarch
2 tbsp. cold water
1 tbsp. soy sauce
2 tsp. salt
1 4 to 5-lb. pork loin roast

Heat oil in saucepan; add garlic. Saute for several minutes. Remove garlic. Drain pineapple, pickles and cherries, reserving about 2 cups combined liquid. Blend cornstarch with cold water; add reserved liquid, soy sauce and salt. Add to oil in saucepan; cook, stirring, until thickened. Set glaze aside. Place roast on rack in shallow roasting pan. Bake in 325-degree oven for 35 to 45 minutes per pound or until meat thermometer registers 170 degrees, basting with part of glaze during last 1 hour and 30 minutes of baking. Add fruits and pickles to remaining glaze; heat. Pour over and around roast on serving platter. Yield: 6-8 servings.

Photograph for this recipe on page 62.

ROAST PORK WITH ANISE

1 5-lb. pork loin with pocket
2 tbsp. anise
1 c. white wine
1/4 c. butter
1 onion, grated
1 tsp. poultry seasoning
1 tsp. sweet marjoram
1 tsp. salt
2 c. fine bread crumbs

Place pork in shallow roasting pan. Combine anise and wine in small saucepan; simmer for several minutes. Combine butter, onion, poultry seasoning, marjoram and salt in large saucepan; blend well. Add crumbs, stirring to mix thoroughly; stuff roast with crumb mixture. Spoon a small amount of wine mixture over roast; seal with foil. Roast at 250 degrees for 4 hours; baste occasionally. Yield: 6-8 servings.

Virginia P. Watt, Corr. Sec.
Xi Alpha Rho X3484
Phoenix, Arizona

SPARERIBS HAWAIIAN

1 40-oz. can pineapple juice
1/2 c. dry ginger
5 to 7 lb. country-style spareribs
1 tbsp. salt
1 16-oz. bottle smoky barbecue sauce

Combine pineapple juice and ginger; pour over ribs. Marinade for about 6 hours; drain and season with salt. Place ribs in flat baking pan. Bake at 375 degrees for about 1 hour or until ribs are done, basting occasionally with barbecue sauce. Garnish with fresh pineapple slices. Yield: 8-10 servings.

Bonita Ellingson, Corr. Sec.
Xi Iota Omicron X2394
Ceres, California

CHINESE SWEET-SOUR SPARERIBS

1 lb. spareribs
1 lg. green pepper
1 can pineapple chunks
1 piece fresh ginger
2 tbsp. sugar
2 tbsp. vinegar
1/2 tsp. salt
2 tbsp. soy sauce
1 tbsp. cornstarch

Cut ribs into 1-inch pieces. Cook ribs in skillet, turning occasionally and pouring off fat, until almost tender. Cut green pepper into 1-inch strips. Add green pepper, pineapple with juice and ginger to pork. Combine sugar, vinegar, salt, soy sauce and cornstarch; pour over rib mixture. Cover; cook for 10 minutes.

Thelma H. Glenn, Rec. Sec.
Xi Alpha X2868
Agana, Guam

ROAST PORK
WITH SAUERKRAUT AND APPLE

1 3 1/2-lb. pork loin roast
Onion salt to taste
Marjoram to taste
Pepper to taste
1 qt. drained sauerkraut
2 red apples, thinly sliced
1/2 c. apple brandy
1 tbsp. light brown sugar
2 tbsp. butter

Sprinkle pork with onion salt, marjoram and pepper; score fatty side. Secure on spit. Insert meat thermometer. Adjust spit about 8 inches from prepared coals, placing foil pan under pork to catch drippings. Roast for 15 to 20 minutes per pound or until meat thermometer registers 185 degrees. Place on heated serving platter; keep warm. Combine sauerkraut, apple slices, brandy, brown sugar and butter in skillet. Simmer, covered, for 5 minutes or until apples are tender. Spoon into serving dish. Garnish with additional apple slices and parsley. Serve with pork.

Photograph for this recipe on page 83.

FILBERT TORTE
WITH STRAWBERRY WHIPPED CREAM

Graham cracker crumbs
2 c. sugar
1/2 tsp. ground allspice
1 lb. filberts, ground
1 tsp. grated lemon peel
6 eggs, separated
1/4 tsp. salt
1 tbsp. light corn syrup
1 tsp. water
1 egg white, slightly beaten

Grease 9-inch 6 1/2-cup ring pan; sprinkle with graham cracker crumbs. Set aside. Mix sugar and allspice together; mix in filberts and lemon peel with tossing motion. Beat egg yolks until thick and lemon colored; blend into filbert mixture, working in well with hands. Beat egg whites until frothy; add salt. Beat until stiff but not dry; fold into filbert mixture. Turn into prepared ring pan. Bake at 350 degrees for 35 to 40 minutes or until cake tests done. Cool for 5 minutes. Loosen cake with spatula; turn out onto ungreased baking sheet. Blend corn syrup and water; brush over top of torte. Brush entire torte with egg white. Bake for 5 minutes longer. Cool; place torte on serving plate.

Strawberry Whipped Cream

2 pt. fresh strawberries
1 1/2 c. heavy cream
3 tbsp. kirsch

Slice strawberries, reserving 1 cup for garnish. Whip cream until stiff, adding kirsch gradually. Fold in sliced strawberries. Mound in center of torte; garnish with reserved strawberries.

Photograph for this recipe on page 83.

HOT POTATO SALAD WITH BACON

4 lb. pared potatoes, sliced
1/2 c. chopped onion
2/3 c. bacon drippings
1/2 c. vinegar
2 tbsp. chopped parsley
2 tsp. sugar
1 tsp. paprika
1/2 tsp. salt
1/4 tsp. pepper
12 slices fried bacon, crumbled

Cook potatoes in saucepan in 2 inches salted water until tender; drain. Saute onion in bacon drippings until tender; stir in vinegar, parsley, sugar, paprika, salt and pepper. Combine potatoes, bacon and onion mixture. Toss gently. Serve warm with pork roast and sauerkraut.

Photograph for this recipe on page 83.

GRILLED CHICKEN WITH KRAUT RELISH

6 c. sauerkraut
1 4-oz. jar pimento
2 med. green peppers, chopped
2 med. onions, chopped
1/4 tsp. paprika
Freshly ground pepper to taste
1 clove of garlic, minced
1/2 c. melted butter
1/4 c. wine vinegar
1/2 c. (firmly packed) dark brown sugar
2 tbsp. Worcestershire sauce
2 tbsp. cornstarch
1/4 c. water
12 chicken legs with thighs

Drain the sauerkraut and reserve liquid. Drain the pimento and chop. Toss sauerkraut with green peppers, pimento, half the onions, paprika and pepper in a bowl and chill. Saute remaining onion and the garlic in butter in a saucepan until golden. Add the vinegar, sugar, Worcestershire sauce, pepper and reserved sauerkraut liquid and stir until sugar is melted. Bring to a boil over medium heat. Blend the cornstarch with water and stir into onion mixture. Boil for 30 seconds, stirring constantly, then remove from heat. Place chicken on grill 7 to 8 inches from source of heat; cook for 10 minutes. Brush with sauce and continue grilling for 10 minutes. Turn chicken and grill an additional 10 minutes or until done, brushing frequently with sauce to glaze. Serve kraut relish with grilled chicken.

Photograph for this recipe on page 84.

OLD-FASHIONED STRAWBERRY SHORTCAKE

2 c. sifted all-purpose flour
4 tsp. baking powder
1/2 tsp. salt
1/2 tsp. cream of tartar
1/4 c. sugar
1/2 c. vegetable shortening
1/3 c. milk
1 egg
Butter
3 pt. fresh California strawberries,
    sliced and sweetened
Whipped cream

Sift flour, baking powder, salt, cream of tartar and sugar together. Cut in shortening until mixture resembles coarse meal. Combine milk with egg; stir into flour mixture with a fork until soft dough is formed. Turn out onto lightly floured board and pat or roll into 8-inch circle, 1/2 inch thick. Place on ungreased baking sheet. Bake in preheated 425-degree oven for 10 to 12 minutes or until golden brown. Split and spread butter on both halves. Pile strawberries and whipped cream between layers and on top. Yield: 8 servings.

Photograph for this recipe on page 84.

VEAL CHOPS WITH GLAZED ONIONS AND POTATOES

4 1-in. thick veal chops
6 tbsp. butter
1/4 c. flour
10 white onions, peeled
8 sm. potatoes, peeled
2/3 c. beef consomme
2 tsp. salt
1/8 tsp. pepper
1 tsp. sugar
1/4 c. chopped parsley

Trim fat from chops. Heat 2 tablespoons butter in 8-inch skillet. Coat chops with flour; brown slowly on both sides. Cover; cook over low heat for about 20 minutes. Melt remaining butter in 12-inch skillet; add onions and potatoes. Cook until golden, shaking pan frequently. Pour off all fat. Add chops and 1/2 cup consomme. Season with salt and pepper; sprinkle sugar over vegetables. Cover; simmer for 20 minutes. Uncover; turn vegetables and chops over. Add remaining consomme. Cover; cook until chops are tender. Remove cover; let juices cook down. Garnish with parsley.Yield: 4 servings.

Pauline Cherry, Pres.
Xi Alpha X167
Terre Haute, Indiana

VEAL FRICASSEE IN PASTRY SHELLS

1 2-lb. veal shoulder
2 tbsp. butter
2 tbsp. flour
1 tsp. salt
1 tbsp. lemon juice or white wine
1 tsp. capers
1 egg yolk
1 tbsp. heavy cream
8 oz. sliced mushrooms
1 pkg. pastry shells

Place veal in enough water to cover in kettle; boil until tender. Remove veal; reserve 1 pint stock. Cut veal into cubes; keep warm. Melt butter in double boiler; stir in flour and salt until smooth. Add reserved stock gradually; cook, stirring, until thickened. Add lemon juice and capers. Beat egg yolk and cream together. Add small amount of hot mixture to egg yolk mixture, blending well. Return egg yolk mixture to double boiler. Cook for about 1 minute longer, stirring constantly. Remove from heat. Saute mushrooms in additional butter; add mushrooms and veal cubes to cream sauce. Keep warm. Prepare pastry shells according to package directions; fill with veal mixture and serve.

Helga Donath
Xi Kappa X4019
Seaford, Delaware

VEAL TARAMINI

2 lg. eggplant
3 eggs, beaten
2 c. soft bread crumbs
Salad oil
2 lb. ground veal
18 oz. tomato sauce
4 tsp. sugar
2 tsp. oregano
1 tsp. basil
1 tsp. salt
1 c. grated Parmesan cheese
1 16-oz. package sliced mozzarella cheese

Pare eggplant; slice 1/4 inch thick. Dip eggplant in eggs; dip in crumbs. Brown in small amount of oil in skillet; drain on paper toweling. Brown veal in skillet over medium heat; stirring to brown evenly. Combine tomato sauce, sugar, oregano, basil and salt in pitcher; blend well. Layer half the eggplant in greased shallow baking dish; cover with half the meat. Pour half the tomato sauce mixture over meat; sprinkle with half the Parmesan cheese. Repeat process. Slice mozzarella cheese into triangles; arrange in pattern over all. Bake at 350 degrees for 30 minutes. May be made ahead of time and frozen or refrigerated until ready to bake.

Beth Maislein Moore, Pres.
Alpha Kappa Lambda No. 8952
Arlington, Texas

VEAL PARMIGIANA

1/4 lb. ground beef
Garlic to taste
Salt and pepper
1 onion, chopped
1 sm. can mushroom pieces
1 can tomato paste
1 lg. can tomato sauce
1/2 c. Parmesan cheese
2 lb. veal cutlets
2 eggs, slightly beaten
1 c. fine bread crumbs
1/3 c. butter
6 slices mozzarella cheese

Brown ground beef in large skillet; add garlic, salt and pepper to taste. Stir in onion, mushroom pieces, tomato paste, tomato sauce and Parmesan cheese. Simmer for 5 to 6 hours. Cut veal into 6 serving pieces; pound until thin. Dip into egg and crumbs. Brown veal in butter in skillet. Season with

3/4 teaspoon salt and 1/4 teaspoon pepper. Place layer of sauce in large shallow baking dish; arrange veal over sauce. Place slice of mozzarella over each cutlet. Pour remaining sauce over all. Bake at 325 degrees for 1 hour. Serve with spaghetti.

Pat Sickinger, W and M Chm.
Beta Tau No. 4835
Eau Claire, Wisconsin

SEVEN-LAYER SANDWICH CAKE

21   4 x 3 3/4-in. slices bread
Softened butter
Tuna Filling
Deviled Ham Filling
Chicken Filling
2 8-oz. packages cream cheese,
*   softened*
1/4 c. sour cream

Trim crusts from bread. Place 3 slices bread side by side on serving platter; spread with

butter. Spread with half the Tuna Filling. Spread another 3 slices bread with butter; place, buttered sides down, on Tuna Filling. Spread tops of bread with butter, then cover with half the Deviled Ham Filling. Spread 3 more slices bread with butter; place, buttered sides down, on ham filling. Spread tops of bread with butter; cover with half the Chicken Filling. Repeat with three more layers of bread and remaining fillings. Butter last 3 slices of bread; place, buttered sides down, to form top of loaf. Blend cream cheese and sour cream. Frost sides and top of loaf with cake decorating tubes, piping on fluting. Garnish with slices of sweet gherkins, cherry tomato roses, radish roses, carrot or pimento. Chill until serving time.

Tuna Filling

1   6 1/2-oz. can tuna
1/3 c. drained sweet pickle relish
2 tbsp. finely chopped radish
1/4 tsp. celery seed
1/4 c. mayonnaise

Drain and flake tuna. Combine all ingredients; chill well.

Deviled Ham Filling

1   4 1/2-oz. can deviled ham
1/3 c. drained sweet pickle relish
1/4 c. minced celery
1 tbsp. grated Parmesan cheese
1 tbsp. catsup
1 tbsp. mayonnaise

Combine all ingredients; chill well.

Chicken Filling

1 c. minced cooked chicken
1/3 c. drained sweet pickle relish
1/4 c. chopped pecans
1 tbsp. grated onion
1/4 tsp. curry powder
1/4 c. mayonnaise

Combine all ingredients; chill well.

ROAST VENISON IN COFFEE

1 venison roast
Cloves of garlic, slivered
Onions, slivered
1 c. vinegar
2 c. coffee
Salt and pepper to taste

Cut slits in venison; insert garlic and onion slivers. Pour vinegar over venison; marinate for 24 to 48 hours, turning occasionally. Brown venison on all sides in Dutch oven. Pour coffee over venison; add 2 cups water. Simmer for 4 hours or until venison is tender. Season well with salt and pepper. Simmer for 20 minutes longer.

Sandye Hedges
Alpha Phi No. 3431
Bentonville, Arkansas

STUFFED VENISON STEAKS

4 thick venison steaks
Salt and pepper to taste
Red pepper to taste
1 clove of garlic, halved
Prepared mustard
1/2 c. chopped green onion
1/2 c. chopped green pepper
1/2 c. diced celery
1/2 c. chopped onion
1/4 c. margarine
2 c. bread crumbs
1 egg, slightly beaten
1/4 c. cooking sherry

Slit steaks on sides; season with salt, pepper and red pepper. Rub with garlic and mustard. Let stand for several hours. Saute vegetables in half the margarine until limp. Add bread crumbs and egg. Stuff each steak with dressing mixture. Hold steaks together by sewing ends or secure with toothpicks. Brown each steak in remaining margarine until golden brown; place in baking dish. Pour sherry over steaks. Bake for about 1 hour at 350 degrees or until tender. Yield: 4 servings.

Edna Dilly
Xi Psi X-2736
Crowley, Louisiana

Seafood

With so much emphasis on creativity by women today, it is only
natural that culinary creativity should show itself in these pages on
gourmet Seafood recipes. Beta Sigma Phis were particularly enthusiastic
in sharing their prized specialities. Several of these recipes, such as
the one for Octopus with Red Wine Sauce, from Canada, border
on the exotic. Other exciting and original recipes are Baked Turtle
and Fried Marinated Frog Legs.

Beta Sigma Phis from all over the world submitted dozens of succulent
crab, lobster, shrimp and scallop recipes for all of us to share.
Each one is different, each one a delight to explore and compare.
And, each one is sure to draw a bounty of compliments.

Whether the mention of seafood evokes memories of a New England
shoreline or a seaside dinner in the glow of a late summer's sun, it
almost invariably calls to mind a savory sweetness that may be explored
in dishes as delicate as a quiche or as hearty as a gumbo. The following
selection of recipes offers the seafood lover several intriguing ideas —
some, old favorites, and others, interesting innovations.

BAKED FLOUNDER FILLETS WITH SHRIMP SAUCE

3 lb. flounder fillets
2 1/4 c. milk
1 1/2 tsp. salt
1/8 tsp. pepper
1/2 c. butter or margarine
1/2 c. all-purpose flour
1/2 lb. process sharp Cheddar
* cheese, coarsely grated*
1/2 c. lemon juice or sherry
1 lb. cleaned cooked shrimp
Paprika

Preheat oven to 350 degrees. Roll up each fillet; stand rolled fillets on end in 12 x 8 x 2-inch baking dish. Pour milk over fish. Sprinkle with salt and pepper. Bake, uncovered, for about 30 minutes or until easily flaked with fork but still moist. Remove from oven; turn oven switch to broil. Remove fish from baking dish; pour milk into large measuring cup to use for sauce. Return fish to baking dish. Melt butter in double boiler. Stir in flour. Stir in milk gradually. Cook until thickened, stirring constantly. Add cheese; stir until melted. Add lemon juice and shrimp. Pour sauce over baked fish. Sprinkle with paprika. Brown quickly under broiler. Two and 1/2 cups canned shrimp may be substituted for fresh shrimp.

Marilyn R. Stephens, VP
Preceptor Gamma
Manchester, Connecticut

BATTER-FRIED FLOUNDER

1 c. flour
1/4 tsp. salt
1 tbsp. dry yeast
6 tbsp. warm water
6 tbsp. beer
1 tbsp. olive oil
1 1/2 lb. flounder

Place flour and salt in warm bowl. Make a well; add yeast, water, beer and oil. Mix well. Cover; place in warm place for 2 to 4 hours. Cut flounder into serving pieces; dredge with additional flour. Dip in batter, draining off excess. Fry in deep fat at 350 degrees until brown.

Elaine Schweter
Xi Zeta Beta X2680
Parma, Ohio

BLUE FLOUNDER

1 c. bread crumbs
2 tsp. chopped parsley
3 tbsp. grated cheese
1/2 tsp. paprika
6 flounder steaks
Creamy bleu cheese or onion
* dressing*

Combine crumbs, parsley, cheese and paprika. Dip flounder into dressing. Dip into crumb mixture; place in buttered baking dish. Bake, uncovered, at 500 degrees for 15 minutes or until flounder flakes easily, depending upon thickness of steaks. Garnish with lemon slices and parsley. Yield: 6 servings.

Bettie Bogarte
Preceptor Delta XP356
Salt Lake City, Utah

FANCY FLOUNDER

4 tbsp. green pepper, chopped
4 tbsp. celery, chopped
1 sm. onion, chopped
2 tbsp. butter
1 1/2 c. flaked crab meat
1 1/2 c. diced shrimp
1 tsp. thyme
Salt and pepper to taste
3/4 c. salad dressing
1/2 c. bread crumbs
4 flounder fillets
1/4 c. melted butter
Lemon juice

Saute pepper, celery and onion in butter in large skillet; remove from heat. Stir in crab meat, shrimp, thyme, salt and pepper; blend well. Add salad dressing and 1/4 cup bread crumbs; mix well. Cut pocket in each fillet. Stuff fillets with shrimp mixture; secure openings. Place fillets in greased baking dish. Sprinkle with melted butter, remaining crumbs and lemon juice. Bake at 350 degrees for 30 minutes or until golden brown. Serve garnished with lemon slices. Yield: 4 servings.

Pamela Lehman, Pres.
Alpha Epsilon Delta, No. 7477
Booker, Texas

SEVICHE

Flounder or halibut fillets,
*   thinly sliced*
Fresh lime juice
1 lg. tomato
1 green pepper
1 sweet red pepper
3/4 c. chopped onion
1 tsp. parsley
1 clove of garlic, pressed
1 or 2 dashes of hot sauce
Vinegar
Salt and pepper to taste
Sugar

Arrange fillets side by side on tray; cover with lime juice. Let stand for 6 to 7 hours in refrigerator. Peel tomato; chop finely. Chop green pepper and red pepper. Combine chopped vegetables. Add parsley, garlic and hot sauce to chopped mixture; add enough vinegar to just cover vegetables. Season with salt, pepper and small amount of sugar. Drain fillets; arrange on serving platter. Spread chopped mixture over top. Serve cold.

Jane Selvig, VP
Xi Delta X0753
Juneau, Alaska

POACHED FISH CHABLIS

1 lb. flounder, sole, haddock or cod
1 med. onion, chopped
1 c. Chablis
Salt and pepper to taste

Butter
3 tbsp. flour
1/2 c. light cream
Grated Swiss and Parmesan cheese

Layer flounder and onion in baking dish. Pour Chablis over all; sprinkle with salt and pepper. Dot with butter. Cover with foil. Bake at 375 degrees for 20 minutes. Remove from oven; drain and reserve liquid. Melt 3 tablespoons butter in saucepan; blend in flour. Add reserved liquid, stirring constantly. Stir in cream. Cook and stir until thickened. Pour over flounder. Sprinkle cheeses over flounder. Bake in 425-degree oven until cheese browns and melts.

Joanne Cicco, Treas.
Iota Upsilon No. 7073
Pittsburgh, Pennsylvania

FILLET OF FLOUNDER VERONIQUE

6 flounder fillets
1 tbsp. minced onion
1 tsp. lemon juice
1/2 c. dry white wine
2 tbsp. butter
2 tbsp. flour
1 c. light cream
Salt and pepper to taste
1 c. seedless white grapes
1/4 c. salted whipped cream

Place fillets in large baking dish; do not overlap. Sprinkle with minced onion and lemon juice; pour wine over fillets. Bake, covered, at 350 degrees for 15 minutes. Melt butter; stir in flour until smooth. Add cream; cook, stirring constantly until thickened. Season with salt and pepper. Pour sauce over fillets; sprinkle white grapes over all. Spread with whipped cream; place under broiler to brown lightly. Fillet of sole may be substituted for flounder. Shrimp may be added to sauce, if desired.

Lela L. McBarron
Preceptor Sigma XP847
New Albany, Indiana

SAUCY PORTIONS

> 6 3-oz. frozen breaded fish
>   fillets
> 2 tbsp. oil
> Paprika to taste
> 1 14 1/2-oz. can green asparagus
>   spears
> 1 can frozen cream of shrimp soup
> 1/3 c. milk
> 1/4 c. grated sharp cheese
> 1 tbsp. horseradish

Place fish fillets on greased cookie sheet; drizzle oil over fish. Sprinkle with paprika. Bake at 500 degrees for 15 to 20 minutes or until fish is brown and flakes easily. Heat asparagus; drain. Combine soup and milk; heat until soup is thawed, stirring occasionally. Add cheese and horseradish; blend well. Arrange asparagus over fish. Pour sauce over asparagus; sprinkle with paprika. Garnish with lemon slices. Yield: 6 servings.

BAKED RED SNAPPER KEY WEST

> 1 5-lb. red snapper
> 4 slices bacon
> Salt and pepper to taste
> 1 lg. onion, chopped
> 1 lg. bell pepper, chopped
> 4 cloves of garlic, chopped
> 1 sm. bottle stuffed olives
> 1 4-oz. bottle olive oil
> 2 sm. cans tomato paste
> 1 No. 2 can tomatoes
> 2 bay leaves
> 1/2 tsp. oregano
> 1 bunch green onions, chopped

Have snapper dressed and ready for baking. Score 4 cuts in side of snapper; place bacon slice in each cut. Sprinkle snapper with salt and pepper. Place in large pan with deep sides. Combine remaining ingredients; pour over snapper. Add 2 cups water and salt and pepper. Bake at 350 degrees for 1 hour to 1 hour and 30 minutes or until snapper flakes easily with a fork, basting occasionally with sauce and adding water, if needed.

Mary Frances Sands, Pres.
Xi Beta Upsilon X2058
Key West, Florida

PESCADO MAZATLECO

3 or 4 slices red snapper
4 c. water
1 lime, thinly sliced
1 green onion, chopped
1/2 tsp. tarragon
Salt
5 peppercorns
3 whole cloves
Pinch of rosemary
Pinch of cinnamon
1/2 bay leaf
1/4 c. olive oil
1 sm. onion, finely chopped
1 clove of garlic, crushed
1 8-oz. can tomatoes
3/4 tsp. chopped parsley
3 tbsp. white wine
Pinch of coriander
Pepper to taste
1 sm. hot pepper, chopped
1 tbsp. cracker crumbs

Place snapper, water, lime, onion, tarragon, 1/2 teaspoon salt, peppercorns, cloves, rosemary, cinnamon and bay leaf in skillet; bring to a boil. Simmer for about 10 minutes; remove from heat. Heat oil in heavy skillet; saute onion and garlic until onion is transparent. Add tomatoes and parsley; cook for 2 to 3 minutes to blend flavors. Add wine and coriander; remove from heat. Place snapper in greased baking dish; top with tomato mixture, salt and pepper to taste, hot pepper and cracker crumbs. Bake at 425 degrees for about 15 minutes or until fish

flakes easily with a fork. Hot pepper may be omitted, if desired.

Mrs. Gerard W. Longhorn
Xi Gamma Nu X-3736
Vashon, Washington

RAINY DAY FISH BAKE

6 pan-dressed fresh or frozen whiting
2 tsp. salt
Dash of pepper
1 c. chopped parsley
1/4 c. butter or margarine,
   softened
1 egg, beaten
1/4 c. milk
3/4 c. toasted dry bread crumbs
1/2 c. grated Swiss cheese

Thaw frozen fish; sprinkle inside with half the salt and pepper. Add parsley to butter; mix thoroughly. Spread inside of each fish with about 1 tablespoon parsley mixture. Combine egg, milk and remaining salt. Combine crumbs and cheese. Dip fish into egg mixture; roll in crumb mixture. Place on a greased cookie sheet. Sprinkle remaining crumb mixture over top of fish. Bake at 500 degrees for 10 to 15 minutes or until fish flakes easily. Garnish with shredded Swiss cheese, lemon, parsley and tomato slices, if desired. Yield: 6 servings.

95

BROOK TROUT STUFFED WITH CRAB MEAT

Butter
1/2 c. flour
2 cans frozen oyster stew, thawed
1 egg yolk, beaten
2 tsp. minced shallots
1/4 c. minced fresh mushrooms
2 tsp. minced parsley
3 tbsp. white wine
1/2 lb. crab meat
6 trout, split and boned
Salt and pepper to taste
Flour
Lemon wedges

Melt 1/4 cup butter in saucepan; stir in flour and oyster stew. Cook over low heat, stirring, until sauce bubbles and thickens. Cool. Beat in egg yolk gradually. Set aside. Melt 2 tablespoons butter in skillet; saute shallots, mushrooms and parsley for about 5 minutes or until soft. Stir in wine. Boil until wine evaporates. Stir in crab meat and oyster sauce. Keep hot over low heat. Sprinkle trout inside and out with salt and pepper. Roll trout in flour. Melt 3/4 cup butter; spoon 1/2 of the butter over bottom of shallow baking pan. Arrange trout in single layer. Bake at 350 degrees for 20 to 25 minutes or until fish flakes easily. Open trout carefully; fill with crab meat stuffing. Close trout. Heat remaining melted butter until golden brown; spoon over trout. Bake for 5 minutes longer. Serve with lemon wedges.

Carrie Wegner, 1st VP, Ventura Co. Coun.
Xi Mu Eta X2924
Oxnard, California

TROUT ON SKEWERS

Fresh lime or lemon juice
6 med. trout, dressed
Soy sauce
Finely chopped green onion
Wine Baste
Tomato wedges
Lime wedges
Pitted ripe olives
Watercress or fresh herb sprigs

Sprinkle lime juice generously inside trout; sprinkle cavities with soy sauce and onion. Place trout on skewers. Place skewers crosswise over shallow pan so trout is held off bottom. Brush with Wine Baste. Bake at 450 degrees for about 20 minutes, brushing frequently with Wine Baste until fish flakes easily. Garnish ends of skewers with wedges of tomato, lime and ripe olives. Tuck sprigs of watercress at end of skewer.

Wine Baste

1/2 c. Chablis, Sauterne or white
table wine
1/4 c. salad oil
1 tbsp. soy sauce
1 tbsp. lime or lemon juice

Combine all ingredients.

Mrs. John Cardmon
Xi Eta Eta X1956
Orange, California

FILLETS OF TROUT EN PAPILLOTE

4 lake trout
1/2 c. water
1/2 c. tarragon vinegar
1 tsp. salt
1 med. onion, chopped
2 tsp. chopped parsley
2 tbsp. butter
1 chopped green onion
1 can mushroom soup

Place trout in skillet; add water, vinegar, 1/2 teaspoon salt, onion and half the parsley. Poach gently for about 10 minutes. Remove from water; cool. Split trout lengthwise; remove backbones. Melt butter in small skillet; add green onion and remaining salt and parsley. Cook until vegetables are tender. Stir in soup; simmer until heated. Cut four 9 x 11-inch pieces of aluminum foil; grease 1 side of each piece well. Place 1 fillet on each piece of foil on greased side; spread with sauce. Top with another fillet. Sprinkle with chopped parsley. Seal squares. Bake at 400 degrees for about 15 minutes. Serve in foil.

Nan G. Weber, Honorary Member
Beta Sigma Phi International
Farmington, Missouri

HERBED SALMON AND ARTICHOKES

6 med. artichokes
12 sm. carrots, sliced
1/2 c. butter or margarine, melted
1 tsp. Worcestershire sauce
1/2 tsp. seasoned salt
1/2 tsp. thyme leaves, crushed
2 tbsp. minced parsley
1 tbsp. lemon juice
1/4 c. dry vermouth or white wine
6 sm. salmon steaks

Remove 2 to 3 layers of outer artichoke leaves. Cut off stem and top half of each artichoke. Cut into quarters; cook in 2 or 3 inches boiling salted water for 15 to 20 minutes or until tender. Drain; remove chokes. Set artichokes aside; keep warm. Cut carrots into 1-inch diagonal slices. Cook in boiling salted water until crisp-tender. Drain; set aside. Blend butter, seasonings, lemon juice and vermouth. Place salmon in large, shallow baking dish; brush on both sides with half the butter mixture. Cover pan with foil. Bake at 350 degrees for 15 minutes. Uncover pan; arrange artichoke quarters and carrots around salmon. Drizzle remaining butter mixture over vegetables. Bake, uncovered, for about 15 minutes longer or until salmon is done and vegetables are hot.

Photograph for this recipe on page 90.

GOURMET SALMON WITH PARSLEY SAUCE

1 onion, chopped
1 stalk celery, chopped
1 sprig of parsley, chopped
1 carrot, chopped
1 tbsp. salad oil
1/2 bay leaf
1 tsp. salt
1/8 tsp. pepper
1 tbsp. vinegar
1 2 1/2-lb. salmon

Saute onion, celery, parsley and carrot in oil in fish poacher for 2 minutes. Add 2 quarts water, bay leaf, salt, pepper and vinegar; bring to a boil. Wrap salmon in cheesecloth; place in water. Reduce heat; simmer for 30 minutes. Remove salmon; discard cheesecloth. Serve salmon on heated platter garnished with lemon slices and parsley.

Parsley Sauce

1 tbsp. butter
1 tbsp. flour
3/4 tsp. salt
1/16 tsp. pepper
1 c. milk
3 tbsp. chopped parsley

Melt butter in small saucepan over low heat; blend in flour, salt and pepper. Add milk gradually, stirring constantly; bring to a boil. Remove from heat; stir in parsley. Serve immediately with salmon.

Fern Woodruff
Xi Alpha Gamma, XO981
Montrose, Colorado

SALMON LOAF

3 c. canned salmon
1/2 c. bread crumbs
1 egg
1/4 c. light cream
4 tbsp. melted butter
1 tbsp. lemon juice
1 tbsp. minced parsley
1 tsp. minced onion
1/2 tsp. salt
Dash of pepper
Buttered crumbs

Place salmon in large bowl; discard skin and bones. Combine bread crumbs, egg, cream, butter, lemon juice, parsley, onion, salt and pepper with salmon; mix well. Shape mixture into loaf; place in greased baking dish. Bake at 350 degrees for 35 minutes; sprinkle with buttered crumbs. Bake for 5 minutes longer or until crumbs are browned.

Billie Jean Towlen, Publ. Chm.
Preceptor Zeta XP550
Winchester, Virginia

SALMON-STUFFED SOLE WHIRLS

4 med. fillets of sole
1 1-lb. can salmon
Juice of 1 lemon
Butter
1/2 tsp. salt
Freshly ground pepper
1/4 lb. mushrooms, sliced
1 tbsp. minced onion
2 tbsp. flour
1 c. light cream
1/2 tsp. dry dillweed
1 tbsp. chopped parsley

Preheat oven to 350 degrees. Cut fillets of sole in half lengthwise; remove bones. Drain salmon, reserving liquid; pour reserved liquid into shallow baking dish. Flake salmon; spread about 2 tablespoons on each sole fillet. Roll up as for jelly roll; secure with wooden picks. Reserve remaining salmon. Arrange fish rolls in baking dish; sprinkle with lemon juice. Dot each roll with 1/2 teaspoon butter; sprinkle with salt and pepper. Cover with foil. Bake for 20 minutes. Saute mushrooms and onion in 3 tablespoons butter in saucepan for 5 minutes. Stir in flour. Stir in cream gradually; cook, stirring, until sauce is smooth and thickened. Add dillweed and chopped parsley; set aside. Transfer fish rolls to warm serving platter. Drain juices from baking pan into sauce; add reserved flaked salmon. Stir over moderate heat until sauce begins to simmer. Garnish rolls with lemon wedges and parsley. Serve sauce separately. Yield: 4 servings.

CRAB MEAT QUICHE

Flour
6 tbsp. butter
2 tbsp. vegetable shortening
3/4 tsp. salt
1/2 lb. Swiss cheese
1 c. crab meat
1/2 c. cooked shrimp
1 1/2 c. light cream
4 eggs, beaten
Dash of pepper
Dash of cayenne pepper
1/4 tsp. nutmeg
2 tbsp. melted butter
2 tbsp. dry sherry

Blend 1 1/2 cups flour, butter, shortening and 1/4 teaspoon salt. Add 3 tablespoons ice water; toss to form pastry. Knead lightly for several seconds; form into ball. Dust with flour; wrap in waxed paper. Chill for 1 hour. Roll out on floured surface; shape in pie pan. Cut Swiss cheese into 1/4-inch thick slices; place on pastry in pie pan. Add crab meat and shrimp. Combine cream, eggs, 1 tablespoon flour, remaining salt, pepper, cayenne pepper, nutmeg, melted butter and sherry; beat well. Pour over crab meat mixture; refrigerate or freeze. Bring to room temperature. Bake at 375 degrees for 40 minutes or until browned; let stand for 20 minutes before serving. May be baked as soon as prepared.

Ruth C. Hartkopf, Honorary Member
Beta Sigma Phi International
Idaho Falls, Idaho

CRAB MEAT DIVAN

1 10-oz. package frozen
*   asparagus spears*
2 7 1/2-oz. cans crab meat
2/3 c. sour cream
1/2 c. bottled French dressing
2 tsp. finely chopped, fresh parsley
2 hard-cooked eggs, sliced
2 slices American cheese, halved

2 tbsp. seasoned fine bread crumbs
Butter or margarine

Preheat oven to 350 degrees. Prepare asparagus according to package directions; arrange in 4 individual casseroles. Drain and flake crab meat. Combine crab meat, sour cream, French dressing and parsley in bowl; mix well. Pour half the crab meat mixture over asparagus; top with egg slices. Pour remaining crab meat mixture over egg slices; top with cheese slices. Sprinkle with bread crumbs; dot with butter. Bake for 15 minutes or until browned and bubbly.

Carol W. Browning, Pres.
Xi Alpha Pi X1532
Fort Pierce, Florida

CRAB NEWBURG SUPREME

1/4 c. butter
4 tbsp. flour
2 c. light cream
4 egg yolks, slightly beaten
1 1-lb. package frozen crab meat,
*   flaked*
1/2 c. sherry
2 tsp. lemon juice
1/2 tsp. salt
Paprika
Patty shells

Melt butter over direct heat in blazer pan of chafing dish. Blend in flour, 1 tablespoon at a time. Add cream gradually. Cook, stirring, until sauce thickens. Place hot water bath under blazer pan. Stir small amount of hot sauce mixture into egg yolks; return to remaining hot mixture. Cook, stirring constantly, until thickened. Add crab meat, sherry, lemon juice and salt. Heat well. Sprinkle with paprika; serve in patty shells. Yield: 4-6 servings.

Betty Carmichael, Treas.
Xi Epsilon X1361
Wilmington, Delaware

CRAB MORNAY

1/4 c. butter
6 tbsp. flour
1 1/2 c. chicken broth

1 1/2 c. evaporated milk
1 lg. can mushrooms, drained
1 sm. onion, minced
3 tbsp. chopped pimento
1/2 lb. Gruyere cheese, grated
1 tbsp. monosodium glutamate
Salt to taste
Red pepper to taste
Dash of hot sauce
Dash of Worcestershire sauce
1 lb. crab meat
Patty shells

Melt butter in large skillet; stir in flour until smooth. Add broth and milk gradually; cook, stirring constantly, until smooth and thickened. Add mushrooms, onion, pimento, cheese, monosodium glutamate, salt, red pepper, hot sauce and Worcestershire sauce; blend well. Fold in crab meat. Fill patty shells with crab meat mixture.

Vallie Jo Sims, Pres.
Preceptor Delta XP287
Montgomery, Alabama

DEVILED CLAMS

24 shelled clams
Bread crumbs
1 tbsp. minced green onions
1 tbsp. minced parsley
3 tbsp. melted butter
Salt and pepper to taste
Worcestershire sauce to taste
Butter
Velveeta cheese cubes

Chop clams, removing hard parts. Measure clams; add half the amount of bread crumbs. Add green onions, parsley and melted butter. Season with salt, pepper and Worcestershire sauce. Spoon clam mixture into greased clam shells or custard cups. Sprinkle with additional bread crumbs; dot with butter and cheese cubes. Bake at 350 degrees until lightly browned. Three small cans drained minced clams may be substituted for fresh clams, if desired.

Meralda Isabel Brennan, Honorary Member
Beta Sigma Phi International
Shenandoah, Pennsylvania

4 egg yolks
Salt and pepper to taste

Cut lobster into bite-sized pieces; saute in butter in saucepan until just tender. Add sherry; simmer, stirring occasionally, until sherry is just absorbed. Add paprika. Heat 1 1/4 cups cream in top of double boiler over hot water. Beat egg yolks; add remaining cream to egg yolks. Blend well. Stir small amount of hot cream into egg yolk mixture; return to hot cream, stirring constantly until smooth. Stir in lobster; heat through. Serve in chafing dish, if desired.

Thelma Pfeiffer, Pres.
Xi Omega No. 1779
Memphis, Tennessee

LOBSTER CARDINALE SOUFFLE

3 tbsp. butter
1/4 c. chopped shallots
4 tbsp. flour
1 c. fish or chicken stock
1/4 c. whipping cream
6 egg yolks
1 tbsp. tomato paste
2 tbsp. cognac
1 c. lobster, shredded
Salt and pepper to taste
8 egg whites
1/8 tsp. cream of tartar
1/4 c. Parmesan cheese

Preheat oven to 400 degrees. Melt butter in saucepan. Add shallots; cook until softened. Stir in flour; add stock and cream gradually. Cook, stirring constantly until smooth and thickened. Remove from heat. Add egg yolks, one at a time, beating well after each addition. Add tomato paste, cognac, lobster, salt and pepper; blend well. Combine egg whites, pinch of salt and cream of tartar in large bowl; beat until stiff peaks form. Fold egg whites into lobster mixture carefully; pour into greased souffle dish. Sprinkle with Parmesan cheese. Place in oven; reduce heat to 375 degrees immediately. Bake for 25 minutes.

Honey Vickers
Omicron No. 4870
Newark, Delaware

ROCK LOBSTER AMERICAINE

1/4 c. butter
1 clove of garlic, crushed
6 shallots, chopped
3 tomatoes, cored and chopped
1/3 c. brandy
1 c. dry white wine
3 8-oz. packages frozen South
   African rock lobster-tails
Salt and pepper

Melt butter in skillet; saute garlic and shallots until golden. Add tomatoes, brandy and wine. Simmer until sauce is thick. Run frozen lobster-tails under hot water. Cut away underside membrane with kitchen shears. Add lobster-tails to sauce; simmer, spooning sauce over lobster-tails, until meat becomes white. Season to taste with salt and pepper. Garnish with parsley. Serve with chunks of French bread, if desired. Yield: 6 servings.

LOBSTER A LA NEWBURG

1 lb. lobster
4 tbsp. butter
1/2 c. sherry
Dash of paprika
1 1/2 c. cream

LOBSTER COCKTAIL

2 lb. cooked lobster meat
1/2 c. lemon juice
6 lettuce leaves
2 c. shredded lettuce
Creole Cocktail Sauce
Lemon wedges

Cut lobster meat into bite-sized pieces; sprinkle with lemon juice. Place 1 lettuce leaf in each of 6 cocktail glasses; arrange 1/3 cup shredded lettuce over each leaf. Place lobster meat over shredded lettuce. Pour Creole Cocktail Sauce over meat. Garnish with lemon wedges.

Creole Cocktail Sauce

2 tbsp. cornstarch
2/3 c. tomato sauce
1/4 c. tomato paste
Dash of pepper
1 tsp. sugar
Pinch of ground cloves
Dash of hot sauce
3 slices bacon
1/3 c. finely chopped onions
1/2 c. finely chopped celery
1/3 c. finely chopped green pepper

Blend cornstarch and 2 tablespoons cold water. Combine cornstarch paste, 1/4 cup hot water, tomato sauce, tomato paste and seasonings in large pot. Bring to a boil; reduce heat. Simmer for 20 minutes. Cook bacon until crisp in frying pan; remove bacon. Add onions, celery and green pepper to bacon drippings; saute for 5 minutes. Add to tomato mixture. Cook over low heat for 10 minutes. Crumble bacon; add to sauce.

Lauren L. Roberts, Pres.
Theta Mu No. 6248
Key West, Florida

LOBSTER THERMIDOR

2 1 1/2 to 2-lb. lobsters, boiled
1/4 c. butter
1/2 tsp. paprika
1/2 c. sherry

2 tbsp. flour
2 egg yolks
2 c. thin cream
1 1/2 c. sliced mushrooms, sauteed
1/2 c. grated cheese

Split lobster shells lengthwise; remove lobster. Wash shells; drain well. Cut lobster into bite-sized pieces. Melt butter in saucepan; stir in paprika, sherry and lobster. Simmer for 1 minute; sprinkle with flour, stirring to blend well. Beat egg yolks; beat in cream. Add egg yolk mixture to lobster mixture, stirring constantly until smooth and thickened; stir in 1 cup mushrooms. Spoon mixture into lobster shells; top with remaining mushrooms and cheese. Broil 6 inches from source of heat until lightly browned. Yield: 4 servings.

Patricia Cobb, Pres.
Alpha Alpha No. 2332
Blytheville, Arkansas

ROCK LOBSTER SUPREME

6 4-oz. frozen rock lobster-tails
1 3-oz. package cream cheese
1/2 c. heavy cream
1/2 c. butter
3 tbsp. flour
1 1/2 c. milk
1 tsp. salt
1/2 tsp. curry powder
1/4 tsp. paprika

Drop frozen lobster-tails into boiling salted water. Let water reboil; cook for 1 minute. Drain immediately; drench with cold water. Remove meat from shell carefully; reserve shells. Cut meat into bite-sized pieces. Blend cream cheese and cream together well. Melt butter; stir in flour. Add milk gradually, stirring constantly; cook until thickened. Add salt, curry powder, paprika and cream cheese mixture, stirring until sauce is smooth. Add lobster meat; simmer gently until heated through. Refill empty shells with lobster mixture; serve immediately. Yield: 6 servings.

Mrs. Addison Eugene Ford
Alpha Lambda No. 2333
Americus, Georgia

BARBECUED OYSTERS

1 pt. oysters
1 can evaporated milk
1 pkg. pancake mix
Cooking oil
1 lg. jar barbecue sauce
1 c. white wine

Drain oysters. Dip into milk, then into pancake mix. Fry oysters in deep oil until brown. Pour barbecue sauce into large electric skillet; add wine. Bring to a simmer. Add oysters; stir until coated. Simmer until oysters are of desired doneness.

Mary Johnson, Rec. Sec.
Epsilon Alpha No. 7047
Colquitt, Georgia

SCALLOPED OYSTERS

1 qt. oysters
2 c. saltine cracker crumbs
1/2 c. butter
1 tbsp. lemon juice
1/4 tsp. salt
1/4 tsp. pepper
1/2 c. (about) cream

Drain oysters; reserve liquor. Wash oysters; drain. Cover bottom of buttered shallow baking dish with half the crumbs; add half the oysters. Melt half the butter; stir in lemon juice. Pour butter mixture over oysters. Add remaining crumbs, then remaining oysters to baking dish. Sprinkle with salt and pepper; dot with remaining butter. Strain 1/4 cup reserved liquor; add cream. Heat through; pour over oysters. Bake at 425 degrees for 20 minutes.

Pauline Barrows, Honorary Member
Beta Sigma Phi International
Newport, Maine

OYSTERS BIENVILLE

1 doz. shrimp
1 2-oz. can mushroom stems and
  pieces
1/4 c. butter

3 tbsp. flour
1 clove of garlic, minced
1 tbsp. onion juice
1 tbsp. Worcestershire sauce
1/4 tsp. celery seed
1 tbsp. sherry
1 1/2 pt. oysters
Grated Parmesan cheese
Paprika
Salt to taste

Cook shrimp in boiling water for 5 minutes. Drain shrimp; reserve liquid. Chop shrimp. Drain mushrooms; add enough reserved shrimp liquid to mushroom liquid to make 3/4 cup liquid. Melt butter; stir in flour, garlic, onion juice, Worcestershire sauce and celery seed. Add mushroom liquid mixture; cook, stirring, until thickened. Add mushrooms, shrimp and sherry; mix well. Drain oysters; place in shallow pan. Broil until edges just curl; pour off liquid. Sprinkle oysters liberally with Parmesan cheese; cover with mushroom sauce. Sprinkle with paprika; broil for 5 to 8 minutes longer or until bubbly. Season with salt. Yield: 4-6 servings.

Sherry Bullock, Pres.
Theta Gamma No. 8845
Ames, Iowa

COQUILLES SAINT JACQUES

2 lb. scallops
2 c. dry white wine
1 c. water
1 tsp. salt
Several celery tops
Sprigs of parsley
1 sm. onion
1/2 lb. mushrooms
6 tbsp. butter or margarine
1 tsp. lemon juice
1/4 c. flour
2 egg yolks
1/4 c. heavy cream
4 tbsp. dry bread crumbs

Mix scallops, wine, water, salt, celery tops and several parsley sprigs; cook over low heat for about 10 minutes or until scallops are tender. Drain scallops. Strain liquid; reserve. Cut scallops into small pieces. Chop onion, mushrooms and several parsley sprigs fine; cook in 2 tablespoons butter and lemon juice for about 10 minutes. Mix with scallops. Melt remaining butter; stir in flour. Add reserved liquid gradually. Cook, stirring constantly, for about 5 minutes or until sauce thickens. Beat egg yolks slightly; add cream. Stir in small amount of hot sauce slowly, then combine all sauce with egg yolks. Cook over low heat, stirring, for 5 minutes longer or until thick. Stir in scallop mixture; spoon into 6 to 8 baking shells. Sprinkle with crumbs; dot with additional butter. Brown under broiler. Mashed potatoes may be substituted for bread crumbs.

L. Joan Novitsky, Pres.
Kappa Sigma No. 8260
Hershey, Pennsylvania

SCALLOPS WITH CHEESE-BREAD CRUMB TOPPING

1 lb. scallops
1 onion, chopped
1 green pepper, chopped
6 stalks celery, sliced thin
6 mushrooms, sliced thin
2 tbsp. butter or margarine
1 can mushroom soup
Salt and paprika to taste
Nutmeg to taste
Lemon juice to taste
Grated Swiss cheese
Bread crumbs

Cut scallops into smaller pieces if large. Saute onion, green pepper, celery and mushrooms in butter till tender. Add scallops; cook over low heat for several minutes. Mix soup with salt, paprika, nutmeg and lemon juice; heat through. Pour over scallop mixture; mix gently. Spoon into ovenproof dish; cover with generous layer of cheese. Cover with bread crumbs. Bake in 350-degree oven for 25 to 30 minutes or until golden brown. Yield: 6 servings.

Jo Pitfield, Dir.
Puerto Rico, Gamma No. 5816
FPO, New York

SCALLONEGG

1 lb. scallops
1   2-lb. eggplant
1/4 c. fine dry bread crumbs
1/4 c. finely chopped parsley
1/2 tsp. thyme
1/2 tsp. celery salt
1/2 c. margarine or butter
1/3 c. chopped onion

Cut scallops into small pieces. Peel eggplant; chop fine. Combine scallops, bread crumbs, parsley, thyme and celery salt. Melt margarine in large frying pan. Add eggplant and onion; cook until eggplant is just tender. Add scallop mixture; toss lightly. Spoon into greased individual ramekins or casserole immediately; place individual ramekins on baking sheet. Bake at 375 degrees for 30 to 35 minutes or until brown and crisp; serve immediately. Yield: 6 servings.

Wilma Yeary, Past Rec. Sec.
Beta Theta No. 5172
Bagdad, Kentucky

ANN'S SECRET SHRIMP AND RICE

3 tbsp. butter
1 c. rice
3 tbsp. chopped onion
3 c. rose wine
3 chicken bouillon cubes
1/8 tsp. curry powder
1 tsp. monosodium glutamate
1 can Danish shrimp
8 preserved kumquats, sliced

Melt butter in small skillet; add rice. Stir over low heat until rice is golden. Add onion; cook until soft. Add rose wine; bring to a boil. Add bouillon cubes; stir until dissolved. Add curry powder and monosodium glutamate. Cook, covered, over low heat for 15 minutes. Stir well; add shrimp and kumquats. Cook, covered, stirring occasionally, for 15 minutes longer or until the liquid is absorbed but rice is moist.

Ann Waller, Pres.
Xi Nu Omicron X-3917
Henderson, Texas

CANTON PINEAPPLE SHRIMP

1   13 1/2-oz. can pineapple chunks
1/2 lb. large shrimp
Garlic salt
1 tbsp. cooking oil
1 sm. onion, cut in wedges
2 stalks celery, sliced diagonally
1/2 green pepper, sliced
2 tbsp. vinegar
1 tbsp. soy sauce
1 tbsp. cornstarch

Drain pineapple, reserving 1/4 cup syrup. Shell and devein shrimp; wash with cold water. Pat dry. Sprinkle shrimp lightly with garlic salt. Cook in hot oil in skillet just until shrimp turn pink. Add onion. Cover; cook for several minutes or until onion is tender. Add celery and green pepper. Cover; cook for several minutes longer or until vegetables are tender but crisp. Combine reserved pineapple syrup, vinegar, soy sauce, 1/2 cup water and cornstarch. Add to shrimp mixture. Cook, stirring, until sauce thickens and becomes clear. Add pineapple chunks; heat for 5 minutes longer. Yield: 4 servings.

Margaret L. Berry, Pres.
Delta Alpha Psi No. 6869
Inglewood, California

SCAMPI ALLA GRIGLIA

2 lb. large shrimp
1/2 c. butter
1/2 c. olive oil
1 tbsp. lemon juice
1/4 c. finely chopped shallots
1 tbsp. chopped garlic
1 tsp. salt
Freshly ground pepper to taste
4 tbsp. chopped parsley
Lemon wedges

Shell and devein shrimp. Preheat broiler. Melt butter in saucepan over low heat; stir in olive oil, lemon juice, shallots, garlic, salt and pepper. Arrange shrimp in shallow baking dish; pour butter mixture over shrimp, turning to coat well. Broil 3 to 4 inches from source of heat for 5 minutes; turn. Broil for 5 minutes longer. Transfer to heated serving platter; pour sauce over shrimp. Sprinkle with parsley; garnish with lemon quarters.

Ivy Baker Priest, Honorary Member
Beta Sigma Phi International
Sacramento, California

SHRIMP CREOLE

1/2 c. chopped onion
1/2 c. chopped celery
1 clove of garlic, minced
3 tbsp. olive oil
1   1-lb. can tomatoes
1   8-oz. can tomato sauce
1 1/2 tsp. salt
1 tsp. sugar
1/2 tsp. chili powder
1 tbsp. Worcestershire sauce
Dash of hot sauce
1 tsp. cornstarch
1 1/2 lb. fresh cleaned shrimp
1/2 c. chopped green pepper

Cook onion, celery and garlic in hot oil until tender; add tomatoes, tomato sauce and seasonings. Simmer for 45 minutes. Mix cornstarch with 2 teaspoons water; stir into sauce. Cook, stirring constantly, until smooth and thickened. Add shrimp and green pepper. Simmer, covered, for 10 minutes. Serve over rice or in a rice ring.

Robyn Story, Pres.
Lambda Alpha No. 7318
Lakeland, Florida

SHRIMP DE JONGHE

1 lb. fresh shrimp
3/4 c. toasted dry bread crumbs
1/4 c. chopped green onion
1/4 c. chopped parsley
3/4 tsp. crushed tarragon
1/4 tsp. crushed garlic
1/4 tsp. nutmeg
1/4 tsp. salt
Dash of pepper
1/2 c. butter or margarine, melted
1/4 c. sherry (opt.)

Remove shells and sand veins from shrimp. Cook in boiling salted water for about 5 minutes or until shrimp turn pink. Combine crumbs, onion, parsley and seasonings. Add butter and sherry; mix thoroughly. Combine crumb mixture and shrimp; toss lightly. Place about 2/3 cup shrimp mixture into each of 6 greased individual shells or 6-ounce custard cups. Bake at 400 degrees for 10 to 15 minutes or until lightly browned. Yield: 6 servings.

Mrs. Christel Conradi, Pres.
Xi Alpha Beta X1282
Tampa, Florida

JAMBALAYA

2 tsp. salt
1 tsp. hot sauce
1 bay leaf
1 stalk celery with leaves
1 lb. shrimp
1/4 c. butter or margarine
1/2 c. chopped onion
1/2 c. chopped green pepper
1 clove of garlic, minced
1 c. rice
1 1-lb. can tomatoes
3/4 c. bouillon
1 1/2 c. diced cooked ham

Combine 3 cups water, half the salt and half the hot sauce in saucepan. Add bay leaf and celery. Bring to a boil; add shrimp. Return to a boil; cook for 5 minutes. Drain shrimp; cool quickly. Shell and clean shrimp. Melt butter in large skillet. Add onion, green pepper and garlic. Cook until onion is tender but not brown. Stir in rice, tomatoes, bouillon, remaining salt and remaining hot sauce. Bring to a boil quickly. Reduce heat; cover skillet. Simmer for 20 minutes. Add ham; cover. Cook for 10 minutes longer or until liquid is absorbed. Yield: 4-6 servings.

Poultry

Brillat-Savarin, a gourmet chef and noted wit, was once reported
to have said, "The discovery of a new dish does more for the happiness
of man than the discovery of a star." Whether or not this is true
will be known the first time that you prepare one of the
superb recipes in this section on poultry.

Turn your culinary talents toward creating unforgettable dishes
featuring versatile chicken, duck, quail, pheasant and Cornish hens.
Chicken a la Reibman is one of these attractive dishes that you'll want
to serve at your next special luncheon or buffet. Beta Sigma Phis
have shared several taste and eye-appealing recipes for turkey,
roasted whole, sliced, diced and cubed, and all delicious.

Italian, Armenian, French and Japanese cookery have been
included in this unusual and diverse collection of elegant main and
side dishes prepared from poultry. Adding an extra measure of flair and
elegance to your dishes are special sauces and stuffings, many of them
created by a Beta Sigma Phi for her family — and for you. These
recipes offer you a chance to serve your family's favorite foods
in a new way — and to earn yourself adulation and praise.

CHICKEN ELEGANTE

1/3 c. flour
2 1/2 tsp. salt
1/8 tsp. pepper
3/4 tsp. tarragon, rosemary or thyme
3 chicken breasts, halved
1/3 c. butter
1 c. sliced fresh mushrooms
1 c. sour cream
1 tbsp. chopped chives

Combine flour and seasonings. Dredge chicken breasts in seasoned flour. Heat butter in frypan over moderate heat. Brown chicken in butter, turning to brown evenly on both sides. Cover; reduce heat. Cook over low heat for 30 to 40 minutes or until chicken is tender. Uncover; cook for about 5 minutes longer or until crisp. Remove chicken from pan. Add mushrooms to pan drippings in frypan. Saute for 2 to 3 minutes or until tender. Remove pan from heat; stir in sour cream and chives. Heat only to serving temperature. Pour sauce into hot serving dish; arrange chicken breasts on top. Yield: 6 servings.

Photograph for this recipe on page 106.

BREAST OF CHICKEN WITH WILD RICE

1 6-oz. package long grain and wild rice mix
4 lg. boned chicken breasts
Salt and pepper to taste
1/4 c. butter or margarine
1/2 c. chopped celery
1/4 lb. fresh mushrooms, sliced
1 can cream of chicken soup
2 tbsp. chopped pimento
3/4 c. sauterne

Prepare rice mix according to package directions in buffet casserole inset. Skin chicken breasts; cut in half lengthwise. Season chicken breasts lightly with salt and pepper. Brown chicken slowly in butter in frypan.

Arrange chicken breasts on cooked rice. Saute celery and mushrooms in drippings in frypan; add soup and pimento. Add sauterne gradually, stirring until smooth. Heat to boiling point. Pour sauce over chicken. Set control at 350 degrees. Cook for 40 to 45 minutes with cover vent open. 1 4-ounce can drained sliced mushrooms may be substituted for fresh mushrooms. Yield: 8 servings.

Fern Holliday, Rec. Sec.
Kappa Iota No. 3651
Vallejo, California

CHICKEN A LA REIBMAN

4 chicken breasts
2 tbsp. butter
2 tbsp. olive oil
1 jar chestnuts in syrup
4 cloves of garlic, minced
3/4 lb. fresh mushrooms, sliced
1 c. chicken broth
Juice of 1 lemon
2 tbsp. cornstarch
3/4 c. Madeira

Remove skin and bones from chicken; split. Saute lightly in butter and oil in skillet until meat is white. Place chicken in casserole. Drain chestnuts, reserving small amount of liquid. Combine garlic, mushrooms and chestnuts in pan drippings in skillet. Saute lightly. Add chicken broth, lemon juice and reserved syrup. Dissolve cornstarch in Madeira; add to mushroom mixture. Cook over low heat, stirring, until thickened. Pour sauce over chicken. Bake at 350 degrees for 30 to 35 minutes. Serve over buttered noodles. Yield: 4 servings.

Jeanette F. Reibman, Honorary Member
Beta Sigma Phi International
Scranton, Pennsylvania

CHICKEN ROLLS

10 oz. mild Cheddar cheese
4 chicken breasts, boned
2 eggs, beaten
3/4 c. cracker crumbs
1/3 c. margarine

1 chicken bouillon cube
1 c. boiling water
1/2 c. chopped onion
1/2 c. chopped green pepper
2 tbsp. flour
1 tsp. salt
1/4 tsp. pepper
2 c. cooked white rice
1 c. cooked wild rice
1 3-oz. can sliced mushrooms,
   drained

Cut cheese in 8 equal sticks. Cut chicken breasts in half. Roll chicken breast around cheese stick. Dip in egg and then in crumbs; brown in 1/2 of the margarine. Dissolve bouillon cube in water. Cook onion and green pepper in remaining margarine until tender. Add flour, seasonings and bouillon; stir until smooth. Add rice and mushrooms. Pour into casserole; top with chicken rolls. Bake, uncovered, at 400 degrees for 20 minutes. Yield: 8 servings.

Jo Laughlin, Corr. Sec.
Xi Alpha Nu X1786
Richland, Washington

DIET CHICKEN BREASTS CACCIATORE

6 chicken breasts
Salt and pepper to taste
Paprika to taste
1 onion, chopped
1 c. tomato juice
1 tsp. oregano
1/2 tsp. crushed bay leaf
1 to 2 green peppers, sliced
1 can mushrooms

Remove skin from chicken breasts; season with salt, pepper and paprika. Brown onion and chicken in Teflon pan. Add tomato juice; sprinkle with oregano and bay leaf. Simmer, covered, for 40 minutes or until tender, adding tomato juice if necessary. Add green peppers and mushrooms; cook for 15 minutes longer.

Donna Fox, Serv. Chm.
Preceptor Alpha Theta XP-555
Houston, Texas

GOURMET RIPE OLIVE POULET

6 whole chicken breasts, boned
2 tbsp. chopped chives
1 1/2 c. pitted California ripe
   olives
Garlic salt to taste
2 tbsp. butter, melted
2 tsp. cornstarch
2 tbsp. lemon juice
2 4 3/4-oz. jars strained apricots
3 tbsp. brandy

Preheat oven to 400 degrees. Place chicken breasts, skin side down, on flat surface. Sprinkle each breast with 1 teaspoon chives. Arrange 4 olives in center of each breast; fold meat around olives. Cut remaining olives in half; set aside. Fasten breasts with small skewers; sprinkle with garlic salt. Pour butter into baking dish. Place chicken, skin side down, in melted butter. Bake for 30 minutes. Combine cornstarch, lemon juice and apricots in saucepan. Bring to a boil, stirring frequently. Stir brandy into apricot sauce. Turn chicken skin side up; spoon sauce over chicken. Bake for 15 minutes longer; add remaining halved olives. Bake for 5 minutes longer. Yield: 6 servings.

GLAZED BUTTERFLY CHICKEN

8 slices bacon, diced
1 lg. onion, chopped
2 tbsp. flour
1 tbsp. curry powder
1 tbsp. sugar
1 tsp. salt
1 tsp. A-1 sauce
2 beef bouillon cubes
3 tbsp. lemon juice
1 lg. jar baby food applesauce and
    apricots
6 tbsp. butter
1 tsp. ground ginger
8 whole chicken breasts
1/4 c. flaked coconut

Cook bacon in frypan; remove bacon. Stir in onion; saute onion until soft. Blend in flour, curry powder, sugar, salt and A-1 sauce; cook until mixture bubbles. Stir in bouillon cubes, 1 cup water, lemon juice and baby food. Bring to a boil, stirring. Simmer, uncovered, for 15 minutes. Sauce may be made ahead and kept refrigerated for as long as 2 days. Melt butter in shallow baking dish; stir in ginger. Roll chicken in ginger mixture; arrange, skin side up, in baking dish. Spoon sauce over chicken. Bake at 350 degrees for 1 hour and 20 minutes. Sprinkle coconut on chicken. Bake for 10 minutes longer.

Sandy Kueser, Pres.
Iota Kappa No. 8562
Kanopolis, Kansas

PARMESAN CHICKEN

1 c. soda cracker crumbs
1 c. grated Parmesan cheese
1 tsp. salt
3 tsp. parsley flakes
6 chicken breasts, halved
1/2 c. melted butter
2 to 3 tbsp. sesame seed

Combine crumbs, cheese, salt and parsley flakes; blend well. Dip chicken into butter; roll in crumb mixture. Arrange chicken in foil-lined shallow baking dish. Dot chicken with additional butter; sprinkle with sesame seed. Bake, covered, at 350 degrees for 30 minutes; remove cover. Bake for 30 minutes longer.

Kay Smith
Preceptor Alpha Delta XP417
Bakersfield, California

LEMONADE CHICKEN

8 lg. chicken breasts
Salt and pepper to taste
1 6-oz. can frozen lemonade
    concentrate, thawed
6 c. crushed corn flakes
1 stick butter
1 clove of garlic

Wash chicken; pat dry. Sprinkle with salt and pepper on all sides. Place chicken in bowl; pour in lemonade, thoroughly coating chicken. Let stand for 1 hour at room temperature. Drain; coat chicken in crumbs. Melt butter. Brush a shallow pan with butter. Cut garlic clove; rub pan thoroughly. Discard used clove. Place chicken in pan in single layer. Drizzle melted butter over chicken. Bake at 350 degrees for 1 hour or until chicken is easily pierced with fork and browned. Serve on platter garnished with parsley sprigs, or on a bed of wild rice. Yield: 6-8 servings.

Nancy B. Rue, Pres.
Xi Beta Sigma X-1925
Auburn, Indiana

SHRIMP-STUFFED CHICKEN

3 whole chicken breasts
1 1/4 c. chopped shrimp
1/4 c. chopped celery
1 1/2 tsp. salt
1/4 c. green onions
1/2 c. softened butter
1 c. mushroom soup
1/2 c. chicken broth
1/2 c. cooking sherry

Bone and halve chicken breasts. Combine shrimp, celery, salt, green onions and butter. Divide shrimp mixture evenly among chicken breasts; roll up, securing with wooden picks. Combine mushroom soup, broth and sherry; blend well. Arrange chicken roll-ups in shallow baking dish; pour sherry sauce over roll-ups. Bake at 350 degrees for 1 hour or until chicken is tender. Serve over wild rice, if desired.

Marilyn McGinley
Pi No. 2421
Williston, North Dakota

BREAST OF CAPON AU BOURBON

2 capon breasts
Butter
6 tbsp. bourbon
1 tsp. salt
1/4 tsp. white pepper
4 med. mushrooms, sliced
2 c. cream
1 tsp. flour

Split breasts in half lengthwise. Melt 6 tablespoons butter in 10-inch skillet; cook breasts in butter for 8 minutes. Turn; cook for 8 minutes longer. Stir in bourbon. Cook, tightly covered, for 15 minutes over low heat. Add salt, white pepper, mushrooms and cream to liquid in skillet; bring to a rolling boil. Remove breasts to heated platter; keep warm. Boil cream mixture rapidly for 5 minutes. Combine flour with 1 teaspoon butter; blend to a paste. Stir flour mixture into cream mixture; boil, stirring constantly, for 3 minutes longer. Return breasts to sauce; simmer for several minutes. Serve with rice.

Mrs. David J. Wright, Soc. Com.
Xi Beta Pi X2384
Des Moines, Iowa

BREAST OF CAPON KIEV

4 lg. capon breasts
Salt and pepper
Monosodium glutamate
1/2 lb. butter
1 or 2 cloves of garlic, minced
1 1/2 tbsp. chopped chives
1 1/2 tbsp. chopped parsley
1 tsp. crumbled rosemary
1/4 tsp. white pepper

1 can cream potato soup
2 tbsp. sherry
1/4 c. cream
Flour
1 egg, well beaten

Split breasts in half; skin and bone. Sprinkle breasts with salt, pepper and monosodium glutamate. Pound breasts between sheets of waxed paper until thin. Combine butter, garlic, chives, parsley, 1 teaspoon salt, rosemary and white pepper; blend well. Divide butter mixture into 8 portions. Place on capon breasts. Roll breasts, enclosing butter completely; secure with string. Chill. Combine soup, sherry and cream in blender container; blend until smooth. Pour into saucepan; heat through. Dip capon rolls into flour; dip into egg. Dip into flour. Fry in deep fat at 350 degrees until golden. Arrange rolls in shallow baking dish. Bake in preheated 350-degree oven for 30 minutes or until tender; spoon sauce over rolls. Serve immediately. May be served over wild rice, if desired.

Odilia Virgin, Pres.
Pi Phi No. 8325
O'Fallon, Illinois

CHICKEN MARENGO

8 lg. chicken pieces
1/4 c. oil
1 tsp. salt
1 can tomatoes
1 tbsp. tomato paste
1/2 c. sherry
2 c. sliced mushrooms
1/2 bay leaf
1 clove of garlic, pressed
1 sm. can cocktail onions, drained
1 can ripe olives, drained

Brown chicken slowly in oil in skillet; sprinkle with salt. Add tomatoes, tomato paste, sherry, mushrooms, bay leaf and garlic. Cover; simmer for 15 to 20 minutes or until chicken is tender. Uncover; add onions and olives. Simmer for about 5 minutes longer. Yield: 6 servings.

Mrs. William A. Glaze, Pres.
Xi Preceptor Omicron XP415
Littleton, Colorado

CHICKEN CROQUETTES

3 tbsp. butter or margarine
1/4 c. flour
1/2 c. milk
1/2 c. chicken broth
1 tbsp. parsley flakes
1 tsp. lemon juice
1 tbsp. minced onion
1/8 tsp. nutmeg
1/8 tsp. pepper
1/8 tsp. paprika
1/4 tsp. salt
2 c. minced cooked chicken
1 c. fine corn flake crumbs
2 eggs, beaten
3 tbsp. water

Melt butter in skillet; blend in flour. Add milk and broth gradually. Cook, stirring, until mixture bubbles and thickens. Cook, stirring constantly, for 1 minute longer. Add parsley flakes, lemon juice, onion and seasonings. Cool. Add chicken; chill well. Shape chicken mixture with wet hands into 8 balls. Roll in crumbs. Shape balls into cones, handling lightly. Combine egg and water; beat well. Dip balls into egg mixture; roll in crumbs. Fry in 365-degree deep fat for about 3 minutes or until golden brown. Drain on paper towels; serve with green peas in cream sauce, if desired. Yield: 4 servings.

Nancy L. Donahoe
Beta No. 471
Rogers, Arkansas

CHICKEN DIVAN

1/4 tsp. nutmeg
2/3 c. white sauce
1/2 c. hollandaise sauce
1/2 c. whipped cream
3 tbsp. sherry
1 tsp. Worcestershire sauce
1 1/2 pkg. frozen broccoli
3/4 lb. sliced cooked chicken
1 c. grated Parmesan cheese

Stir nutmeg into white sauce. Combine white sauce, hollandaise sauce and whipped cream; add sherry and Worcestershire sauce. Cook broccoli according to package direc-

tions; drain. Arrange broccoli on greased deep ovenproof platter; place chicken on broccoli. Pour sauce over chicken; sprinkle generously with cheese. Place under broiler about 5 inches from source of heat. Broil until brown and bubbly, watching carefully. Yield: 4 servings.

Angela Shrawder, Prog. Chm.
Preceptor Delta Rho XP1027
Hemet, California

CHICKEN TETRAZZINI

1 3-lb. frying chicken
Melted butter
1/3 c. sifted flour
2 c. light cream
3 tsp. salt
4 tbsp. sauterne
1 4-oz. package broad noodles
2 tbsp. grated Parmesan cheese
1/2 lb. mushrooms, sliced
Pepper to taste
1 clove of garlic, slivered

Steam chicken in 2 cups boiling water for 1 hour or until tender. Drain chicken; reserve broth. Bone chicken; cut into thin slices. Combine 1/4 cup melted butter with flour in saucepan; stir in cream gradually, stirring constantly until smooth and thickened. Add 1 cup reserved broth, stirring constantly until smooth. Add 1 1/2 teaspoons salt and sauterne. Simmer, stirring constantly, for 5 minutes. Prepare noodles according to package directions, using unsalted water. Cook until just tender; drain well. Place noodles in bowl; stir in 1 teaspoon salt, 1 tablespoon melted butter, cheese and 1 cup cream sauce. Saute mushrooms in 2 tablespoons melted butter in medium skillet for 5 minutes; stir occasionally. Season with 1/2 teaspoon salt, pepper and garlic. Cook, stirring, for several minutes longer. Pour noodle mixture into greased large shallow baking dish. Spoon mushrooms over noodles; pour small amount of cream sauce over mushrooms. Arrange chicken slices over top; sprinkle with additional salt and pepper. Pour remaining sauce over chicken. Sprinkle with additional Parmesan cheese. Bake at 350 degrees for 30 minutes. Broil 5 to 6 inches from source of heat for 5 minutes or until golden. Yield: 6 servings.

Marty McMaster, Corr. Sec.
Preceptor Alpha Omega XP599
San Jose, California

CHICKEN STRATA

1/4 c. butter
1/2 lb. mushrooms
9 slices bread
4 c. diced cooked chicken
1 8-oz. can water chestnuts, sliced
1/2 c. mayonnaise
9 slices sharp process cheese
4 eggs, well beaten
2 c. milk
1 tsp. salt
1 can mushroom soup
1 can celery soup
Buttered bread crumbs

Melt butter in saucepan; saute mushrooms for 3 to 4 minutes. Remove crust from bread. Line large shallow buttered pan with bread; top with chicken. Spoon mushrooms and water chestnuts over chicken. Dot with mayonnaise; top with cheese. Combine eggs, milk and salt in small bowl. Pour over cheese. Combine soups; spread over top. Cover with foil; refrigerate overnight. Bake at 350 degrees for 45 minutes. Sprinkle with crumbs; bake for 15 minutes longer or until brown.

Mrs. James Schwartz, Past Pres.
Xi Beta Phi X2102
Kokomo, Indiana

COLD CHICKEN WITH GINGER

Salt
1 sm. piece of gingerroot
1 4-lb. chicken
3/4 c. salad oil
1 clove of garlic, minced
1/3 c. minced gingerroot
1/3 c. minced green onions
1/4 tsp. monosodium glutamate
1 tbsp. chopped parsley

Bring 2 quarts water, 1 tablespoon salt and piece of gingerroot to a boil; add chicken. Reduce heat. Simmer, covered, over lowest heat for 25 minutes; turn chicken over. Simmer, covered, over lowest heat for 25 minutes longer. Remove chicken from broth; rinse in cold water. Drain well. Freeze broth for later use, if desired. Skin and bone chicken; cut into 1 x 2-inch pieces. Place chicken in serving dish. Heat oil; add 1/2 teaspoon salt, stirring until salt is dissolved. Cool. Stir garlic, minced gingerroot, green onions and monosodium glutamate into oil mixture; blend well. Pour over chicken; garnish with parsley. Yield: 6 servings.

Cindy Kawabata, Corr. Sec.
Gamma Beta No. 7778
Seattle, Washington

COUNTRY CAPTAIN

1/4 c. flour
1 tsp. salt
1/4 tsp. pepper
1 2 1/2-lb. frying chicken
4 to 5 tbsp. butter
1/3 c. chopped onion
1/3 c. chopped green pepper
1 clove of garlic, crushed
1 1/2 tsp. curry powder
1/2 tsp. dried thyme
1 1-lb. can stewed tomatoes
3 tbsp. dried currants
Blanched toasted almonds
Chutney

Mix flour, salt and pepper together. Cut chicken into serving pieces; coat with flour mixture. Heat butter in large heavy skillet until hot; add chicken, browning well on all sides. Add additional butter if necessary. Remove chicken from skillet; set aside. Add onion, green pepper, garlic, curry powder and thyme to pan drippings in skillet. Cook for several minutes over low heat, scraping up brown particles in skillet. Add tomatoes. Return chicken to skillet, skin side up; cover. Cook slowly for 20 to 30 minutes or until tender. Stir in currants carefully. Serve with blanched toasted almonds and chuntney.

Elsie M. Price
Exemplar Preceptor Mu XP829
Luray, Virginia

COLD CURRIED CHICKEN

1/4 c. butter
1 5-lb. roasting chicken,
*   disjointed*
2 tbsp. cognac
1 lg. Bermuda onion
1 1/2 tsp. salt
Freshly ground pepper to taste
1 tbsp. curry powder
1 c. heavy cream

Melt butter in Dutch oven; cook chicken until brown. Warm cognac; pour over chicken pieces. Ignite at once. Peel and slice onion. Place onion slices over chicken when flame dies. Sprinkle with salt and pepper. Pour in 1/4 cup water. Cover; simmer for about 1 hour or until meat falls from bone. Sprinkle curry powder over chicken. Cool in stock. Remove skin and bones; arrange chicken in square or oblong dish. Stir cream into chicken stock; bring just to boiling point. Strain over chicken in dish. Cool. Chill in refrigerator for several hours or until jelled. Unmold and garnish as desired. Yield: 6 servings.

Floretta W. Hanson, Pres.
Kappa Zeta No. 6850
Sumterville, Florida

CURRIED CHICKEN A LA TRINIDAD

1 chicken
Salt and pepper to taste
2 med. onions, sliced
2 tomatoes, thinly sliced
4 tbsp. catsup
2 tbsp. mustard
Garlic powder to taste
1/2 c. cooking oil
1 tbsp. curry powder
4 potatoes, cubed
Cooked white rice

Cut chicken into serving pieces; sprinkle with salt and pepper. Place in shallow casserole. Cover with onions, tomatoes, catsup, mustard and garlic. Let marinate for about 1

hour. Heat oil in large skillet until almost burning. Mix curry with water to form a paste, then add to hot oil, stirring for 30 seconds. Add chicken ,1 piece at a time. Cook over high heat until chicken is cooked through, adding water to prevent sticking. Add potatoes; cook until potatoes are well done and chicken almost falls off bones. Serve over rice.

Fay Scordato, Treas.
Xi Alpha Xi X3519
Cantonment, Florida

CHICKEN SUPREME IN RAISIN SAUCE

1 tsp. paprika
1/2 tsp. instant coffee
1 1/2 tsp. seasoned salt
1/4 c. flour
1 4-lb. fryer chicken, disjointed
1/4 c. shortening
1 10 1/2-oz. can bouillon
2 sliced stalks celery
1 sliced onion
1 lg. carrot, sliced
1/2 c. seedless raisins

Combine paprika, coffee, salt and flour; coat chicken with seasoned flour. Brown chicken in hot shortening in skillet over low heat on

both sides. Drain off excess fat. Add bouillon and vegetables. Cover tightly; simmer over low heat for about 1 hour or until chicken is tender. Remove chicken to chafing dish; keep warm. Strain out and discard vegetables. Measure remaining liquid; skim off excess fat. Add additional water or bouillon, if necessary, to make 1 1/4 cups liquid. Add to chicken. Add raisins. Correct seasonings, if necessary. Heat gently for about 5 to 10 minutes longer. May thicken sauce slightly with small amount of cornstarch mixed with cold water, if desired. Yield: 4 servings.

CHICKEN LIVERS PORTUGAL

  5 tbsp. butter or margarine
  1 clove of garlic, minced
  2 tbsp. minced onion
  6 tbsp. all-purpose flour
  1 c. beef broth
  1/2 tsp. salt
  Dash of pepper
  1 lb. chicken livers
  3 tbsp. Madeira or Marsala

Melt 3 tablespoons butter in heavy skillet; add garlic and onion. Cook until onion is tender, but not brown. Blend in 2 tablespoons flour. Add beef broth; cook and stir till sauce is smooth and thickened. Combine remaining flour, salt and pepper; coat livers with flour mixture. Melt remaining butter in medium skillet; add livers. Brown over high heat. Stir livers and Madeira into sauce. Heat through; serve with wild rice. Yield: 4 servings.

Nancy Samuels
Xi Omega X1381
Martinsburg, West Virginia

RUMAKI SKILLET

  1 tbsp. butter or margarine
  1 lb. chicken livers
  1 lg. onion, sliced
  1 8 1/2-oz. can water chestnuts,
    drained
  1 tbsp. cornstarch

  1/3 c. soy sauce
  1 tbsp. sherry
  2 tbsp. sugar
  Dash of salt
  Dash of pepper
  1 to 2 tbsp. cooked crumbled bacon
  Cooked rice

Melt butter; add livers, onion and water chestnuts. Cook until livers are tender. Combine cornstarch, soy sauce, sherry, sugar, salt and pepper; stir until smooth. Add sauce to liver mixture; cook and stir until thickened and smooth. Stir in bacon. Serve over hot rice.

Jackie Powers, Pres.
Preceptor Gamma Eta XP-789
Temple City, California

POULET NORMANDIE

  1 pkg. herb-seasoned stuffing mix
  1 stick margarine, melted
  1 c. chicken broth
  2 1/2 c. cooked diced chicken
  1/4 c. chopped green onion tops
  1/2 c. chopped onions
  1 c. chopped celery
  3/4 tsp. salt
  1/2 c. mayonnaise
  2 eggs, lightly beaten
  1 1/2 c. milk
  1 can cream of mushroom soup
  Grated cheese

Combine stuffing mix, margarine and broth in large bowl; mix lightly. Pat half the mixture in buttered 12 x 8-inch casserole. Combine chicken, onion tops, onions, celery, salt and mayonnaise in large bowl; mix well. Spoon over stuffing layer in casserole; top with remaining stuffing mixture. Combine eggs and milk; mix well. Pour evenly over stuffing mixture. Cover with foil; refrigerate overnight. Remove from refrigerator 1 hour before baking. Spread soup over top. Bake, uncovered, in 325-degree oven for 40 minutes. Sprinkle with cheese. Bake for 10 minutes longer.

Mrs. Sybil Huskins, Pres.
Preceptor Alpha Epsilon XP0813
Palm Bay, Florida

115

HERBED ROAST CHICKEN

1   2 1/2 to 3-lb. chicken
1 carrot
Thyme to taste
Salt to taste
3 tbsp. butter
3 slices bacon
Paprika to taste
1/2 c. beef bouillon
Juice of 1 lemon

Wash chicken; drain well. Place carrot, 1 tea-spoon thyme, 1/3 teaspoon salt and 1 table-spoon butter into chicken cavity; truss. Place chicken in shallow roasting pan; cover breast with bacon slices. Dot chicken with remaining butter; sprinkle with thyme, salt and paprika. Bake at 450 degrees for 15 minutes or until lightly browned; reduce oven temperature to 350 degrees. Bake for 1 hour and 45 minutes longer or until tender. Combine bouillon with 1/4 cup water; baste chicken every 15 minutes with bouillon mixture. Remove chicken to heated platter; remove strings. Add lemon juice to pan drippings; heat through, stirring constantly. Season to taste; serve with chicken. Yield: 4 servings.

Ruth Ann Rihel, Pres.
Gamma Upsilon No. 6437
Weirton, West Virginia

ROAST CHICKEN WITH STUFFED ARTICHOKES

6 artichokes
Juice of 1 lemon
1/2 c. butter
1   5-lb. roasting chicken
Salt and pepper to taste
1/4 c. chopped onion
1 clove of garlic, minced
3/4 c. chopped celery
1/2   8-oz. package herb-seasoned
  stuffing mix
1/4 c. chopped parsley
1/2 c. chicken bouillon
1/2 c. chopped toasted pecans

Wash artichokes; cut off and discard upper third of leaves. Trim base. Open center; pull out yellowish leaves. Scrape and remove choke from center. Place artichokes in boiling salted water with lemon juice. Bring to a boil; reduce heat. Simmer, covered, for 40 minutes or until inner leaf comes out easily; invert and drain well. Melt 1/4 cup butter; brush over chicken. Sprinkle with salt and pepper; place chicken in roaster. Bake at 375 degrees for 2 hours and 15 minutes. Melt remaining butter in skillet over medium heat; saute onion and garlic in butter until onion is tender. Stir in celery; saute until onion is just golden. Remove from heat; stir in stuffing mix, parsley, bouillon and pecans. Fill artichokes with stuffing mixture. Arrange artichokes around chicken. Bake for 15 minutes longer. Serve pan drippings or melted butter with artichokes, if desired. Yield: 6 servings.

Regina Jankiewicz, City Coun. Pres.
Beta No. 397
Columbus, Georgia

STIR-FRIED CHICKEN WITH WATER CHESTNUTS

4 to 6 dried black mushrooms
1   2-lb. chicken
1 c. water chestnuts
1/2 c. almonds
1 tsp. salt
1/4 tsp. pepper
3 to 4 tbsp. oil
1 tbsp. soy sauce
1/4 c. stock

Soak dried mushrooms; drain. Skin and bone chicken; slice thin. Slice water chestnuts and mushrooms. Blanch and mince almonds. Combine with salt and pepper. Dip chicken slices in almonds; coat well. Heat oil in large skillet over medium heat; brown chicken slices. Stir in mushrooms, water chestnuts, soy sauce and stock. Bring to a boil; reduce heat. Cook, covered, over medium heat for 2 to 3 minutes or until chicken is tender. Yield: 8-10 servings.

Winafred N. Borough, Pres.
Xi Alpha Psi X2054
Renton, Washington

STRAWBERRY MOCHA CREAM TARTLETS

4 c. sifted all-purpose flour
2 tsp. salt
1 1/2 c. vegetable shortening
2 pt. fresh strawberries
Light corn syrup
1/2 c. strong coffee
1/2 c. sugar
6 egg yolks
1 tbsp. instant coffee powder
2 tbsp. cocoa
1 c. softened sweet butter

Combine the flour and salt in bowl. Cut in the shortening until uniform but coarse. Sprinkle with 1/2 cup water; toss with fork, then press into ball. Roll out 1/2 of the dough at a time on a lightly floured surface to a 1/8-inch thickness. Cut into 3-inch circles, then fit inside 2 1/4-inch tart pans. Prick with fork. Place on a baking sheet. Bake in a 425-degree oven for 10 minutes or until lightly browned. Cool; remove from tart pans. Brush the strawberries with corn syrup and let dry on racks. Combine the coffee and sugar; boil to the thread stage or until candy thermometer registers 234 degrees. Beat the egg yolks with the instant coffee powder and cocoa until fluffy and thick. Add the hot syrup gradually to yolks, pouring in a thin steady stream and beating constantly. Continue beating until light in color and cold, then beat in butter. Chill slightly, if necessary. Pipe a ring of the butter mixture around the inside edge of each cooled tartlet shell. Place a strawberry in each shell and chill until served. Yield: 50 servings.

Photograph for this recipe on page 117.

BLACK BEANS AND RICE

1 6-oz. package herb rice
1/4 c. chopped onion
1 c. cooked black beans or kidney beans
1 tomato, cut in wedges
Finely chopped parsley

Cook rice according to package directions, adding onion at beginning of cooking. Stir in part of the beans. Turn out onto a large square of heavy-duty aluminum foil. Top with tomato; add remaining beans. Fold foil over top, sealing to make a tight package. Place on grill for 10 to 15 minutes or until heated through. Sprinkle with parsley when ready to serve. Rice mixture may be cooked the day before and chilled, if desired. Yield: 6 servings.

Photograph for this recipe on page 118.

SEAFOOD CREAM WITH AVOCADO HALVES

1 lb. fresh mushrooms, sliced
1 c. sliced onion
1 c. butter or margarine
2/3 c. flour
2 1/2 tsp. salt
1 tsp. monosodium glutamate
1/2 tsp. dry mustard
1/2 tsp. pepper
1/4 tsp. thyme leaves
5 c. milk
2 c. light cream
2 eggs, slightly beaten
2 c. grated Swiss cheese
8 7-oz. cans solid white tuna
1 c. sauterne
2 tsp. grated lemon peel
Lemon juice
6 5-oz. cans lobster, drained
2/3 c. chopped toasted blanched almonds
12 ripe avocados
Watercress

Saute the mushrooms and onion in butter until lightly browned; remove with slotted spoon. Quickly stir in the flour and seasonings. Stir in the milk and cream gradually. Cook and stir until the sauce boils for 1 minute. Stir a small amount of hot sauce into eggs, then return to the saucepan. Stir the cheese into hot sauce over low heat until melted. Drain the tuna; separate into large pieces. Add sauterne, lemon peel, 2 tablespoons lemon juice, tuna, lobster, almonds, sauteed mushrooms and onion to the sauce. Heat to serving temperature. Cut the avocados in half lengthwise, twisting gently to separate halves. Whack a sharp knife directly into seeds and twist to lift out. Peel avocado halves and brush with lemon juice. Arrange on a serving platter with watercress. Garnish with lime slices. Serve hot seafood mixture over avocado halves. Garnish with buttered, toasted fine bread crumbs and sliced truffles. Yield: 24 servings.

Photograph for this recipe on page 117.

BAHAMIAN-BARBECUED CHICKEN

1/4 c. lime juice
1/4 c. honey
1/4 c. light rum
4 1/2 tsp. monosodium glutamate
1/4 c. salad oil
2 tbsp. soy sauce
1/2 tsp. dried leaf tarragon
4 broiler-fryer chickens, halved
4 tsp. salt
1 tsp. pepper
Lime slices (opt.)

Line bottom of grill with heavy-duty aluminum foil and prepare fire. Blend the lime juice and honey in a bowl. Warm the rum slightly, then ignite. Add to honey mixture when flame has burned out. Add 1/2 teaspoon monosodium glutamate, oil, soy sauce and tarragon and beat until blended. Sprinkle both sides of chickens with the salt, pepper and remaining monosodium glutamate. Place chickens, skin side up, on grate 6 inches from heat and cook, turning occasionally, for 45 minutes to 1 hour and 15 minutes depending on weight of chicken. Brush with barbecue sauce during last 30 minutes of cooking time. Chicken leg should twist easily out of thigh joint and pieces should feel tender when probed with a fork when done. Garnish chicken with lime slices.

Photograph for this recipe on page 118.

TROPICAL FRUIT BAKE

1/2 c. (packed) brown sugar
1/4 c. butter, melted
1 tsp. grated lemon rind
2 tbsp. lemon juice
1/8 tsp. nutmeg
3 bananas
1 papaya
1 c. honeydew melon balls
1 c. cantaloupe balls
Flaked coconut

Combine brown sugar, butter, lemon rind and juice and nutmeg. Peel bananas; cut in half crosswise and lengthwise. Peel papaya; discard seeds and cube fruit. Combine all fruits; divide among 6 squares of heavy-duty aluminum foil. Sprinkle brown sugar mixture over each and sprinkle with coconut. Seal foil to make tight packages. Place on grill for 10 to 15 minutes or until heated through. Yield: 6 servings.

Photograph for this recipe on page 118.

HERBED PINWHEELS

1 c. butter, softened
1/4 c. chopped parsley
1/2 tsp. oregano leaves
1/4 tsp. tarragon leaves
1/4 tsp. ground thyme
1/8 tsp. pepper
4 c. sifted all-purpose flour
2 tbsp. baking powder
2 tsp. salt
2/3 c. vegetable shortening
1 1/2 c. milk
1 egg

Whip the butter with parsley, oregano, tarragon, thyme and pepper; let stand for 1 hour to blend flavors. Mix the flour, baking powder and salt in a bowl; cut in shortening until mixture looks like coarse meal. Stir in the milk. Knead about 10 times on a floured board and divide the dough in half. Roll out each half into a 12 x 10-inch rectangle. Spread half the herb mixture on each rectangle; roll up each rectangle from 12-inch side and seal edge. Cut each roll into 24 1/2-inch pinwheels and place pinwheels in ungreased muffin pans. Beat the egg with 2 tablespoons water and brush over pinwheels. Bake in a 425-degree oven for 10 to 15 minutes or until golden brown.

Photograph for this recipe on page 117.

CORNISH HENS
WITH HARVEST STUFFING

4 Cornish hens
2 tbsp. shortening
1/3 c. diced onion
1 c. grated carrots
1/2 c. finely diced celery
2 c. cooked rice
1/2 c. evaporated milk
3/4 tsp. poultry seasoning
1 1/3 tsp. salt
1/8 tsp. pepper
2 tsp. onion salt
1/4 tsp. garlic salt
2 tsp. celery salt
1 c. melted butter

Salt hens well. Melt shortening in heavy skillet; add onion, carrots and celery. Cook, covered, for 5 minutes. Combine rice, milk, poultry seasoning, salt and pepper with onion mixture. Stuff hens; truss, securing opening with wooden picks. Place hens in shallow baking pan with water to depth of 1 inch. Combine onion salt, garlic salt and celery salt with butter. Brush on hens. Bake, basting frequently with butter mixture, at 350 degrees for 1 hour.

Mrs. Miles Winship
Delta No. 478
Mitchell, South Dakota

ORIENTAL CORNISH HENS

2 1-lb. Cornish hens
1/4 c. soy sauce
1/4 c. sherry
1/4 c. pineapple juice
1 clove of garlic, crushed
1/2 tsp. curry powder
1/4 tsp. dry mustard

Split hens in half; arrange, skin side down, in 12 x 8 x 2-inch baking dish. Combine soy sauce, sherry, pineapple juice, garlic, curry powder and mustard; blend well. Pour sherry mixture over hens. Marinate, refrigerated, for 4 to 6 hours; turn occasionally, brushing with marinade. Drain hens, reserving marinade. Arrange hens in baking dish, skin side down. Bake, covered, at 375 degrees for 40 minutes or until tender. Turn every 10 minutes; brush with marinade. Yield: 4 servings.

Lillie Gilligan, City Coun. Pres.
Xi Kappa Phi X3185
Laredo, Texas

ROAST CORNISH HENS
IN WINE SAUCE

1 c. chopped onion
1 c. chopped green pepper
3 tbsp. bacon drippings
6 slices crisp bacon, crumbled
3 c. small dried bread cubes
1 c. coarsely chopped walnuts
4 tsp. salt
1/2 tsp. dried thyme
1 tsp. rubbed sage
6 1-lb. Cornish hens
1/2 c. butter or margarine
1 1/2 c. white wine
1 clove of garlic, crushed
3 tbsp. flour
1 c. currant jelly
1 tsp. dry mustard

Saute onion and green pepper in bacon drippings in skillet until tender. Combine bacon, bread cubes, walnuts, 1 1/2 teaspoons salt, thyme and 1/2 teaspoon sage in large bowl; stir in onion mixture lightly. Stuff hens; truss, securing openings with wooden picks. Preheat oven to 400 degrees. Arrange hens, breast side up, in shallow baking pan. Combine butter, 1/2 cup wine, garlic, 1 1/2 teaspoons salt and remaining sage in small skillet over low heat; blend well. Brush hens with butter mixture. Bake for 1 hour, brushing occasionally with butter mixture. Remove hens to heated platter; keep warm. Pour off pan drippings; reserve 2/3 cup drippings. Combine reserved drippings with flour in baking pan; stir until smooth. Add remaining wine gradually, stirring until thickened. Stir in jelly, mustard and remaining salt. Bring sauce to a boil, stirring constantly. Reduce heat; simmer, stirring occasionally, until jelly is melted and sauce is smooth. Serve with Cornish hens.

Judy Bello, Pres.
Gamma Mu No. 1504
Santa Rosa, California

ROCK CORNISH HENS BOMBAY

3 Cornish hens
1/4 tsp. celery salt
1 tsp. onion flakes
1 pkg. chicken-flavored rice
2 tbsp. salad oil
2 tsp. soy sauce
1/8 tsp. ground ginger
1/3 c. white wine

Remove giblets from hens. Combine giblets with celery salt, onion flakes and 2 cups water in saucepan; simmer until tender. Chop giblets; reserve broth. Prepare rice according to package directions,using reserved broth and giblets. Stuff hens with rice mixture; truss, securing opening with wooden picks. Combine oil, soy sauce, ginger and wine; blend well. Place hens in roasting bag in shallow roasting pan. Pour wine mixture over hens; seal bag. Bake at 350 degrees for 1 hour and 15 minutes or until tender.

Della Gould Emmons, Honorary Member
Beta Sigma Phi International
Tacoma, Washington

APPLE-GLAZED CORNISH HEN

6 frozen Cornish hens
Salt and pepper to taste
1 1/4 c. applesauce
1/2 c. corn flake crumbs
1/2 c. raisins
2 c. apple juice
1 c. currant jelly
Grated rind and juice of 1 lemon

Thaw Cornish hens; dry. Sprinkle inside and out with salt and pepper. Mix applesauce with crumbs and raisins; place 1/3 cup crumb mixture in each hen. Close opening with skewers. Place hens on rack in baking pan, breast side up. Bake in 350-degree oven for 30 minutes. Combine apple juice, jelly and lemon rind and juice in saucepan; heat until jelly melts. Bake hens for 1 hour longer, basting frequently with jelly mixture. Baste hens with pan drippings before serving.

Mary E. Imle, W and M Chm.
Xi Zeta No. 223
Denver, Colorado

ROAST GINGER DUCKLING WITH WILD RICE

1 5 to 6-lb. duckling
Salt and pepper
1 c. honey
1 tbsp. ground ginger
1 c. wild rice
3 beef bouillon cubes
1 onion, diced
1 stalk celery, sliced

Score duckling front and back; rub inside and outside with salt and pepper. Place duckling, breast side down, on wire rack in shallow pan. Roast at 450 degrees for 30 minutes. Turn; roast for 30 minutes. Reduce temperature to 350 degrees; roast for 30 minutes. Mix honey and ginger; spread on duckling. Roast for 30 minutes longer. Place rice in 2 cups boiling water. Add bouillon cubes, onion and celery; bring to boiling point. Reduce heat; simmer for 1 hour. Place rice on heated platter; place duckling on rice.

Barbara Lee Nolan, W and M Chm.
Preceptor Alpha Mu XP470
San Jose, California

DUCKS WITH WINE SAUCE

2 4-lb. ducks
Salt and pepper
Thyme
Apple wedges
Pinch of marjoram
1 c. orange juice
1 tbsp. cornstarch
1/2 c. marmalade
3/4 c. port or sherry
1/2 to 1 c. sugar or honey
Grated rind of 1 orange
1/4 c. brandy

Place ducks in roasting pan; sprinkle inside and out with salt, pepper and thyme. Fill cavities with apple; sprinkle breasts with marjoram. Roast in 400-degree oven for 30 minutes. Reduce temperature to 325 degrees; roast for 1 hour. Drain off fat. Cook remaining ingredients except brandy until thickened; spread some of the mixture on ducks. Roast for 30 minutes to 1 hour or until ducks are tender, basting once more with sauce. Heat remaining sauce. Add brandy; ignite. Serve with ducks.

Mrs. Inga Moore, Serv. Chm.
Preceptor Epsilon XP1123
Prince Albert, Saskatchewan, Canada

ROAST DUCK WITH SWEDISH RAISIN STUFFING

1/2 c. dark raisins
2 c. cold cooked rice
1/8 tsp. ground cardamom
1 tsp. grated orange peel
2 1/4 tsp. salt
1 tbsp. instant minced onion
2 tbsp. melted butter
1 c. grated fresh apple
1   4-lb. duck
1/3 c. sifted flour
Parsley sprigs
Orange slices

Combine raisins, rice, cardamom, orange peel, 3/4 teaspoon salt, onion, butter and apple. Mix lightly. Stuff raisin mixture loosely into body cavity of duck; close opening with lacing pins and string. Place duck in baking pan. Bake at 325 degrees for about 2 hours and 30 minutes. Transfer duck to hot platter. Skim all fat from pan drippings in baking pan, reserving 1/2 cup. Blend reserved fat with flour; add 2 cups water and liquid from pan. Cook, stirring constantly, until mixture thickens. Season with remaining salt. Cut duck into quarters with kitchen scissors. Pile hot stuffing on platter. Arrange duck pieces over stuffing. Top with small amount of gravy; serve remaining gravy separately in bowl. Garnish platter with parsley and orange slices. Stuffing may be baked separately in greased baking dish, if desired. Bake at 350 degrees for about 1 hour. Yield: 4 servings.

ROAST PHEASANT WITH WILD RICE STUFFING

2 2 1/2 to 3-lb. pheasant with
*   livers*
Salt and pepper to taste
Softened butter
3/4 c. wild rice
1/4 c. finely chopped onion
1/4 lb. fresh mushrooms, chopped
2 tbsp. chopped celery
1/4 c. coarsely chopped pecans
2 tbsp. chopped parsley
1/4 tsp. thyme
1/4 tsp. marjoram
8 to 12 bacon strips
Toasted Bread Croutons
Creamed Pan Sauce

Season cavities of pheasant with salt and pepper; coat each cavity with 1 teaspoon butter. Rinse rice 3 or 4 times in cold water; cook in large kettle of boiling, salted water for 20 minutes. Drain in colander. Place colander over pan containing about 1 inch boiling water; cover. Steam for 20 to 25 minutes or until dry. Transfer rice to bowl. Add 1 tablespoon butter; fluff rice with fork. Chop pheasant livers. Saute onion and livers in 1 1/2 tablespoons butter in skillet over low heat for 2 minutes. Add mushrooms and celery; saute over moderate heat for 3 to 4 minutes or until mushrooms are tender. Add to rice. Add pecans, parsley, thyme, marjoram, salt and pepper; mix well. Cool; fill cavities of pheasant. Truss pheasant tightly; rub skin with butter. Cover each breast with 4 to 6 bacon strips; secure bacon strips with string. Place pheasant on sides in roasting pan. Roast in 425-degree oven for 15 to 20 minutes. Turn pheasant to other sides; roast for 15 to 20 minutes. Cut strings securing bacon; remove bacon. Turn pheasant, breast side up; baste with drippings. Roast for 15 minutes longer or until done. Remove trussing; place each pheasant on hot Toasted Bread Crouton on heated serving dish. Keep warm. Serve with Creamed Pan Sauce; garnish platter with cranberry-filled lemon baskets.

Toasted Bread Croutons

1 loaf unsliced sandwich bread
Melted butter

Preheat oven to 300 degrees. Remove crusts from bread; cut in half lengthwise. Trim halves to size of pheasant; brush on all sides with butter. Place on baking sheet. Bake until browned.

Creamed Pan Sauce

1/4 c. minced carrot
1/4 c. minced onion
3 tbsp. flour
1/4 tsp. thyme
2 1/4 c. hot chicken broth
1/2 c. heavy cream
1/4 c. dry sherry
Salt and pepper to taste

Skim off all except 3 tablespoons fat from roasting pan; heat pan drippings over low heat. Add carrot and onion to drippings; saute for 1 minute. Add flour and thyme; cook, stirring, for 2 minutes. Remove pan from heat; stir in chicken broth, cream and sherry. Bring to a boil, stirring; simmer for 5 minutes or until thickened. Season with salt and pepper; strain into sauceboat.

Judith E. Johnson, W and M Chm.
Alpha Kappa No. 1452
Beloit, Wisconsin

QUAIL BAKED IN WINE

1/2 c. fat
2 sm. onions, minced
2 whole cloves
1 tsp. peppercorns
2 cloves of garlic, cut fine
1/2 bay leaf
6 quail, cleaned and trussed
2 c. white wine
1/2 tsp. salt
1/8 tsp. pepper
Dash of cayenne pepper
1 tsp. minced chives
2 c. cream or evaporated milk

Melt fat in skillet; add onions, cloves, peppercorns, garlic and bay leaf. Cook for several minutes. Add quail; brown on all sides. Add wine, salt, pepper, cayenne pepper and chives; simmer for about 30 minutes or until tender. Strain sauce; add cream. Heat to boiling point. Pour over quail. Yield: 6 servings.

Mrs. Nancy Schuler, Coun. Pres.
Xi Beta Upsilon X913
Dixon, Illinois

CHINESE TURKEY

1/4 lb. sliced bacon
1/2 c. chopped celery
1/2 c. chopped onion
1/2 c. slivered almonds
1 c. chopped cooked turkey
1 tbsp. cornstarch
1 tbsp. soy sauce
1 tsp. lemon juice
1 No. 2 can pineapple chunks
1/4 tsp. salt
1 c. chopped carrots

Fry bacon until crisp; crumble. Pour off drippings, reserving 2 tablespoons in skillet. Add celery, onion and almonds to reserved bacon drippings; saute. Add turkey. Mix cornstarch, soy sauce and lemon juice. Drain pineapple; add enough water to syrup to make 1 1/4 cups liquid. Mix pineapple liquid into cornstarch mixture. Add salt and turkey mixture; cook, stirring, until thickened. Add carrots and pineapple chunks. Cover; simmer for 20 minutes. Serve over fried noodles or rice; sprinkle with bacon. Yield: 6 servings.

Vera Meinert
Alpha Pi No. 1000
Leavenworth, Kansas

TURKEY CASSEROLE DELUXE

1/4 c. melted butter
5 tbsp. flour
1 tsp. salt
1/4 tsp. onion salt or juice
2 1/2 c. milk
1 1/2 c. instant rice
1 1/2 c. turkey broth
1/2 c. grated cheese
1 1/2 c. cooked cut asparagus
2 c. sliced cooked turkey
2 tbsp. slivered almonds

Melt butter in skillet; add flour, salt and onion salt, mixing well. Add milk gradually; cook, stirring constantly, until thickened. Pour rice into greased 2-quart casserole. Pour broth over rice; sprinkle with cheese. Arrange asparagus over cheese; top with turkey. Pour white sauce over turkey mixture. Cover. Bake at 375 degrees for 30 minutes. Sprinkle with almonds before serving.

Irene Winjum, Pres.
Preceptor Alpha XP-125
Fargo, North Dakota

SPANISH-STYLE TURKEY WITH CHESTNUTS

24 chestnuts
Oil
3/4 c. blanched almonds
Juice of 2 lemons
1 sm. uncooked turkey, cubed
Salt and pepper to taste
1 lg. onion, minced
3/4 c. cubed uncooked ham
1 1/2 c. turkey or chicken broth
3/4 c. dry sherry

Cut 1 slit in each chestnut. Pour small amount of oil into heavy frying pan. Add chestnuts; cook over low heat, shaking pan, for about 10 minutes. Remove shells and skins with sharp knife. Process chestnuts and almonds through food grinder. Pour lemon juice over turkey; sprinkle with salt and pepper. Heat 1/2 cup oil in skillet; brown turkey mixture. Add onion, ham, broth and sherry; cover. Cook over low heat until almost done. Combine processed chestnuts and almonds; add to turkey mixture. Cook until turkey is tender.

Teresa C. Griffin, Rec. Sec.
Alpha Theta No. 3358
Albuquerque, New Mexico

Vegetables, Eggs and Side Dishes

Vegetables, the underrated step-child of many cooks, are making
a stirring come-back as main and side-dishes. More and more gourmets
are ignoring the old adage of "don't ever drain the cooking water
from the vegetables" and are learning the "French chefs"
secrets of blanching the vegetables, and then quickly refreshing
them under cold water to stop the cooking process. Vegetables cooked
in this manner are comparable to those served in the finest French
restaurants on the Champs Elysee in Paris.

Also included in this section on Vegetables, are Egg and Side Dish
recipes. Some of these delectable recipes are quiches, casseroles,
souffles and tarts. All are guaranteed to please the gourmets
in your family.

ARTICHOKES MILANESE

1/2 c. butter
2 c. sliced fresh mushrooms
1 tsp. salt
1 tsp. crushed sweet basil
1/2 tsp. crushed oregano
1/4 tsp. garlic powder
1 tbsp. fine dry bread crumbs
2 tbsp. fresh lemon juice
2 8-oz. packages frozen artichoke
*   hearts, thawed*
1/2 c. Parmesan cheese

Melt butter in large, heavy skillet; saute mushrooms in butter until golden. Sprinkle with salt, sweet basil, oregano and garlic powder during cooking. Stir in bread crumbs and lemon juice; mix well. Arrange artichoke hearts in greased shallow baking dish. Spoon mushroom mixture over artichokes. Sprinkle cheese over all. Bake at 350 degrees for 25 minutes or until bubbly and cheese is browned. Yield: 8 servings.

Shirley Ayers, Pres.
Xi Gamma Rho X3864
Federal Way, Washington

ASPARAGUS FROMAGE

8 mushroom caps
2 tbsp. butter or margarine
2 tbsp. flour
1 c. milk
1/2 tsp. salt
1/8 tsp. dry mustard
2 tbsp. sherry
2 10-oz. packages frozen asparagus
*   spears*
1/2 c. almond halves, toasted
1/4 c. grated American cheese

Saute mushroom caps in butter in a 10-inch heavy skillet over low heat. Remove mushrooms; blend flour into remaining butter. Stir in milk gradually. Cook, stirring constantly, over medium heat until sauce is thickened. Add salt, mustard and sherry. Prepare asparagus according to package directions; drain. Arrange on ovenproof serving platter. Cover with toasted almonds; top with mushrooms. Pour sauce over mushrooms; sprinkle with cheese. Broil 5 to 6 inches from source of heat until cheese is melted. Yield: 8-10 servings.

Maxine D. Steinbrook, Pres.
Alpha Chi No. 7430
Columbus, Ohio

BAKED BROCCOLI PARMESAN

2 pkg. frozen broccoli
1/4 c. shortening
1 lg. clove of garlic, minced
1/2 lb. mushrooms
1 can Italian-style tomato paste
1/4 c. sifted flour
1 tsp. salt
1/4 tsp. nutmeg
1/4 tsp. pepper
1/4 c. grated Parmesan cheese

Prepare broccoli according to package directions; drain, reserving 1 cup liquid. Slice broccoli thinly lengthwise; arrange in greased 10 x 11 x 2-inch shallow baking dish. Melt shortening in saucepan; stir in garlic. Saute for several minutes. Slice mushrooms; add to garlic mixture. Saute for 5 minutes; stir frequently. Stir in tomato paste, reserved liquid and flour; blend well. Season with salt, nutmeg and pepper; stir in cheese. Simmer, covered, for 15 minutes; pour over broccoli. Sprinkle with additional Parmesan cheese. Bake at 350 degrees for 30 minutes. Fresh broccoli may be used, if desired, adding 1 teaspoon salt to cooking water. Yield: 6 servings.

Lena Galanti, Spon.
Xi Alpha Omega X2649
Alexandria, Virginia

BARBECUED BAKED BEANS

1 lg. onion, chopped
8 to 10 slices bacon, chopped
1 lg. green pepper, chopped
2 1-lb. cans pork and beans

1 can tomatoes, chopped
1/2 c. barbecue sauce
1/3 c. catsup
1/4 c. (packed) brown sugar
1/8 c. molasses
1 clove of garlic, minced
Salt and pepper to taste

Place onion and bacon in large skillet; stir in green pepper. Cook, stirring constantly, until bacon and onion are golden; add beans. Combine tomatoes, barbecue sauce, catsup, brown sugar, molasses, garlic, salt and pepper; blend well. Combine bean mixture with tomato mixture; pour into large heavy casserole. Bake, covered, at 300 degrees for 4 to 5 hours; stir occasionally. Yield: 15-20 servings.

Carolyn Benham, Pres.
Beta Mu No. 4614
Grants, New Mexico

SWISS-STYLE GREEN BEANS

2 tbsp. butter
2 tbsp. flour
1 tsp. salt
1/4 tsp. pepper
1 tsp. (heaping) sugar
1/2 tsp. grated onion
1 c. sour cream
4 c. fresh cooked green beans
1/4 lb. processed Swiss cheese,
  grated
2 c. corn flakes, slightly crushed
2 tsp. melted butter

Melt butter in skillet; stir in flour, salt, pepper, sugar and onion until smooth. Add sour cream, stirring constantly, until thickened. Fold in green beans. Pour into greased 2-quart casserole; sprinkle with cheese. Combine corn flakes and butter; sprinkle over cheese. Bake at 400 degrees for 20 minutes. May be refrigerated and baked for 10 minutes longer. Canned green beans may be substituted for fresh green beans, if desired.

Ruth S. Davis, Corr. Sec.
Xi Gamma Iota X1409
Bay Village, Ohio

WALNUT-MUSTARD SAUCE WITH CAULIFLOWER

1/2 c. plain or toasted California
  walnuts
1 tbsp. butter
1 egg, beaten
2 tbsp. sugar
2 tbsp. (packed) brown sugar
2 tbsp. prepared mustard
1/4 c. cider vinegar
2 tsp. cornstarch
1/2 c. whipping cream
1 cooked cauliflower, drained

Chop walnuts fine. Melt butter in small saucepan. Combine egg, sugars and mustard; combine vinegar and cornstarch. Blend both mixtures into melted butter. Cook, stirring, until mixture boils and begins to thicken. Stir in cream; continue cooking over moderate heat until thickened and smooth. Add walnuts; spoon hot sauce over hot cauliflower. Sprinkle additional walnuts over top, if desired. Yield: 5-6 servings.

CAULIFLOWER WITH GREEN GRAPES AND ALMONDS

1 lg. head cauliflower
3 tsp. salt
2 tbsp. butter or margarine
1 c. white seedless grapes
1/2 c. slivered toasted almonds

Break cauliflower into flowerets. Combine 1 1/2 cups water and salt in saucepan; add cauliflower. Simmer, covered, for 5 minutes or until tender; drain. Add butter, grapes and almonds, tossing well. Yield: 6 servings.

Louise Mitchell, VP
Preceptor Delta Tau XP 1030
China Lake, California

CELERY-CHEESE CASSEROLE

3 c. chopped celery
1 lg. onion, chopped
1 clove of garlic, minced
1 bay leaf
Salt
2 tbsp. butter
1 tbsp. (heaping) flour
1/2 c. milk
2 oz. blue cheese
1 can mushroom soup
1 hard-boiled egg, chopped
1 beaten egg
1 wine glass sherry
Chow mein noodles
Cheddarins
Grated Cheddar cheese

Combine celery, onion, garlic, bay leaf and 1/4 teaspoon salt in water to cover in saucepan. Simmer until celery is tender. Drain, reserving 1/2 cup liquid. Melt butter in skillet; blend in flour until smooth. Add milk and reserved liquid gradually. Cook, stirring constantly, until thickened. Season with salt to taste. Stir in blue cheese and soup; heat through, mixing well. Combine celery mixture and sauce. Add hard-boiled egg, beaten egg and sherry. Line bottom of greased casserole with noodles; spoon celery mixture into casserole. Top with Cheddarins; sprinkle with Cheddar cheese. Bake at 350 degrees for 30 minutes or until mixture bubbles and cheese is melted. Garnish with sprig of parsley. Cheese-flavored spiral snack crackers may be substituted for Cheddarins, if desired. Yield: 4-6 servings.

Lady Robinson, Honorary Member
Beta Sigma Phi International
Toronto, Ontario, Canada

CORN SOUFFLE

1 can cream-style corn
3 eggs, separated
1/4 c. butter, melted
1/4 c. flour
2/3 c. milk
1/2 c. grated Cheddar cheese
Salt and pepper to taste

Preheat oven to 300 degrees. Force corn through colander or coarse sieve. Beat egg yolks slightly. Beat egg white until stiff peaks form. Combine corn, butter, flour, milk, egg yolks, cheese, salt and pepper in large bowl; blend thoroughly. Fold in egg whites gently. Pour into greased casserole. Bake for 10 minutes. Increase oven temperature to 350 degrees; bake for 50 minutes longer or until souffle tests done.

Jean Blanton, Pres.
Xi Nu X0639
Springfield, Missouri

SHRIMP-STUFFED EGGPLANT

1 1 1/4-lb. eggplant
1/4 lb. mushrooms, sliced
1/2 c. chopped onions
1/4 c. melted butter or margarine
1 tsp. salt
1/8 tsp. pepper
1 lb. shelled cleaned shrimp,
   cooked
2 tbsp. packaged bread crumbs
1 tbsp. grated Parmesan cheese

Cut eggplant in half lengthwise. Scoop out pulp, leaving 1/2-inch shell. Parboil shells for 5 minutes; drain. Chop pulp. Saute chopped eggplant, mushrooms and onions in butter over medium heat for 10 minutes, stirring occasionally. Add salt, pepper and shrimp. Pile stuffing into eggplant shells; top with bread crumbs and cheese. Place shells in baking pan. Bake at 375 degrees for 25 minutes. Yield: 4 servings.

Photograph for this recipe on page 126.

ITALIAN EGGPLANT

1 9-oz. can tomato sauce
1 med. onion, quartered
1/2 lg. green pepper, chopped
1 clove of garlic, peeled
3 tbsp. butter or margarine
1/2 tsp. oregano
1/4 lb. mozzarella cheese, cubed
8 slices dry bread
1/4 c. milk
1 egg
1 med. pared eggplant, sliced
Flour
Salad oil
Grated Parmesan cheese

Combine tomato sauce, onion, green pepper, garlic, butter and oregano in blender container; cover. Blend until smooth. Spoon into saucepan; bring to a boil. Simmer for 15 minutes. Place several cubes mozzarella cheese in blender container; cover. Blend until all cheese is grated. Place 2 slices bread in blender container at a time; blend to fine crumbs. Set aside. Combine milk and egg in container; blend until mixed. Set aside. Roll eggplant slices in flour; dip in egg mixture. Coat with crumbs. Fry in shallow hot oil until tender and lightly browned on both sides. Arrange eggplant slices in large baking dish. Cover with hot tomato sauce mixture. Sprinkle with grated mozzarella cheese and grated Parmesan cheese. Place under broiler for 3 to 5 minutes or until cheese melts. Yield: 6-8 servings.

Mrs. Mary Andress, Treas.
Epsilon No. 4888
Lakeland, Florida

BRAISED STUFFED CUCUMBERS

2 long thin cucumbers
1/2 c. ground pork
1/2 c. dry bread crumbs
1/8 tsp. slivered fresh gingerroot
1 tbsp. red wine vinegar
1 tbsp. soy sauce
1 tsp. salt
1/4 tsp. sugar
1/4 tsp. monosodium glutamate
1 to 2 tbsp. cooking oil

Peel cucumbers; cut crosswise into 1 1/2-inch thick slices. Hollow out centers. Mix remaining ingredients except oil; pack into cucumbers. Heat oil in skillet. Stand stuffed cucumbers in oil; cook gently until tinged with brown. Turn; brown other end. Add 1/4 cup water. Cover; turn heat to low. Cook for 8 to 10 minutes longer or until cucumbers are tender and pork is done. Yield: 6 servings.

Helen Helton
Preceptor Alpha XP-130
Colorado Springs, Colorado

CREAMED SPINACH
WITH BACON

1 10-oz. package frozen spinach
2 slices bacon, finely chopped
1/2 c. finely chopped onion
2 tbsp. flour
1 tsp. seasoned salt
1/4 tsp. seasoned pepper
1 clove of garlic, minced
1 c. milk

Prepare spinach according to package directions; drain well. Saute bacon and onions until onions are tender and bacon is crisp. Remove from heat; stir in flour, seasoned salt, seasoned pepper and garlic, blending well. Add milk gradually; return to heat. Cook, stirring constantly, until thickened. Add spinach; mix thoroughly. Yield: 4 servings.

Charlene Swan, Pres.
Delta Delta Epsilon No. 7825
Cypress, California

1/4 c. chopped onion
1 clove of garlic, crushed
1 c. wild rice, cooked
3 tbsp. chopped parsley
1/4 tsp. thyme
1/2 tsp. salt
1/4 tsp. pepper
1/3 c. slivered almonds
1/4 c. grated Cheddar cheese
1 tbsp. sesame seed
3/4 c. cream

Remove mushroom stems; set aside. Place caps, hollow side up, in greased shallow baking dish. Chop stems; saute in butter with onion and garlic until onion is tender. Add rice, parsley, thyme, salt, pepper and almonds. Mix well; heap into mushroom caps. Press down firmly. Sprinkle with grated cheese and sesame seed. Pour cream over mushrooms. Bake, covered, at 350 degrees for 30 to 45 minutes, basting once or twice with cream.

Delores Schmidt, Pres.
Preceptor Tau XP 873
Silver City, New Mexico

CARAWAY-CREAMED MUSHROOMS

4 c. sliced fresh mushrooms
1/2 c. thinly sliced onion
2 tsp. caraway seed
1/3 c. butter
3 tbsp. flour
1 tsp. salt
1/8 tsp. pepper
1 tall can evaporated milk
1 tbsp. lemon juice

Saute mushrooms, onion and caraway seed in butter in skillet over low heat until onion is tender. Remove from heat; stir in flour, salt and pepper. Stir in milk gradually. Cook over medium heat, stirring occasionally, until thickened. Stir in lemon juice just before serving. Serve over waffles, toast or in patty shells. Yield: 6 servings.

WILD RICE-STUFFED MUSHROOMS

1 lb. large fresh mushrooms
1/4 c. butter or margarine

PARTY CARROTS AND ONIONS

1 lb. carrots
1 lb. sm. white onions
1 can mushroom soup
1 tbsp. chopped parsley
1/4 tsp. paprika

Pare carrots; halve lengthwise. Cut carrots into 3-inch pieces; peel onions. Place carrots and onions in water to cover in saucepan. Simmer, covered, for 30 minutes or until tender; drain well. Stir in soup, 1/2 cup water, parsley and paprika; heat through, stirring occasionally. Garnish with toasted slivered almonds. Yield: 6-8 servings.

Marilyn Gustafson, Coun. Pres.
Xi Alpha Psi X2054
Seattle, Washington

JENNY LIND'S ONION MEDLEY CUP

3 sweet Spanish onions
1 1/2 tsp. melted butter

1 chicken bouillon cube
1 10-oz. package frozen peas
1 2-oz. can sliced mushrooms,
   drained
1/4 c. sliced water chestnuts,
   drained
1 tsp. soy sauce

Peel and halve onions. Place in large skillet in 1 1/2-inch boiling salted water. Bring to a boil, cover. Simmer for 20 to 25 minutes or until tender. Drain; remove center sections. Brush onions with butter; keep warm. Dissolve bouillon cube in 1/2 cup boiling water; add peas, mushrooms, water chestnuts and soy sauce. Bring to a boil; cover. Simmer for 5 minutes. Spoon vegetables into onion cups; serve immediately. Yield: 6 servings.

Janet Lind, City Coun. Pres.
Eta Nu No. 3526
Waukegan, Illinois

SPINACH-STUFFED ONIONS

1 10-oz. package frozen chopped
   spinach
1 3-oz. package cream cheese,
   softened
1 egg
1/2 c. soft bread crumbs
1/4 c. grated Parmesan cheese
1/4 c. milk
1/4 tsp. salt
Dash of pepper
1 lg. white onion

Prepare spinach according to package directions; drain well. Beat cream cheese and egg until light; stir in crumbs, cheese, milk, salt, pepper and spinach. Peel onion; cut in half crosswise. Separate onion slices to form shells; arrange larger shells in 9 x 9 x 2-inch baking dish. Arrange smaller onion pieces in shells; spoon mixture into shells. Bake at 350 degrees for 35 minutes or until onions are tender and filling is set. May be frozen for baking at a later time.

Virginia Landuyt, Past Pres.
Iota Eta No. 3332
Sebastopol, California

POTATOES STUFFED WITH CHIPPED BEEF

6 baked potatoes
1/2 lb. shredded chipped beef
6 tbsp. butter
1/4 c. flour
2 to 2 1/2 c. scalded milk
Pepper to taste

Cut thick slice from each potato, scoop out pulp, reserving shells. Place pulp in blender container; puree. Saute chipped beef in butter for 5 minutes; stir in flour. Cook, stirring constantly, for 2 minutes; add milk gradually, stirring constantly. Cook for 5 minutes. Combine potato puree with chipped beef mixture; stir in pepper. Heap mixture into reserved shells. Arrange potatoes in shallow baking dish. Bake at 350 degrees for 10 minutes or until heated through. Serve topped with herb butter, if desired.

Fleeta P. Bass, Pres.
Preceptor Iota XP278
Cleburne, Texas

RICE-STUFFED TOMATOES

6 lg. firm tomatoes
1/2 c. chopped onion
1/4 c. olive oil
1/2 c. uncooked rice
2 tsp. salt
1/4 tsp. pepper
1/2 tsp. basil
1/2 c. grated mozzarella cheese

Slice tops from stem ends of tomatoes. Scoop out pulp; reserve pulp and shells. Drain shells inverted. Saute onion in 2 tablespoons oil in skillet; stir in rice, cooking until rice is translucent. Add reserved pulp, 1/2 cup hot water, salt, pepper and basil. Simmer, covered, for 10 minutes; cool. Stir in cheese; place rice mixture in reserved shells. Arrange tomatoes in greased baking dish; sprinkle with remaining oil. Bake, covered, at 350 degrees for 35 minutes; remove cover. Bake for 10 minutes longer. May be served hot or cold.

Connie M. McGinley, Sec.
Alpha Rho No. 3057
Norfolk, Virginia

1/2 c. raisins
6 tbsp. butter
1/3 c. dry sherry
1/4 c. chopped walnuts

Cook potatoes until tender; peel and halve lengthwise. Arrange potatoes in 9 x ¹3-inch baking pan; sprinkle with salt. Combine brown sugar and cornstarch in saucepan; blend in orange peel and juice. Add raisins; cook over low heat, stirring constantly, until thick and bubbly. Add butter, sherry and walnuts, stirring until butter is melted. Pour sauce over potatoes. Bake at 325 degrees for 30 minutes or until potatoes are glazed. Baste occasionally. Yield: 8 servings.

Mrs. Philip W. Jean, Honorary Member
Beta Sigma Phi International
Vancouver, British Columbia, Canada

GOURMET PEAS
IN SOUR CREAM SAUCE

1 lg. peeled cucumber
1/4 tsp. dried tarragon leaves
1   10-oz. package frozen sweet
*   green peas*
1 tsp. salt
1/2 c. sour cream
1/2 c. cooked salad dressing or
*   mayonnaise*
1 tbsp. lemon juice

Cut cucumber into 1/4-inch slices. Soak tarragon leaves in 2 tablespoons warm water for 10 minutes. Place peas, cucumber, salt and tarragon in saucepan. Bring to a boil. Cover; simmer for 5 minutes. Drain well. Combine sour cream, salad dressing and lemon juice. Place in saucepan over low heat; stir constantly until thoroughly heated. Serve sauce with vegetables.

SHERRIED SWEET POTATOES

8 med. sweet potatoes
1/2 tsp. salt
1 c. (packed) brown sugar
2 tbsp. cornstarch
1 tsp. grated orange peel
2 c. orange juice

SNOW PEAS
WITH WATER CHESTNUTS

1 lb. fresh Chinese pea pods
1 tbsp. salad oil
1 tsp. soy sauce
1 med. clove of garlic, minced
1   5-oz. can bamboo shoots, drained
1   5-oz. can sliced water chestnuts,
*   drained*
1 chicken bouillon cube
1 tsp. cornstarch

Wash peas; remove tips and strings. Combine salad oil, soy sauce and garlic in wok or skillet; cook over low heat until garlic has browned. Add peas, bamboo shoots and water chestnuts. Cook, stirring, over high heat for 1 minute. Dissolve bouillon cube in 1/4 cup boiling water; add to peas. Cover wok; cook over medium heat for 4 minutes. Combine cornstarch and 1 teaspoon cold water; stir into pea mixture. Cook, uncovered, for about 1 minute over high heat until sauce thickens. Two 7-ounce packages frozen pea pods may be substituted for fresh pea pods.

Sandy Cepica, Pres.
Alpha Theta Zeta No. 8409
Houston, Texas

CRAB-STUFFED SQUASH

6 to 8 med. squash
2 6 1/2-oz. cans crab meat, drained
1 c. shredded Swiss cheese
1/3 c. chopped green pepper
1/4 c. finely chopped onion
Salt to taste
1/2 c. mayonnaise
Lemon juice to taste
1/3 c. crushed crackers (opt.)

Boil squash in water to cover just until tender; drain. Cut squash into halves lengthwise; scoop out centers, reserving pulp and shells. Combine crab meat, cheese, green pepper, onion and salt; mix well. Blend mayonnaise with lemon juice; stir into crab meat mixture. Add cracker crumbs and reserved pulp, if desired. Heap crab meat mixture into reserved shells. Arrange squash in greased shallow baking dish. Bake at 350 degrees for 20 minutes or until heated through and cheese is melted.

Laura Spencer
Epsilon Lambda No. 2218
Greenville, Texas

ZUCCHINI-CORN CASSEROLE

1 3-lb. zucchini
1 med. onion, minced
1/2 c. butter
2 eggs, lightly beaten
2 1/2 c. soft bread crumbs
1 No. 2 can cream-style corn
Salt and pepper to taste
1 1/4 c. grated Cheddar cheese
1/4 c. corn flake crumbs

Peel zucchini; boil in salted water until tender. Drain and mash. Saute onion in 1/2 of the butter in large skillet until soft. Add zucchini, eggs, bread crumbs, corn, seasonings and remaining butter. Mix well. Spoon into greased baking dish. Sprinkle with cheese and corn flake crumbs. Bake at 350 degrees for 45 minutes or until knife inserted in center comes out clean.

Barbara MacTavish, Serv. Chm.
Xi Xi X2314
Laramie, Wyoming

DOUBLE CHEESE-STUFFED ZUCCHINI

4 med. zucchini
1/2 c. instant rice, cooked
1 egg, beaten
1 c. cottage cheese
1 sm. onion, chopped
1/2 tsp. salt
Coarsely ground pepper to taste
1 tbsp. chopped parsley
4 slices American cheese

Halve zucchini lengthwise. Boil in salted water until just tender; scoop out centers. Chop pulp. Arrange shells in shallow baking dish. Combine pulp, rice, egg, cottage cheese, onion, seasonings and parsley. Stuff zucchini shells, mounding filling. Bake at 375 degrees for 30 minutes. Cut each cheese slice into 8 strips. Place strips crisscross fashion over filling. Bake for 5 minutes or until cheese melts. Yield: 4 servings.

Betty Jane Jenkin, Pres.
Xi Alpha Nu X3154
Kearny, Arizona

SCOTCH EGGS

1 lb. bulk pork sausage
1 tbsp. prepared mustard
Pepper to taste
6 hard-cooked eggs
3/4 c. fine dry bread crumbs
1 egg, beaten
1 tbsp. water
Chili sauce or mustard mayonnaise

Combine sausage, mustard and pepper. Divide into 6 equal portions; wrap 1 portion around each egg. Roll in bread crumbs. Mix egg and water; dip sausage mixture in egg. Roll in bread crumbs again; place in buttered shallow baking dish. Bake at 400 degrees for about 30 minutes or until browned, turning once during baking. Cut into halves lengthwise; serve hot or cold with chili sauce. Yield: 6 servings.

Vernial Wood
Preceptor Beta XP252
Calgary, Alberta, Canada

JAVANESE OMELET

4 slices bacon
1 onion
Butter
Sliced tomatoes
Snipped parsley
Salt and pepper to taste
Hungarian paprika
4 eggs
1 tbsp. milk
Soy sauce to taste

Fry bacon in heavy frypan until crisp; remove from frypan. Pour off excess grease. Slice onion thin; place in frypan. Add small amount of butter, if needed; cook over low heat until golden brown. Add layer of sliced tomatoes; sprinkle with generous amount of snipped parsley. Cut bacon into large pieces; place on parsley. Sprinkle with salt and pepper; sprinkle with generous amount of paprika. Beat eggs and milk with fork; pour over paprika. Do not disturb layers. Reduce heat as low as possible; cover frypan. Cook for about 20 minutes or until eggs are set; sprinkle with soy sauce. Cut into serving portions. Yield: 2-4 servings.

Virginia D. Smith, Honorary Member
Beta Sigma Phi International
Chappell, Nebraska

EGGS PRINCESS WITH HAM

4 mushrooms
3 tbsp. butter
1/4 lb. cooked ham or tongue, chopped
1 tbsp. freshly chopped parsley
3 tbsp. light cream
1 egg yolk
Pinch of cayenne pepper
1 tbsp. lemon juice
Salt to taste
4 eggs, fried in butter

Slice mushrooms; saute in 1 tablespoon butter in skillet until tender. Add ham and about 2/3 of the parsley; heat through over low heat. Mix cream, egg yolk, remaining

butter, cayenne pepper and lemon juice in double boiler; cook, stirring with spoon or whisk, until thick. Season with salt. Heap ham mixture in serving dish; arrange eggs on ham mixture. Spoon sauce over eggs; sprinkle with remaining parsley. Yield: 4 servings.

Mrs. Joseph Kelby
Xi Zeta Zeta X1753
Dunsmuir, California

EGGS BENEDICT

6 c. water
1 tbsp. vinegar
4 eggs
4 tsp. soft butter
2 English muffins, split
4 slices Canadian bacon or ham
Hollandaise Sauce

Bring water and vinegar to a boil in a stainless steel skillet. Add eggs; reduce heat. Cook until eggs are done; remove eggs to warm dish. Spread butter on muffins; toast until brown. Broil Canadian bacon until done; place on toasted muffins. Top with poached eggs; cover with Hollandaise Sauce.

Hollandaise Sauce

3 egg yolks
1 tsp. lemon juice
1/4 tsp. salt
Pinch of pepper
1/2 c. butter

Place egg yolks in blender; blend until light and thick. Add lemon juice, salt and pepper. Melt butter; add to egg mixture, small amount at a time, while blending.

Mary Kaufman, Treas.
Preceptor Alpha XP 113
Little Rock, Arkansas

QUICHE LORRAINE

1 pkg. pastry mix
12 slices lean bacon
4 eggs

2 c. heavy cream
3/4 tsp. salt
1/8 tsp. powdered nutmeg
1/8 tsp. sugar
1/16 tsp. cayenne pepper
1/8 tsp. pepper
1 tbsp. softened butter or margarine
1/4 lb. Swiss cheese, grated

Prepare pastry according to package directions; fit into 9-inch pie plate. Chill for about 30 minutes. Fry bacon until crisp; drain on paper towels. Crumble. Beat eggs with cream, salt, nutmeg, sugar, cayenne pepper and pepper. Rub pie shell with butter. Sprinkle bacon and cheese into pie shell; pour cream mixture over bacon mixture. Bake in preheated 425-degree oven for 15 minutes. Reduce temperature to 300 degrees; bake for 40 minutes longer or until knife inserted in center comes out clean. Remove from oven; let stand for 5 minutes. Cut into wedges; serve at once. May be cooled, cut into small squares and served as hors d'oeuvres.

Mrs. Alan Avilla, Pres.
Xi Delta Kappa X 1405
Daly City, California

BAKED NOODLES PAPRIKA

1/2 lb. wide egg noodles
2 tbsp. butter or margarine
2 tbsp. flour
1 c. sour cream
1 c. dry sherry
1 c. cottage cheese
1 tsp. Worcestershire sauce
1 tsp. paprika
Dash of garlic powder
Salt and pepper to taste
2 tbsp. grated Parmesan cheese

Cook noodles in boiling water until tender; drain. Melt butter; stir in flour. Add sour cream and sherry; bring to a boil, stirring constantly. Remove from heat; add cottage cheese, Worcestershire sauce, paprika, garlic powder, salt and pepper. Combine with noodles; turn into greased baking dish. Sprinkle with Parmesan cheese. Bake, uncovered, in 350-degree oven for 40 minutes. Yield: 6 servings.

Linda Jones, Pres.
Phi Zeta P620
Moundsville, West Virginia

NOODLES ALFREDO

1/4 c. salt
8 to 12 qt. boiling water
2 lb. medium egg noodles
1 lb. sweet butter, softened
4 c. grated Parmesan cheese
1 c. heavy cream, at room
   temperature

Add salt to boiling water. Add noodles gradually so that water continues to boil. Cook, uncovered, stirring occasionally, until tender. Drain in colander. Place butter in hot 4-quart casserole; add noodles, tossing gently. Add cheese; toss again. Pour in cream; toss well. Sprinkle with freshly ground pepper, if desired. Yield: 12-16 servings.

CALIFORNIA CASSEROLE

1 c. converted rice
1 1/2 tsp. salt
1 c. chopped onion
1/4 c. butter or margarine
2 c. sour cream
1 c. creamed cottage cheese
1 bay leaf, crumbled
1/8 tsp. pepper
3 cans green chilies, drained
2 c. grated Cheddar cheese
Chopped parsley

Bring 2 1/2 cups water to a boil in large saucepan. Add rice and 1 teaspoon salt; cover tightly. Cook over low heat for about 25 minutes or until all water is absorbed. Saute onion in butter until golden; remove from heat. Stir in rice, sour cream, cottage cheese, bay leaf, remaining salt and pepper; toss to mix well. Place half the rice mixture in greased 12 x 8 x 2-inch pan. Cut green chilies in half; place half the chilies on rice mixture. Sprinkle with half the cheese; repeat layers. Bake, uncovered, at 350 degrees for 25 minutes or until bubbly and hot; sprinkle with parsley.

Lynn Archer, VP
Gamma Tau No. 6631
El Dorado, Arkansas

GREEN RICE

1 c. long grain rice
4 c. boiling water
1 tsp. salt
3 lg. eggs
2 c. light cream
1/2 c. melted butter
1 c. grated sharp Cheddar cheese
2 c. finely minced parsley
1 med. onion, grated
2 cloves of garlic, minced
Salt and pepper to taste

Cook rice in boiling water with salt until tender but firm. Drain; keep hot. Beat eggs until light; add cream. Add butter, cheese, parsley, onion, garlic and seasonings; mix well. Stir into rice; place in buttered casserole.

Bake at 350 degrees for about 1 hour or until firm. Unmold on hot serving plate. Yield: 12 servings.

Lois Keener Thome, Honorary Member
Beta Sigma Phi International
Corona, California

POLYNESIAN RICE MINGLE

1 c. wild rice
1 c. rice
3 tbsp. minced onion
3 tbsp. soy sauce
4 chicken bouillon cubes
4 c. boiling water
1 1/2 c. macadamia nuts, coarsely
*   chopped (opt.)*
1/4 c. snipped parsley (opt.)

Combine wild rice, rice, onion and soy sauce in 2-quart casserole. Dissolve bouillon cubes in boiling water; stir into rice mixture. Bake, covered, in 350-degree oven for 45 minutes. Cool; refrigerate. Let stand at room temperature for 20 minutes. Bake in preheated 350-degree oven for 15 minutes or until heated through. Sprinkle with macadamia nuts and parsley just before serving. May be served after preparing, if desired. Yield: 4-6 servings.

Jamet Glock, Pres.
Zeta Kappa No. 5126
Albany, New York

SAVANNAH RED RICE

1/4 lb. sliced bacon
1/2 c. chopped onion
2 c. rice, washed
2 c. tomatoes
1/2 tsp. salt
1/4 tsp. pepper
1/8 tsp. hot sauce

Fry bacon until crisp; remove from pan. Crumble. Cook onion in bacon fat until tender. Add rice, tomatoes, seasonings and bacon; cook over low heat for about 10 minutes. Pour into 1-quart casserole; cover tightly. Bake at 350 degrees for 1 hour, stirring with fork several times. Yield: 6-8 servings.

Vivian Turner Howard, Pres.
Zeta Iota No. 8816
Savannah, Georgia

HAZEL'S DRESSING FOR CORNISH HENS

1 1/2 c. diced apples
3 1/2 c. bread crumbs
1/2 c. seedless raisins
2 tbsp. sugar
3/4 tsp. salt
1/4 c. melted butter
1/4 tsp. cinnamon
1/4 c. chopped nutmeats

Combine all ingredients; add enough hot water to moisten. Yield: Stuffing for 4 Cornish hens.

Jacqueline Shafar
Zeta Iota No. 4732
Creston, Iowa

OYSTER DRESSING

1 lg. onion, chopped
1/2 c. butter
Pinch of saffron
1 c. milk
1 loaf bread
18 lg. oysters
1 tsp. salt

Saute onion in butter in medium saucepan until onion is soft. Add saffron and milk; place over low heat. Cut bread into small cubes; place in large mixing bowl. Chop oysters with kitchen shears or in blender; add oysters and liquid to bread cubes. Add salt and milk mixture; mix well. Mixture should be very moist; add more milk, if needed. Place in buttered 2-quart casserole. Bake in 400-degree oven for about 1 hour or until brown.

Alice Garrett, Pres.
Delta Xi No. 7104
Sterling, Virginia

STUFFING FOR 15-POUND TURKEY

Turkey gizzard, heart and liver
1 lg. onion, diced
6 tbsp. butter or margarine
2 lb. ground round steak
4 c. mashed potatoes or cooked rice
1 c. seedless raisins
2 tsp. poultry seasoning
1/2 tsp. salt
1/2 tsp. pepper

Dice gizzard, heart and liver. Cook onion in butter until wilted. Add giblets and ground steak; cook until ground steak is almost done. Cool. Add potatoes and raisins. Add seasonings; mix well. Use to stuff into cavity of turkey. Stuffing may be made in advance; refrigerate until ready to stuff turkey.

Helena Hatzes, Honorary Member
Beta Sigma Phi International
Sandy Spring, Maryland

SAUSAGE AND RAISIN STUFFING

2 c. fresh bread crumbs
1 1/3 c. milk
1/2 c. minced onion
2 tbsp. butter
1/2 lb. bulk sausage
3/4 c. chopped celery
1/4 c. raisins
1/4 c. chopped fresh cranberries
2 tart apples, peeled and diced
Salt and pepper to taste
Sage and thyme to taste

Moisten bread crumbs with milk; squeeze dry. Saute onion in butter till soft, not brown. Add crumbled sausage, celery, raisins, cranberries and apples; cook for 5 minutes. Place in large bowl. Add bread; mix well. Season with salt, pepper, sage and thyme; place in baking pan. Bake at 350 degrees for 20 minutes. Bake for 1 hour if in center of meat or poultry; excellent stuffed in crown roast of pork.

Mrs. John Van Wyk, Contact Chm.
Delta Mu No. 4102
Leisure City, Florida

Breads

Often called the staff of life, bread is another food, along with
accompaniments and desserts, which inspires the creativity of every
homemaker. The preparation, kneading and baking give any
woman a glowing feeling of accomplishment. There is something
about the smell of fresh yeast dough baking that reminds one of years
gone by and of a heritage that will always live on — through the
tradition of breadmaking.

Included in this section are family recipes that Beta Sigma Phis are
passing on to you. Many of these recipes have been handed down from
mother to daughter, generation after generation. Creative cooks
from Maryland to California have turned their considerable talents
towards creating quick breads, muffins, biscuit and roll recipes
that will soon become your family favorites. Whenever you need
a versatile bread recipe, be sure to turn to these pages and introduce
your family to some delicious Beta Sigma Phi recipes.

ALABAMA BISCUITS

1 pkg. dry yeast
1 c. warm milk
2 c. flour
1 tbsp. baking powder
2 tbsp. sugar
1/2 tsp. salt
2 tbsp. melted shortening

Dissolve yeast in milk; add flour, baking powder, sugar, salt and shortening. Knead until well mixed. Roll out 1/4-inch thick; cut in desired shape. Dip in melted butter; stack 2 biscuits. Let rise for 1 hour. Bake at 400 degrees for 10 minutes.

Pizza Dough

Mix recipe as for biscuits; let rise for 1 hour. Flatten in 2 pans; let set for 10 to 15 minutes. Add sauce, meat and cheese. Bake for 12 minutes at 425 degrees.

Jeannie Rice, Pres.
Zeta Rho No. 5622
Salina, Kansas

SOURDOUGH BISCUITS

1 1/2 c. sifted all-purpose flour
2 tsp. baking powder
1/4 tsp. soda
1/2 tsp. salt
1/4 c. butter or margarine
1 c. Sourdough Starter
Melted butter

Sift dry ingredients together; cut in butter with pastry blender. Add starter; mix well. Turn dough out on lightly floured board. Knead lightly until satiny. Roll dough 1/2-inch thick. Cut with floured 2 1/2-inch cutter. Place biscuits in well-greased 9-inch square pan. Brush with melted butter. Let rise for about 1 hour in a warm place. Bake at 425 degrees for 20 minutes. Yield: 10 biscuits.

Sourdough Starter

1 pkg. dry yeast
2 c. sifted all-purpose flour

2 tbsp. sugar
2 1/2 c. water

Combine in stone crock or glass or pottery bowl. Beat well. Cover with cheesecloth; let stand for 2 days in warm place. Stir in 2 cups warm water and 2 cups flour to replenish starter as needed.

Thearon T. Russell, Treas.
Nu Gamma No. 6410
Kankakee, Illinois

PINEAPPLE-SOUR CREAM BRUNCH RING

1 1-lb. 4 1/2-oz. can crushed
*   pineapple*
2 tbsp. sliced almonds
1 3-oz. package cream cheese
1 c. sugar
2 tsp. vanilla
1 egg
2 c. sifted flour
1 tsp. soda
1 tsp. salt
1/2 c. sour cream
1 tbsp. soft butter
1 c. sifted confectioners' sugar

Drain pineapple, reserving 1/2 cup for glaze. Grease 9-inch tube pan or mold; sprinkle

with almonds. Beat cream cheese until soft. Beat in sugar and vanilla; blend in egg well. Sift flour, soda and salt together; add to egg mixture alternately with sour cream. Stir in pineapple. Turn batter into prepared pan. Bake at 350 degrees for 45 minutes or until bread tests done. Remove to wire rack; let stand for 10 minutes. Turn out on cake plate. Combine reserved pineapple, soft butter and confectioners' sugar. Spread glaze over warm bread.

BLUEBERRY COFFEE CAKE

2 c. flour
1 c. sugar
3 tsp. baking powder
1/4 tsp. salt
1/2 c. shortening
2 eggs, beaten
1 c. milk
1 1/2 c. fresh blueberries
1 1/3 c. flaked coconut

Sift flour, sugar, baking powder and salt together; cut in shortening with pastry blender. Combine eggs and milk; stir into flour mixture. Fold in blueberries. Place in 2 greased 9-inch cake pans; sprinkle coconut evenly over tops. Bake at 375 degrees for 25 minutes.

Thelma Huhta
Preceptor Eta XP598
Ithaca, New York

CINNAMON COFFEE CAKE

1/2 c. shortening
3/4 c. sugar
1 tsp. vanilla
3 eggs
2 c. sifted flour
1 tsp. baking powder
1 tsp. soda
1/2 pt. sour cream
6 tbsp. softened butter
1 c. (firmly packed) brown sugar
2 tsp. cinnamon
1 c. chopped nuts

Cream shortening, sugar and vanilla thoroughly. Add eggs, one at a time, beating well after each addition. Sift flour, baking powder and soda together. Add to creamed mixture alternately with sour cream, blending well after each addition. Spread half the batter in greased and waxed paper-lined 10-inch tube pan. Cream butter, brown sugar and cinnamon together. Add nuts; mix well. Dot batter in pan evenly with half the nut mixture; cover with remaining batter. Dot with remaining nut mixture. Bake at 350 degrees for about 50 minutes. Cool for 10 minutes; remove from pan.

Sandra J. Lange
Zeta Delta No. 8668
Chamblee, Georgia

FRENCH COFFEE CAKE

1/2 c. butter
1/2 c. vegetable shortening
1 1/2 c. sugar
3 eggs
3 c. sifted cake flour
3 tsp. baking powder
1 tsp. soda
1/2 tsp. salt
1 c. sour cream
1 tsp. almond extract
1 tsp. vanilla
1/4 c. cocoa
1/2 c. chopped pecans

Cream butter and shortening; beat in 1 cup sugar gradually. Add eggs, one at a time, beating well after each addition. Sift flour, baking powder, soda and salt together. Mix sour cream, almond extract and vanilla. Add flour mixture to creamed mixture alternately with sour cream mixture. Pour half the batter into greased tube pan. Mix remaining sugar, cocoa and pecans; sprinkle half the mixture over batter in pan. Add remaining batter; sprinkle with remaining cocoa mixture. Run knife through batter to marble. Bake at 350 degrees for about 1 hour; cool in pan.

Virginia Butterfield, Pres.
Preceptor Epsilon XP0446
Windsor, Connecticut

SOUR CREAM-PECAN COFFEE CAKE

1/2 c. butter
1 1/4 c. sugar
2 eggs
1 tsp. soda
2 c. flour
1 tsp. baking powder
1/2 tsp. salt
1 c. sour cream
1 tsp. vanilla
1/3 c. (packed) brown sugar
1 tsp. cinnamon
1 c. chopped pecans

Cream butter and 1 cup sugar. Add eggs, one at a time, beating well after each addition. Sift dry ingredients together; add to creamed mixture alternately with sour cream, beginning and ending with flour mixture. Stir in vanilla. Pour half the batter into buttered deep 9 x 9-inch or 9 x 13-inch baking pan. Mix brown sugar, remaining sugar, cinnamon and pecans; sprinkle half the mixture over batter in pan. Pour remaining batter over pecan mixture; top with remaining pecan mixture. Bake at 325 degrees for 30 to 35 minutes. May be made day before, covered and refrigerated until ready to bake.

Mildred Williams
Beta Beta No. 576
DeWitt, Iowa

MEXICAN CORN BREAD

1 lb. ground beef
1 med. onion, chopped fine
1 med. green bell pepper, chopped
fine
1/2 c. finely chopped celery
1 can whole kernel corn, drained
Salt and pepper to taste
1 recipe corn bread batter
Hot sauce to taste
1 c. grated hoop cheese

Brown beef, onion, green pepper and celery in large iron skillet, stirring frequently. Add corn, salt and pepper; heat through. Pour 1/2 of the corn bread batter into large baking pan; spread beef mixture on batter. Sprinkle with hot sauce; cover with cheese. Pour remaining batter over cheese. Bake at 350 degrees for 45 minutes.

Vivienne Stringer, Pres.
Alpha Sigma No. 7414
Mobile, Alabama

SOUTHERN SPOON BREAD

1 c. white cornmeal
1 tsp. salt
1 c. butter
1 tsp. sugar
7 eggs, separated

Stir cornmeal and salt into 2 cups boiling water gradually; reduce heat. Simmer, stirring constantly, until smooth and thickened. Remove from heat. Stir in butter and sugar; blend thoroughly. Cool. Beat egg yolks until thick and lemony. Add to cornmeal mixture; blend well. Beat egg whites until stiff peaks form; fold into cornmeal mixture. Pour into greased 2-quart casserole. Bake at 350 degrees for 1 hour or until knife inserted in center comes out clean. Yield: 8-10 servings.

Mary Clare Dinneen
Preceptor Iota Chap.
Richmond, Virginia

GERMAN FURDENS

1 pkg. dry yeast
1/2 c. butter
1 1/2 c. warm milk
4 eggs, separated
1/4 c. sugar
1/4 tsp. salt
1/4 tsp. cinnamon
4 c. flour
1/2 c. raisins
1/2 c. whiskey
Grated rind of 1/2 lemon
6 cardamom seeds, pounded
Sugar

Dissolve yeast and butter in warm milk; let cool. Beat egg yolks; add beaten yolks, sugar and salt to milk mixture. Add remaining dry ingredients to egg yolk mixture. Beat egg whites until soft peaks form; fold into batter. Soak raisins in whiskey until plump; add raisins, lemon rind and cardamom seeds to batter. Let rise until doubled in bulk. Place iron Furden pan over low flame on top of stove; add grease to each mold. Place small amount of batter in each mold; cook slowly until brown, turning occasionally with 2 forks. Remove; sprinkle with sugar or powdered sugar. Serve warm.

Alice Hebbel, Rec. Sec.
Xi Zeta X0150
Davenport, Iowa

RAISED DOUGHNUTS

1 c. shortening
2 tsp. salt
1 c. sugar
1 lg. can evaporated milk
1 cake yeast
3 eggs, well beaten
8 c. flour
1 1-lb. box confectioners' sugar
1 tsp. vanilla

Combine shortening, salt and sugar in large bowl. Blend milk with 1 milk can water in saucepan; scald. Stir into sugar mixture until shortening is melted; cool mixture to lukewarm. Stir in crumbled yeast until dissolved; add eggs. Stir in flour gradually; knead into smooth dough. Let rise, covered, for 2 hours or until doubled in bulk; punch down. Roll out 1/2 inch thick; cut with doughnut cutter. Place in greased baking pans; let rise in warm place until doubled in bulk. Fry in deep fat at 360 degrees, turning once, until golden; drain on paper toweling. Mix confectioners' sugar, vanilla and 1/2 cup water. Blend well. Dip warm doughnuts into glaze; stand on edge to drain. Yield: 4-6 dozen doughnuts.

Shirley J. Lewis, Pres.
Phi No. 4742
Cody, Wyoming

LEMON CUSTARD FRENCH TOAST

3 eggs, separated
Grated rind and juice of 1 lemon

Sugar
3 tbsp. butter or margarine
1/4 tsp. salt
1/2 c. milk
1/4 tsp. nutmeg
1/2 tsp. vanilla
Sliced bread

Combine slightly beaten egg whites, lemon rind and juice, 1 cup sugar and 1 tablespoon butter in top of double boiler. Cook over boiling water, stirring constantly, until thick; keep warm. Mix beaten egg yolks, salt and 1 tablespoon sugar. Add milk, nutmeg and vanilla; beat well. Melt remaining butter in skillet. Dip slices of bread into egg yolk mixture; fry in skillet till browned on both sides. Serve with lemon custard.

Lee Cook, Pres.-Elect
Gamma Omicron No. 6110
Albuquerque, New Mexico

COFFEE CAN BREAD

4 c. flour
1 pkg. yeast
1/2 c. milk
1/2 c. vegetable oil
1/4 c. sugar
1 tsp. salt
2 eggs

Measure 1 1/2 cups flour into mixing bowl; blend yeast into flour. Place 1/2 cup water into saucepan; add milk, oil, sugar and salt; heat until warm. Add to flour mixture; beat until smooth. Stir in eggs and remaining flour; beat until smooth and elastic. Divide mixture between two buttered 1-pound coffee cans; cover with plastic lids. Let rise in warm place for 35 minutes. Dough should rise almost to top of cans; remove lids. Bake at 375 degrees for 35 minutes or until browned. Let stand in cans until bread shrinks slightly from sides and is easily removed.

Thelma J. Evans, City Coun. Pres.
Xi Kappa X0770
Corvallis, Oregon

CELERY ROLLS IN A LOAF

1 sm. loaf unsliced bread
1/2 c. butter or margarine,
  softened
1 tsp. celery seed
1/4 tsp. salt
Dash of cayenne pepper
1/4 tsp. paprika

Trim crusts from top, sides and ends of loaf. Cut down through center of loaf lengthwise, almost to bottom. Cut at 1-inch intervals, crosswise, almost to bottom. Combine butter, celery seed, salt, cayenne pepper and paprika. Spread butter mixture over entire surface of cuts. Place on baking sheet; refrigerate, covered, with waxed paper. Bake at 400 degrees for 15 to 18 minutes or until golden. Yield: 6 servings.

Rochelle Dolan, Corr. Sec.
Iota Theta No. 3348
Walnut Creek, California

DELICIOUS WHOLE WHEAT BREAD

3 c. milk, scalded
1 c. sugar
1/2 c. margarine
2 tsp. salt
6 c. flour
2 pkg. dry yeast
2 eggs, slightly beaten
6 c. whole wheat flour

Pour scalded milk over sugar, margarine and salt in large bowl. Stir until margarine is melted. Add 4 cups flour. Cool to lukewarm. Dissolve yeast in 1/2 cup lukewarm water. Add yeast mixture and eggs to batter. Beat well; stir in remaining flour and whole wheat flour. Knead well on dough board or cloth. Let rise in warm place for 45 minutes. Shape into 5 medium loaves; place in greased loaf pans. Let rise until doubled in bulk. Bake at 350 degrees for 30 minutes or until brown on top.

Glenda Raby, 2nd VP
Gamma Psi No. 6933
Las Cruces, New Mexico

FRENCH BREAD

1 pkg. dry yeast
1 tbsp. sugar
1 1/2 tsp. salt
1 tbsp. cooking oil
4 c. flour

Dissolve yeast in 1/2 cup warm water; add sugar, salt, 1 cup warm water and oil. Add flour. Let rise for 10 minutes, working spoon through dough 5 times. Divide into 2 balls; let rest for 10 minutes, covered. Roll out into 2 rectangles; roll up as for jelly roll. Place on ungreased cookie sheet. Score top with sharp knife. Let rise, uncovered, for 1 hour and 30 minutes. Bake at 400 degrees for 30 to 35 minutes.

Freda L. Price, Corr. Sec.
Sigma Kappa No. 5038
San Jose, California

MONKEY BREAD

1 c. milk
1/2 c. sugar
1 tsp. salt
1 c. butter, melted
1 pkg. dry yeast
1 egg
4 c. flour

Scald milk; stir in sugar, salt, and 1/2 cup butter. Cool to lukewarm. Place 1/4 cup warm water in large heated bowl; add yeast, stirring until dissolved. Add milk mixture, egg, and half the flour. Beat with electric mixer until smooth. Add remaining flour to form stiff batter. Cover loosely with foil; refrigerate for at least 2 hours. Divide dough into 24 pieces; dip each piece into remaining melted butter. Place 12 pieces in well greased tube pan; arrange remaining pieces over top. Let rise, covered, in warm place until doubled in bulk. Bake at 375 degrees for 40 minutes. Each piece may be rolled in brown sugar and bread drizzled with glaze when cooked.

Tanya Hatley, Pres.
Gamma Kappa No. 5525
Eunice, New Mexico

DILLY CASSEROLE BREAD

1 pkg. dry yeast
1 c. creamed cottage cheese
2 tbsp. sugar
1 tbsp. instant minced onion
1 tbsp. butter
2 tsp. dillseed
1 1/2 tsp. salt
1/4 tsp. soda
1 egg
2 1/4 to 2 1/2 c. flour

Sprinkle yeast over 1/4 cup lukewarm water. Heat cottage cheese to lukewarm; add sugar, onion, butter, dillseed, salt, soda, egg and yeast mixture. Add enough flour to form stiff dough. Cover; let rise in warm place until doubled in bulk. Stir down. Turn into greased pan or 1 1/4-quart casserole. Let rise for 30 to 40 minutes or until light. Bake at 350 degrees until brown. Brush with additional butter; sprinkle with additional salt.

Ruth Dominise
Xi Alpha Zeta X1074
Sterling, Colorado

HERB-CHEESE BREAD

1 pkg. yeast
1 egg, slightly beaten
3 tbsp. margarine, melted
2 tbsp. sugar
1 tsp. salt
1 tsp. oregano
1 tsp. basil
3 c. flour
1/2 c. minced onion
1/2 lb. Swiss cheese, grated

Dissolve yeast in 1 cup warm water in large mixing bowl. Stir in egg, margarine, sugar, salt, 1/2 teaspoon oregano and 1/2 teaspoon basil. Blend in flour; knead until well mixed. Place dough in greased bowl, turning to grease top. Let rise, covered, in warm place for 1 hour or until doubled in bulk; punch down. Place dough in greased 3-quart round baking dish; let rise until doubled in bulk. Combine remaining oregano and basil with onion and Swiss cheese; sprinkle over dough.

Preheat oven to 375 degrees. Bake for 45 minutes; slice while warm.

Marchelle Bohon
Theta No. 1035
Carlsbad, New Mexico

ALOHA LOAF

1 7 1/4-oz. package Hawaiian
pineapple frosting mix
Orange juice
2 pkg. dry yeast
1/2 c. cooking oil
1 tbsp. salt
8 to 8 1/2 c. flour
1 c. sifted confectioners' sugar
1 tbsp. soft butter

Combine 1 1/2 cups boiling water and frosting mix packet in large bowl. Add can of pineapple from package and 1 cup orange juice. Cool to lukewarm. Stir in yeast, oil and salt. Add 4 cups flour; beat well. Add enough remaining flour gradually to form stiff dough, beating well after each addition. Knead on floured surface for 5 to 7 minutes or until smooth and elastic. Place dough in greased bowl; cover. Let rise in warm place for 1 hour to 1 hour and 30 minutes or until doubled in bulk. Shape into 3 loaves. Place loaves in 3 well-greased 9 x 5-inch pans. Cover; let rise in warm place for 45 minutes to 1 hour or until light. Bake at 375 degrees for 35 to 40 minutes. Combine confectioners' sugar, butter and 1 to 2 tablespoons orange juice. Remove bread from pans; spread glaze over warm loaves.

147

MEDITERRANEAN FEAST BREAD

1 pkg. dry yeast
1/2 c. milk, scalded
2 tbsp. softened butter or margarine
1/4 c. sugar
1 tsp. salt
1 egg, slightly beaten
3 1/2 to 3 3/4 c. sifted all-purpose
  flour
1/2 c. chopped red maraschino
  cherries
1 tbsp. grated lemon peel

Pour 1/4 cup warm water into large bowl; add yeast, stirring until dissolved. Cool milk to lukewarm; stir into yeast mixture. Add butter, sugar, salt and egg. Stir in half the flour, cherries and lemon peel; mix well. Add remaining flour gradually; mix until dough can be handled easily. Knead on lightly floured board for 10 minutes or until smooth and elastic. Shape into ball; place in greased bowl. Cover with towel. Let rise in warm place for about 1 hour and 30 minutes to 2 hours or until doubled in bulk. Punch down; shape into 3 round loaves. Place on lightly greased baking sheet 1/2 inch apart to form 3-leaf clover. Cover with towel; let rise until doubled in bulk. Bake at 350 degrees for 30 to 35 minutes. Frost with thin confectioners' sugar glaze and garnish each loaf with 3 red glace cherry halves to form flower and red glace cherry slice to form stem, if desired.

Photograph for this recipe on page 140.

PANETTONE

2 c. milk
2 tsp. salt
1 1/4 c. sugar
1/2 c. butter or margarine, softened
2 pkg. dry yeast
2 eggs
1 egg yolk
8 3/4 c. (about) all-purpose flour
2 tbsp. dark rum
2 4-oz. jars mixed candied fruits
1 c. red glace cherries, chopped

Scald milk; pour 1 1/2 cups milk into large bowl. Stir in salt, sugar and butter; cool to lukewarm. Cool remaining milk to lukewarm; add yeast, stirring to dissolve. Combine eggs and egg yolk; beat lightly. Add 5 cups flour to sugar mixture alternately with yeast mixture and eggs; beat until smooth. Cover bowl with towel; allow to stand for 1 hour. Combine rum, candied fruits and cherries; let stand for 1 hour, stirring frequently. Add remaining flour and fruits to dough; beat well. Turn out onto lightly floured board; knead for about 10 minutes or until smooth and elastic. Place in lightly greased bowl; cover with towel. Let rise in warm place for about 3 hours or until doubled in bulk. Punch down. Divide dough; place in 3 greased 1 1/2-quart fluted molds or 9 x 5 x 3-inch loaf pans. Cover with towel; let rise again in warm place until doubled in bulk. Bake at 350 degrees for about 50 minutes. Frost with thin confectioners' sugar glaze and garnish with whole red maraschino cherries with stems, if desired.

Photograph for this recipe on page 140.

CHOCOLATE TEA BREAD

1/4 c. butter
2/3 c. sugar
1 egg
2 c. sifted cake flour
1 tsp. soda
3/4 tsp. salt
1/3 c. cocoa
1 tsp. cinnamon
1 c. buttermilk
1 c. raisins
3/4 c. chopped walnuts

Cream butter; add sugar gradually, creaming well after each addition. Add egg; beat well. Sift flour, soda, salt, cocoa and cinnamon together. Add to creamed mixture alternately with buttermilk, beating until blended after each addition. Stir in raisins and walnuts. Turn into greased 9 x 5 x 2 3/4-inch bread pan. Bake at 350 degrees for 1 hour. Cool on wire rack. Spread with softened cream cheese, if desired.

Emma Lee Goodrick, Pres.
Xi Gamma Alpha X 2810
Dubuque, Iowa

CHOCOLATE-WALNUT-DATE LOAF

1 6-oz. package semisweet
  chocolate morsels
1/4 c. butter or shortening
1/3 c. sugar
1 c. sliced pitted dates
1 egg, beaten
1 tsp. vanilla
3/4 c. milk
2 3/4 c. sifted all-purpose flour
1 1/2 tsp. salt
1 tsp. baking powder
1 tsp. soda
1 c. coarsely chopped California
  walnuts

Melt chocolate and butter together over hot water. Add sugar; mix well. Set aside to cool. Pour 3/4 cup boiling water over dates; cool. Stir egg and vanilla into cooled chocolate mixture. Add milk and dates with water. Sift flour, salt, baking powder and soda together; add to chocolate mixture, stirring just until flour is moistened. Add walnuts; mix lightly. Turn into greased 9 x 5 x 3-inch loaf pan. Let stand for 20 minutes. Bake at 350 degrees for 1 hour and 5 minutes to 1 hour and 15 minutes or until pick inserted in center comes out clean. Cool for 5 to 10 minutes; turn out onto wire rack. Cool completely.

CHOCOLATE POMPADOUR

1 pkg. yeast
Sugar
3 c. sifted flour
3/4 c. scalded milk, cooled
3/4 c. butter or margarine
3 eggs
1 tsp. vanilla
2/3 c. unsweetened cocoa
1/2 tsp. salt
1 tsp. soda
1/2 tsp. cinnamon
1 c. chopped blanched almonds
Confectioners' sugar

Dissolve yeast in medium bowl in 1/4 cup warm water, stirring until dissolved; add 1 tablespoon sugar, 2 cups flour and milk. Beat until dough is smooth and elastic. Let rise, covered, in warm place for 40 minutes or until doubled in bulk. Beat butter in large bowl with electric mixture at medium speed; add 2 cups sugar, eggs and vanilla, beating until fluffy. Dissolve cocoa in 1/2 cup warm water; beat into egg mixture. Combine remaining flour with salt, soda and cinnamon. Reduce mixer speed to low; add yeast mixture and flour mixture. Beat for 5 minutes; fold in almonds. Pour into greased bundt pan. Let rise, covered, in warm place until doubled in bulk. Preheat oven to 350 degrees. Bake pompadour for 1 hour or until tester inserted in center comes out clean. Let stand for 30 minutes. Loosen side and center; invert on wire rack. Cool completely. Sprinkle lightly with confectioners' sugar. May be served as coffee cake or dessert. Yield: 16 servings.

Aurelia R. Hawkins, Rec. Sec.
Xi Beta Theta X2353
South Glens Falls, New York

OATMEAL BREAD

1 1/2 c. whole wheat flour
1 1/4 c. oatmeal
1 pkg. dry yeast
1 1/4 c. milk
1/4 c. margarine
1/4 c. honey
2 tsp. salt

2 eggs
1 1/2 c. all-purpose flour

Combine whole wheat flour, 1 cup oatmeal and yeast in large mixer bowl. Pour milk, margarine, honey and salt in small saucepan; heat over medium heat, stirring until margarine is melted. Add to dry ingredients with 1 egg plus 1 egg yolk. Beat at low speed for 30 seconds, scraping sides of bowl to blend. Beat for 3 minutes at high speed. Stir in remaining flour. Dough should be soft. Beat by hand until smooth. Cover; let rise for 1 hour and 30 minutes to 2 hours or until doubled in bulk. Stir dough down. Sprinkle 2-quart greased casserole with 2 tablespoons oatmeal. Place dough into casserole; let rise for about 45 minutes to 1 hour. Brush with slightly beaten egg white; sprinkle with remaining oatmeal. Bake for 45 to 50 minutes at 350 degrees. Let cool for 15 minutes on rack, then remove from casserole.

Margaret Husband, Treas.
Xi Upsilon X1665
Salt Lake City, Utah

CRANBERRY FRUIT BREAD

2 c. sifted flour
1 c. sugar
1 1/2 tsp. baking powder
1/2 tsp. soda
1 tsp. salt
1/4 c. shortening
3/4 c. orange juice
1 tbsp. grated orange rind
1 egg, beaten
1/2 c. chopped nuts
1 to 1 1/2 c. chopped fresh
  cranberries

Sift flour, sugar, baking powder, soda and salt. Cut in shortening. Combine juice, rind and egg. Pour all at once into dry ingredients. Mix until dampened. Fold in nuts and cranberries. Spoon into greased loaf pan. Spread sides and corners higher than middle of pan. Bake at 350 degrees for 1 hour. Store overnight for easy slicing.

Dorothy J. Hall, Pres.
Xi Alpha Pi X2152
Williamsburg, Virginia

PATE MAISON

1/2 env. unflavored gelatin
1/2 c. bouillon or consomme
Pimento
Capers
Truffles and ripe olives
1 lb. chicken livers
1/2 tsp. monosodium glutamate
2 tbsp. minced onion
6 tbsp. butter or margarine
1/2 tsp. salt
1 tsp. dry mustard
1/4 tsp. cloves
1/8 tsp. nutmeg
2 tbsp. brandy

Sprinkle gelatin over bouillon in saucepan. Place over low heat, stirring constantly, until gelatin is dissolved. Pour thin layer of bouillon mixture in bottom of 8 x 4 x 2 1/2-inch pan. Chill until thickened. Press a design of pimento, capers, truffles and ripe olives into thickened bouillon. Pour remaining bouillon mixture over design and chill while preparing pate. Sprinkle chicken livers with monosodium glutamate. Saute with onion in 2 tablespoons butter for 6 to 7 minutes. Remove from heat. Turn into blender. Sprinkle with salt, dry mustard, cloves and nutmeg. Blend until smooth. Add remaining butter and brandy. Blend until smooth. Turn into prepared pan. Chill. Dip quickly into pan of hot water up to top to unmold. Loosen with sharp knife. Turn onto platter. Yield: 24 servings.

Photograph for this recipe on page 152.

RIPE OLIVE RIGOLETTOS

2 c. canned pitted ripe olives
2 8-oz. packages cream cheese
1 tsp. salt
6 drops of hot sauce
2 tbsp. lemon juice
2 tbsp. tomato paste
1/2 c. mashed avocado
8 candied cherries, chopped
1 tbsp. chopped sugared ginger
1/4 c. chopped nuts
1 bunch hearts of celery
1 cucumber
1 green pepper
1 tomato
1 red onion
1 pkg. Cheddar cheese

Chop 1 1/2 cups ripe olives very fine. Cut remaining olives into halves, quarters and rings for garnish. Soften the cream cheese in a bowl. Add the chopped olives, salt, hot sauce and lemon juice and mix well. Spoon equal amounts into 3 bowls. Add tomato paste to 1 bowl, mashed avocado to 1 bowl and cherries, ginger and nuts to remaining bowl. Stuff celery with cherry mixture and press together to form bunch. Roll in waxed paper and chill. Cut the cucumber into slices. Cut green pepper and tomato into wedges, scooping out seeds and membrane. Cut the onion into wedges and separate. Cut cheese into triangles. Pipe cream cheese mixtures onto canape bases with a pastry tube and garnish with reserved ripe olives. Cut celery into slices. Chill all canapes well before serving.

Photograph for this recipe on page 151.

LOBSTER BARQUETTES

1 10-oz. package pie crust mix
1 tbsp. butter
1 5-oz. can lobster, finely chopped
1 tbsp. chopped onion
1 tbsp. chopped parsley
2 tbsp. brandy
1/2 tsp. monosodium glutamate
2 tsp. lemon juice
1/3 c. warm light cream
1 egg yolk
Grated Parmesan cheese
Buttered bread crumbs

Prepare pie crust mix according to package directions. Roll dough on lightly floured board to 1/8-inch thickness. Invert 3-inch barquette molds on dough. Cut 1/3 inch around each mold with knife. Fit piece of pastry into each mold; press to bottom and sides. Trim excess around rim of mold. Prick bottom with a fork. Fill pastry shells with rice to prevent pastry from bubbling. Bake at 375 degrees for 10 to 12 minutes or until shells are golden brown. Remove rice. Cool. Melt butter in a skillet. Add lobster, onion and parsley. Cook until onion is tender but not brown. Stir in brandy. Sprinkle with monosodium glutamate and lemon juice. Combine cream and egg yolk; stir into skillet. Spoon mixture into baked barquettes. Sprinkle with Parmesan cheese and bread crumbs. Brown under broiler to serve immediately. Refrigerate until ready to serve if prepared in advance. Reheat in a 350-degree oven for 15 minutes. Brown lightly under broiler.

Photograph for this recipe on page 152.

CRAB MEAT QUICHE

1 8-in. unbaked pie shell
2 eggs
1 c. light cream
1 tsp. monosodium glutamate
3/4 tsp. salt
Dash of cayenne pepper
3 oz. Swiss cheese, grated
3 oz. Gruyere cheese, grated
1 tbsp. flour
1 6 1/2-oz. can crab meat, flaked

Prick bottom and sides of pie shell with fork. Bake in a 450-degree oven for about 10 minutes or until delicate brown. Combine eggs, cream, monosodium glutamate, salt and cayenne pepper; beat well. Combine cheeses, flour and crab meat; sprinkle evenly in pie shell. Pour in cream mixture. Bake at 325 degrees for 45 minutes to 1 hour or until tip of knife inserted in center comes out clean. Cut into small wedges.

Photograph for this recipe on page 152.

ALMOND MUSHROOMS

18 lg. mushrooms
Monosodium glutamate
1/3 c. fine dry bread crumbs
2 tsp. lemon juice
1/8 tsp. rosemary
1 tsp. marjoram
1/4 tsp. salt
1/4 c. finely chopped almonds
1 tbsp. capers
3 tbsp. butter
3 tbsp. chopped parsley

Wash mushrooms and remove stems. Sprinkle inside of mushroom caps with monosodium glutamate. Chop stems finely; combine with bread crumbs, lemon juice, herbs, salt, almonds and capers. Spoon mixture into caps. Place in greased shallow baking pan. Dot each mushroom with butter. Bake at 350 degrees for 20 to 25 minutes. Sprinkle with parsley.

Photograph for this recipe on page 152.

RIPE OLIVE QUICHE

1 10-oz. package frozen patty shells
1 8-oz. package cream cheese
2 eggs
2 c. canned pitted ripe olives, drained
1 2-oz. can rolled anchovies with capers
1/2 c. grated Fontina or imported
   Swiss cheese
1/2 c. grated Parmesan cheese

Thaw patty shells in refrigerator. Knead patty shells together and roll out. Press into 10-inch fluted tart pan. Mix cream cheese with eggs; pour into pastry. Cut olives into halves and chunks. Sprinkle evenly over cheese filling. Arrange anchovies on top; sprinkle with cheeses. Bake in 400-degree oven for 40 minutes or until brown. Serve warm or cold.

Photograph for this recipe on page 151.

VEGETABLES VINAIGRETTE

White Beans

3 c. cooked white beans
1/2 tsp. monosodium glutamate
1 onion, chopped
2 tbsp. chopped parsley
1/2 c. French dressing
1 clove of garlic, slashed

Place beans in a large bowl; add remaining ingredients. Mix well. Chill for several hours. Remove garlic before serving.

Cucumbers

3 cucumbers
1/2 tsp. monosodium glutamate
1/2 c. vinegar
2 tbsp. sugar
1 clove of garlic, slashed
Chopped dill

Peel cucumbers and slice thinly. Sprinkle with monosodium glutamate. Combine vinegar, sugar and 2 tablespoons water; pour over cucumbers. Add garlic. Sprinkle with dill. Chill. Remove garlic before serving.

Artichoke Hearts

2 1-lb. cans artichoke hearts
1 tsp. monosodium glutamate
1/2 c. French dressing
2 tbsp. lemon juice

Drain artichoke hearts and place in bowl. Sprinkle with monosodium glutamate. Add dressing and lemon juice. Marinate for several hours. Garnish with diced pimento and capers.

Photograph for this recipe on page 152.

IRISH BREAD

3 c. flour
2/3 c. sugar
2 tbsp. baking powder
1 1/2 tsp. salt
1 tbsp. (heaping) caraway seed
1/3 c. shortening
1 c. raisins
3/4 c. (about) milk

Combine dry ingredients in large bowl; mix well. Cut in shortening with 2 knives to consistency of peas. Add raisins and enough milk to hold dough together. Knead well; place in greased 8-inch square cake pan. Bake at 400 degrees for 35 to 40 minutes. Cool in pan for 10 minutes.

Patricia R. Stewart, Rec. Sec., Corr. Sec.
Xi Epsilon X733
Hartford, Connecticut

GUMDROP BREAD

3 c. sifted all-purpose flour
1 tsp. salt
3 1/2 tsp. baking powder
3/4 c. sugar
1/2 c. (about) nutmeats
1/2 c. white raisins or dates
1 1/4 c. cut gumdrops
1 beaten egg
2 tbsp. melted shortening
1 1/2 c. milk

Sift flour, salt, baking powder and sugar together into large bowl. Stir in nutmeats, raisins and gumdrops. Add egg, shortening and milk; mix only until dry ingredients are moistened. Turn into paper-lined loaf pan. Bake at 350 degrees for 1 hour. Omit black gumdrops.

Betty J. Scholl, Pres.
Xi Iota X 227
Canal Winchester, Ohio

FRENCH BANANA TEA BREAD

1 1/2 c. sifted all-purpose flour
1 tsp. soda
1/2 tsp. salt
1/2 c. butter
1 c. sugar
2 eggs
1 tsp. vanilla
1/2 tsp. lemon extract
1 c. mashed bananas
1/2 c. thick sour cream
1/2 c. chopped nuts

Sift flour, soda and salt together. Combine butter, sugar, eggs and flavorings; cream until smooth. Add bananas, sour cream, nuts and flour mixture. Beat until well blended. Turn into greased loaf pan. Bake at 350 degrees for 1 hour or until done. One-fourth cup buttermilk may be substituted for sour cream.

Irene M. Woods, Pres.
Ohio Pi Iota No. 7817
Napoleon, Ohio

STEWART'S ORANGE BREAD

4 c. flour
2 tbsp. baking powder
1 2/3 c. sugar
1/2 tsp. salt
1 1/2 c. milk
2 eggs
1/2 c. cooking oil
1 orange

Sift flour, baking powder, sugar and salt into large mixing bowl; make well in center of dry ingredients. Pour milk, eggs and cooking oil into well. Grind whole orange; place 1 cup of orange into well. Beat batter thoroughly by hand for 4 minutes. Pour batter into 3 greased and floured loaf pans; allow to stand 20 minutes before baking. Bake at 350 degrees for 30 minutes; score tops with sharp knife. Bake for 30 minutes longer or until tester inserted in center comes out clean. Remove to wire rack; let stand for 5 minutes. Remove from pans; allow to cool thoroughly.

Barbara Krueger, Pres.
Xi Alpha Theta X1029
Jamestown, New York

PARADISE PINEAPPLE-NUT BREAD

1 c. chopped nuts
Sugar
1/2 c. butter
1/4 tsp. grated lemon peel
1 beaten egg
2 1/2 c. sifted flour
2 tsp. baking powder
1 tsp. salt
1/2 tsp. soda
1 8 1/2-oz. can crushed pineapple
1/4 c. milk

Place nuts in heavily greased loaf pan and shake to coat bottom and sides. Shake out excess nuts and reserve. Sprinkle pan with sugar. Blend butter and lemon peel until soft; add 3/4 cup sugar. Beat until fluffy. Beat in egg. Sift flour, baking powder, salt and soda together. Add reserved nuts. Add to egg mixture alternately with undrained pineapple and milk; mix well. Spoon batter into loaf pan; let stand for 15 minutes. Bake at 350 degrees for 50 minutes or until bread tests done. Cool for 10 minutes; turn out on rack. Cool completely.

Donna A. Moryas, Rec. Sec.
Xi Beta Exemplar X190
East Chicago, Indiana

QUICK AND EASY CINNAMON BREAD

2 pkg. yeast
1 1/4 c. buttermilk
3 eggs
6 c. flour
1/2 c. margarine
1/2 c. sugar
2 tsp. baking powder
2 tsp. salt
3 tbsp. melted margarine
3/4 c. (packed) brown sugar
1 1/2 tsp. cinnamon
1 tbsp. milk

Dissolve yeast in 1/2 cup warm water. Combine yeast mixture with buttermilk, 2 eggs,

flour, margarine, sugar, baking powder and salt in large bowl; mix well. Turn out on lightly floured board; knead for 5 minutes. Roll out to rectangle. Combine melted margarine, brown sugar and cinnamon. Preheat oven just to warm. Brush dough with cinnamon mixture; roll up jelly roll fashion. Place on baking sheet; let rise in oven for 30 minutes. Increase oven temperature to 350 degrees. Combine remaining egg with milk. Make slashes in dough; brush with egg mixture. Bake for 20 minutes. Cool slightly in pan; invert on wire rack. Cool thoroughly.

Kay Norris, Pres.
Xi Alpha X104
Albuquerque, New Mexico

WALCHER BREAD

3 c. sifted all-purpose flour
1 c. sugar
4 tsp. baking powder
2 tsp. salt (opt.)
1 egg, slightly beaten
1/2 c. melted margarine
1 1/2 c. milk
1 tsp. vanilla
1 1/2 c. chopped walnuts
3/4 c. chopped cherries

Sift flour, sugar, baking powder and salt together; add egg, margarine, milk and vanilla. Stir just until flour is moistened. Stir in walnuts and cherries. Turn into greased 9 x 5 x 3-inch loaf pan. Bake at 350 degrees for about 1 hour and 20 minutes.

Betty Jo Adams, C. C. 2nd VP
Alpha Zeta No. 3333
Los Alamos, New Mexico

YULETIDE ORANGE BREAD

2 cans 12-count refrigerator
*   biscuits*
1/4 c. butter or margarine
1 6-oz. can frozen orange juice
*   concentrate, thawed*
1 c. sugar

Place biscuits upright on sides in greased ring mold. Melt margarine; add orange juice and sugar, stirring to blend. Pour over biscuits. Bake at 400 degrees for 25 minutes.

Carolyn Atkinson, VP
Xi Theta X992
Durham, North Carolina

BUTTERSCOTCH PECAN BISCUITS

1/3 c. melted butter
3/4 c. (packed) brown sugar
2 tbsp. cream
1 c. pecans
2 c. flour
2 tbsp. sugar
3 tsp. baking powder
1 tsp. salt
1/3 c. shortening
3/4 c. milk

Combine butter, brown sugar and cream; place 2 teaspoons mixture in 18 muffin cups. Arrange pecans over mix. Mix flour, sugar, baking powder and salt; cut in shortening. Stir in milk; knead gently. Drop dough into muffin cups. Bake at 425 degrees for 15 minutes or until golden. Turn out of pan immediately.

Jeanette Bush, Pres.
Zeta Omega No. 6951
Stillwater, Oklahoma

CHEDDAR BRAN MUFFINS

1 1/4 c. buttermilk
1 c. whole bran
1/4 c. shortening
1/3 c. sugar
1 egg
1 1/2 c. sifted all-purpose flour
1 1/2 tsp. baking powder
1/2 tsp. salt
1/4 tsp. soda
1 c. shredded sharp Cheddar cheese

Pour buttermilk over bran in small bowl; let stand till bran is softened. Cream shortening and sugar until fluffy; beat in egg. Sift flour, baking powder, salt and soda; add to creamed mixture alternately with bran mixture. Stir in shredded cheese. Fill greased muffin pans 2/3 full. Bake at 400 degrees for 30 minutes or until golden brown. Serve immediately.

Frances Brown, Pres.
Xi Delta Gamma X3065
Raytown, Missouri

FRENCH BREAKFAST PUFFS

1 c. sugar
1/3 c. shortening
1 egg
1 1/2 c. sifted flour
1 1/2 tsp. baking powder
1/2 tsp. salt
1/4 tsp. ground nutmeg
1/2 c. milk
1 tsp. ground cinnamon
6 tbsp. butter or margarine,
melted

Cream 1/2 cup sugar, shortening and egg in mixer bowl. Sift flour, baking powder, salt and nutmeg; add to creamed mixture alternately with milk, beating well after each addition. Fill 12 greased muffin cups 2/3 full. Bake at 350 degrees for 20 minutes or until golden. Combine remaining sugar and cinnamon; blend well. Remove muffins from cups. Dip into melted butter; dip into cinnamon mixture. Serve immediately.

Carol Boyer, Pres.
Theta Alpha No. 6098
Seymour, Indiana

BLUEBERRY FLAPJACKS

2 c. prepared biscuit mix
2 tbsp. sugar
1 c. blueberries

Combine biscuit mix with sugar and 1 1/3 cups water; blend well. Fold in blueberries carefully. Bake on lightly greased hot griddle; turn once to brown both sides. Yield: 16 flapjacks.

Rita Lynch, Pres.
Xi Beta Rho X4086
Clendenin, West Virginia

FRENCH PANCAKES

3 eggs, separated
1 tbsp. sugar
1/4 tsp. salt
1 c. milk
3/4 c. flour
1 tbsp. melted butter
Jelly
Confectioners' sugar

Beat egg yolks until thick and lemon-colored; add sugar, salt and 1/2 cup milk. Sift flour; add to egg mixture with remaining milk and butter. Beat egg whites until stiff peaks form; fold into flour mixture carefully. Bake on hot griddle, turning griddle to spread batter thinly; turn pancakes to brown both sides. Spread each cake with jelly and roll while hot. Place on heated platter; sprinkle with confectioners' sugar. Serve immediately.

Lillian Potts, Pres.
Gamma Chi No. 8692
Merritt, British Columbia, Canada

SAN ANTONIO SOUR CREAM HOT CAKES

2 eggs, beaten
2 tbsp. flour
2 tbsp. sugar
1/4 tsp. soda
Dash of salt
1 c. sour cream

Combine eggs, flour, sugar, soda, salt and sour cream; mix well. Spoon onto hot grill; turn once to brown on both sides. Yield: 4 servings.

Linda L. Schlegel, Pres.
Delta Delta Xi No. 8075
Richmond, California

YUM-YUM GRIDDLE CAKES

1 beaten egg
1 c. milk
2 tbsp. melted shortening
1 1/4 c. sifted flour
1 tbsp. baking powder
1 tbsp. sugar
1/2 tsp. salt

Combine egg, milk and shortening. Sift flour, baking powder, sugar and salt into egg mixture. Stir just to moisten dry ingredients. Bake on hot griddle, turning once to brown both sides. May add 1/2 cup blueberries, 1/2 cup drained crushed pineapple, 1/2 cup sliced fresh bananas or 1/2 cup sliced fresh strawberries, if desired.

Mary Eileen Schulte, Prog. Chm.
Xi Chi X783
Jefferson City, Missouri

RICE WAFFLES

1 c. flour, sifted
2 tsp. baking powder
1/2 tsp. salt
1 tbsp. sugar
3 eggs, separated
1 1/2 c. buttermilk
1/3 c. melted shortening
1 c. cooked rice
1/2 c. butter
1 c. maple syrup

Sift flour, baking powder, salt and sugar into large bowl. Beat egg yolks until lemony; combine with buttermilk and shortening, blending well. Combine flour mixture with buttermilk mixture; blend well. Fold in rice. Beat egg whites until stiff peaks form; fold into rice mixture gently. Bake in hot waffle iron until golden. Beat butter at high speed in medium bowl, adding syrup gradually, until mixture is light and fluffy. Serve with waffles. Remaining maple butter may be stored in refrigerator for later use.

Nancy Black, Philanthropic Chm.
Xi Iota Sigma X2427
La Canada, California

EASY REFRIGERATOR ROLLS

2 pkg. dry yeast
1/2 c. sugar
2 tsp. salt
5 1/2 to 7 c. sifted flour
1/4 c. shortening
1 egg, slightly beaten
Melted butter

Dissolve yeast in 2 cups warm water; add sugar and salt. Add half the flour, mixing well. Melt shortening; cool to lukewarm. Add egg and shortening to flour mixture, blending well. Work in remaining flour to make easily handled dough. Place dough in large greased bowl; cover with damp cloth. Place in refrigerator for at least 2 hours. Punch dough down; shape into 1-inch balls. Place 3 balls in each cup of greased muffin pans. Brush with melted butter; cover. Let rise in warm place until doubled in bulk. Preheat oven to 400 degrees. Bake rolls for 12 to 15 minutes. Butter tops before serving. Dough may be kept in covered bowl for 3 or 4 days.

Rachel Stover
Delta Beta No. 6974
Ravenswood, West Virginia

HONEY DINNER ROLLS

6 tbsp. lard
2 pkg. dry yeast
1/2 c. sugar
2 tsp. salt
8 to 12 c. sifted flour
Soft butter or margarine
Honey

Melt lard in 2 cups boiling water; cool to lukewarm. Dissolve yeast in 1/4 cup warm water. Combine lard mixture and yeast mixture in large bowl. Add sugar and salt. Work in enough flour to make soft easily handled dough. Place on cloth; cover with waxed paper. Let rise in warm place until doubled in bulk. Punch down; knead well. Roll out half the dough on floured surface to 1/4-inch thick rectangle. Spread dough with layer of butter and heavy layer of honey. Roll as for jelly roll; cut into individual slices. Place 1/4-inch apart on greased baking sheet. Let rise, covered, until doubled in bulk. Bake at 375 degrees for 20 to 25 minutes. Remove from sheet immediately. Repeat process with remaining dough.

Carolyn La Grange, Pres.
Xi Gamma Psi X3975
Tremont, Illinois

REFRIGERATOR POTATO ROLLS

2 pkg. dry yeast
1/2 c. sugar
1 tbsp. salt
2 eggs, slightly beaten
Soft butter or margarine
1/2 c. unseasoned warm mashed
*   potatoes*
6 1/2 c. unsifted all-purpose flour
Poppy or sesame seed

Pour 1 1/2 cups warm water in warmed bowl; sprinkle yeast over water. Add sugar and salt. Stir until dissolved. Let stand for several minutes until mixture bubbles slightly. Add eggs, 1/2 cup butter, potatoes and 3 cups flour. Beat with electric mixer until smooth. Add 2 cups flour, beating with wooden spoon until flour is absorbed. Add remaining flour; knead until dough is smooth and stiff. Brush top of dough with 1 tablespoon butter. Cover with waxed paper and tea towel. Let rise in refrigerator for 2 hours or until doubled in bulk. Punch down. Refrigerate for 1 to 3 days. Punch down once a day. Shape into desired rolls. Cover with towel; let rise in warm place until doubled in bulk. Preheat oven to 400 degrees. Brush with butter; sprinkle with poppy seed. Bake for 12 minutes or until golden brown. Serve warm. Yield: 36 rolls.

Virginia Reindahl, Pres.
Xi Chi X4058
Story, Wyoming

SCOTCH SHORTBREAD

1 lb. butter
1 c. sugar
4 c. all-purpose flour

Cream butter and sugar until smooth. Add flour gradually, mixing well. Divide into 4 pieces; pat each piece into pie pan. Prick with a fork. Bake at 350 degrees for 25 to 30 minutes.

Martha C. Janson, Pres.
Mu Epsilon No. 7992
Fort Lauderdale, Florida

Desserts

Elegant . . . lavish . . . gourmet . . . these are some of the words used
to describe one of the most beautiful and creative areas of cooking —
desserts. The most renowned chefs have gained considerable
fame creating magnificent desserts. Pots de Creame au Chocolat,
Lane Cake and Raspberry-Peach Chantilly are a few of the famous
gourmet desserts that await the creative cook in this section.

Wonderful things can happen when a woman decides to create
a new dessert in her kitchen or recreate a family favorite. Each one
of the recipes in this diverse and innovative section has been
painstakenly prepared, adapted and perfected by a Beta Sigma Phi
for her family — and for you.

Meringues, souffles, tortes, ices, parfaits and pies . . . the list of
desserts is virtually endless. There are desserts for every occasion,
holiday or celebration. When it comes time to crown a meal,
choose your dessert with care and forethought. Your family and
friends are sure to be pleased with your creative effort, and
it will be the "frosting on the cake" at your dinner.

BLUEBERRY GATEAU

3/4 c. butter
Sugar
3 eggs, separated
2 c. flour
1/2 tsp. salt
1/2 tsp. cinnamon
3 tbsp. quick-cooking tapioca
1 qt. blueberries
2 tbsp. lemon juice
3 tbsp. heavy cream
1/8 tsp. cream of tartar

Cream butter and 1/4 cup sugar until light and fluffy. Add 2 egg yolks; mix. Stir in flour and salt; press on bottom and 3/4 of the way up sides of 9-inch springform pan. Chill. Combine cinnamon, tapioca and 3/4 cup sugar; sprinkle over blueberries. Add lemon juice; let stand for 15 minutes. Mix remaining egg yolk and cream; stir into blueberry mixture. Pour into chilled crust. Bake in 425-degree oven for 15 minutes. Reduce temperature to 375 degrees; bake for 35 minutes. Beat egg whites and cream of tartar until fluffy. Add 6 tablespoons sugar gradually; beat until stiff. Spread over blueberry mixture. Increase oven temperature to 400 degrees; bake for 8 to 10 minutes or until golden. Cool before serving. Yield: 8-10 servings.

Marceline L. Martin, Pres.
Preceptor Gamma XP 861
St. Paul, Minnesota

PEAR-BLUEBERRY COMPOTE

1 c. sour cream
2 tbsp. sugar
1/2 tsp. ground cinnamon
8 med. pears
2 c. (packed) brown sugar
1 1/4 c. water
1/4 c. lemon juice
1/4 c. butter
2 packages frozen blueberries

Mix sour cream, sugar and cinnamon; chill. Core pears, leaving stems on; place in baking pan. Mix brown sugar, water, lemon juice and butter; bring to a boil. Pour over pears; cover. Bake at 350 degrees for 1 hour to 1 hour and 5 minutes. Uncover; bake for 10 minutes longer. Place pears in individual dishes. Pour syrup from baking pan into saucepan; bring to a boil. Cook for 15 minutes. Add blueberries; cook for 15 minutes longer. Spoon over pears; top with sour cream mixture. Serve warm.

Dorothy Condone, Pres.
Gamma Tau No. 7314
Long Branch, New Jersey

BANANA SPLIT CAKE

2 c. graham cracker crumbs
1/4 c. melted butter
1/4 c. sugar
2 c. confectioners' sugar
1/2 c. butter, softened
1 egg
1 tsp. vanilla
4 bananas
2 10-oz. packages frozen
*   strawberries, thawed*
1 med. can crushed pineapple
2 c. whipped cream
1 c. chopped walnuts

Combine crumbs, melted butter and sugar; mix well. Press into 13 x 9 x 2-inch baking dish; chill for 1 hour. Cream confectioners' sugar and butter; add egg and vanilla. Blend well. Spread evenly over crumb layer; chill for 1 hour longer. Slice bananas; drain strawberries and pineapple well. Place bananas over cake; add strawberries, then pineapple. Spread whipped cream over pineapple; top with walnuts. Chill until ready to serve. Yield: 12 servings.

Judith A. Corso, VP
Nu Upsilon No. 6776
Sandusky, Ohio

BANANA-WHIPPED CREAM CAKE

2 1/4 c. flour
2 1/2 tsp. baking powder
1/2 tsp. soda
1/2 tsp. salt

1 1/4 c. sugar
1/2 c. soft shortening
1 c. mashed ripe bananas
1 tsp. vanilla
2 eggs
1/2 c. buttermilk
2 c. heavy cream, whipped
3 tbsp. confectioners' sugar
2 or 3 thinly sliced bananas

Preheat oven to 350 degrees. Sift flour, baking powder, soda, salt and sugar together into large mixer bowl. Add shortening, mashed bananas and vanilla. Beat with electric mixer at low speed until combined. Beat at medium speed for 2 minutes. Add eggs and buttermilk; beat for 2 minutes longer. Pour batter into 2 greased 8-inch cake pans. Bake for 30 to 35 minutes or until cake tests done. Cool for 1 hour. Split both cake layers in half. Sweeten cream with confectioners' sugar. Spread first layer with whipped cream; arrange sliced bananas over cream. Repeat with next 2 layers. Place remaining layer on top; frost cake with remaining whipped cream. Refrigerate for several hours before serving.

Claudia Silva, Treas.
Alpha Omega No. 5651
Springerville, Arizona

DELUXE RED VELVET CAKE

1 1/2 c. sugar
1/2 c. shortening
2 eggs
2 1/2 c. flour
1 c. buttermilk
2 oz. red food coloring
2 tbsp. cocoa
1/2 tsp. salt
1 tsp. vanilla
1 tsp. soda
1 tbsp. vinegar

Cream sugar and shortening; beat in eggs. Add flour and buttermilk alternately. Combine food coloring, cocoa, salt and vanilla; add to egg mixture. Dissolve soda in vinegar; add to batter. Pour into 2 greased 10-inch cake pans or 3 greased 8-inch cake pans.

Bake at 350 degrees for 20 minutes or until cake tests done.

Icing

7 1/2 tbsp. flour
1 c. milk
1 1/2 c. sugar
1/2 c. butter or shortening
1 1/2 tsp. vanilla

Combine flour and milk in saucepan; cook, stirring constantly, until thickened. Cool. Cream sugar, butter and vanilla until fluffy. Combine milk mixture with sugar mixture; blend well. Spread between layers and over top and side of cake. Sprinkle with coconut, if desired.

Evelyn Wilson, Treas.
Xi Kappa Upsilon X3184
Waxahachie, Texas

GEORGE HARDIKIAN'S ALL-PURPOSE CAKE

2 c. (packed) brown sugar
2 c. flour, sifted
1/2 c. butter
1 c. sour cream
1 tsp. soda
1 egg, beaten
1 tsp. nutmeg
Chopped nuts
Cinnamon

Blend brown sugar, flour and butter as for pie crust; set aside 1/2 of the mixture. Mix sour cream and soda in bowl; add egg and nutmeg. Add to remaining crumb mixture. Grease 9-inch square or rectangular pan. Spread reserved crumb mixture evenly over bottom of pan. Spread sour cream mixture over crumbs; sprinkle top with chopped nuts and cinnamon. Bake at 350 degrees for about 40 minutes. Do not open oven door for 30 minutes while cake is baking. Cake will bake a hard caramel base. Yield: 15 servings.

Dorothy Gill, Honorary Member
Beta Sigma Phi International
Halifax, Nova Scotia, Canada

QUEEN'S CHOCOLATE POUND CAKE

1 c. butter
1/2 c. shortening
2 1/2 c. sugar
5 lg. eggs
3 c. flour
1/2 c. cocoa
1/2 tsp. baking powder
1/2 tsp. salt
1 1/4 c. milk
2 tsp. vanilla

Cream butter, shortening and sugar until fluffy. Beat in eggs, one at a time, beating well after each addition. Sift flour with cocoa, baking powder and salt. Add flour mixture alternately with milk to egg mixture; blend well. Pour into greased 10-inch tube pan. Bake in preheated 350-degree oven for 1 hour and 20 minutes or until cake tests done. Let cool; invert on wire rack. Cool completely. Baking time is for 1-mile altitude.

Icing

1 oz. unsweetened chocolate
1 c. sugar
1/4 c. milk
1/3 c. butter
Dash of salt
1 tsp. vanilla

Combine all ingredients in saucepan; bring to a boil. Boil for 1 minute; beat to spreading consistency. Spread over top and side of cake.

Virginia Weller, Pres.
Preceptor Kappa XP0332
Montrose, Colorado

PECAN AND FRUITCAKE DELUXE

1 lb. butter
2 1/2 c. sugar
12 eggs
4 c. flour
1 tsp. nutmeg
1 tsp. salt
1 c. bourbon or brandy

1 tsp. almond extract
1 tsp. lemon extract
1 tsp. vanilla
1 lb. white raisins
1/4 lb. chopped candied citron
1/2 lb. chopped candied pineapple
2 doz. candied cherries, chopped
2 lb. broken pecans

Cream butter; add sugar gradually, beating until fluffy. Beat in eggs, one at a time, beating well after each addition. Combine flour, nutmeg and salt; add to creamed mixture alternately with bourbon and flavorings. Combine fruits and pecans; mix with small amount of additional flour. Fold fruit mixture into batter. Divide batter evenly between 2 greased and floured tube pans. Bake at 325 degrees for 1 to 2 hours or until cakes test done. Cool. Garnish with candied fruits and nutmeats. Store in airtight containers. Sprinkle cakes with additional whiskey or brandy occasionally.

Mrs. Victor Shaw, Honorary Member
Beta Sigma Phi International
Fairmont, West Virginia

WILLIAMSBURG WHITE FRUITCAKE

1 c. butter or margarine, softened
2 1/3 c. sugar
4 eggs, separated
4 c. sifted all-purpose flour
California sherry
4 1/4 c. chopped walnuts
1   15-oz. package light seedless raisins
1 1/3 c. finely chopped red glace cherries
1 c. cubed preserved pineapple
1 c. diced preserved citron
1   7-oz. package grated coconut
Almond Paste
Royal Icing

Cream butter and sugar. Beat in egg yolks, 1 cup flour and 1/2 cup sherry. Combine remaining flour, walnuts, raisins, cherries, pineapple, citron and coconut; stir. Add fruit mixture to egg yolk mixture. Beat egg whites until stiff but not dry; fold into batter. Turn into greased and floured 10-inch tube pan lined with heavy brown paper. Bake in 300-degree oven for 2 hours and 30 minutes. Cool; turn out of pan. Saturate cheesecloth with sherry; wrap around cake. Wrap cake tightly in aluminum foil. Remove foil at 2-week intervals. Moisten cheesecloth with sherry; rewrap cake. Apply Almond Paste day before serving; let dry at room temperature for about 4 hours. Reserve 1 cup Royal Icing for piping; spread remaining icing on top and side of cake. Decorate cake with reserved icing, using pastry tube; garnish cake with coconut and red and green cherries. Let icing dry at room temperature for about 4 hours.

Almond Paste

4 c. ground blanched almonds
1 1-lb. box confectioners' sugar,
* sifted*
2 egg whites
1 tbsp. lemon juice
1/2 tsp. orange extract
1/2 tsp. vanilla

Mix almonds, confectioners' sugar, 1 egg white, lemon juice, orange extract and vanilla thoroughly; press into ball. Roll out 1/3 of the almond paste on waxed paper dusted with additional confectioners' sugar into 8-inch circle. Roll remaining almond paste into 28 x 4-inch strip; cut into 8 pieces. Brush top and side of cake with remaining slightly beaten egg white. Arrange circle of almond paste on top of cake; place pieces of almond paste on side and press firmly.

Royal Icing

6 c. sifted confectioners' sugar
2 egg whites
2 tbsp. lemon juice

Blend sugar, egg whites and lemon juice.

Mary Clare Dinneen
Preceptor Iota Chap.
Richmond, Virginia

HARVEST CAKE

4 med. crisp apples
2 c. sugar
3 c. flour
2 tsp. soda
1/2 tsp. salt
2 eggs
1 c. salad oil
1/2 c. chopped black walnuts
1/2 c. chopped English walnuts
1 tsp. vanilla

Peel, core and dice apples finely. Stir apples into sugar in large bowl. Let stand for 1 hour. Combine flour, soda and salt; add to apple mixture. Beat eggs; beat in oil until blended. Combine egg mixture and apple mixture; blend thoroughly. Stir in nuts and vanilla. Pour into tube pan or 2 loaf pans. Bake at 325 degrees for 1 hour or until cake tests done. Cake may be frozen for later use, if desired.

Mary A. Gibala, Honorary Member
Beta Sigma Phi International
Silver Spring, Maryland

COCONUT-SOUR CREAM POUND CAKE

2 sticks whipped margarine
3 c. sugar
6 eggs
1/4 tsp. soda
3 c. flour
1 c. sour cream
1 sm. can coconut
1/2 tsp. coconut flavoring
1/2 tsp. butter flavoring

Cream margarine with sugar; add eggs, one at a time, beating well after each addition. Combine soda with flour. Add flour mixture and sour cream to egg mixture alternately, beating well after each addition. Stir in coconut, coconut flavoring and butter flavoring. Pour into tube pan. Bake at 350 degrees for 1 hour and 20 minutes or until cake tests done.

Jo Ann Sutton, Pres.
Xi Alpha Lambda X4124
Ariton, Alabama

Desserts

LANE CAKE

3 1/4 c. sifted flour
3 1/2 tsp. baking powder
1/2 tsp. salt
1 c. butter or margarine
2 c. sugar
1 tsp. vanilla
1 c. milk
8 egg whites

Preheat oven to 375 degrees. Grease four 9-inch layer cake pans; line with waxed paper. Sift flour with baking powder and salt. Cream butter with sugar in larger mixer bowl. Beat with mixer at medium speed until light and fluffy; add vanilla. Reduce to low speed; add flour mixture and milk alternately, beating after each addition until just smooth. Beat egg whites in large bowl until stiff peaks form; fold into batter carefully. Pour batter into prepared pans to depth of 1 inch. Bake for 15 minutes or until cake tests done. Cool for 5 minutes; remove from pans to wire racks. Remove waxed paper; cool completely.

Lane Filling

8 egg yolks
1 1/4 c. sugar
1 c. butter or margarine
1 c. chopped pecans
1 c. grated coconut
1 c. cut-up candied cherries
1/3 c. whiskey or wine
1 c. finely chopped seedless raisins

Place egg yolks in heavy saucepan; beat slightly. Add sugar and butter. Cook over low heat, stirring constantly, for 5 minutes or until slightly thickened. Stir in remaining ingredients; blend well. Cool. Spread between cake layers.

Lane Frosting

1 1/3 c. dark corn syrup
2 egg whites
Dash of salt
1 tsp. vanilla

Bring corn syrup to a boil in small saucepan; remove from heat. Beat egg whites until soft

peaks form; add salt. Add corn syrup gradually, beating until fluffy and stiff peaks form when beaters are raised; fold in vanilla. Spread frosting over top and side of cake.

Marilyn Gross, Pres.
Xi Theta Zeta X3710
Joliet, Illinois

WHIPPED CREAM POUND CAKE

1 c. shortening
3 c. sugar
6 eggs
3 c. cake flour
1/2 pt. whipping cream
2 tsp. vanilla

Cream shortening and sugar until fluffy; add eggs, one at a time, beating well after each addition. Add flour and whipping cream alternately. Stir in vanilla. Place in cold oven. Bake at 300 degrees for 1 hour and 20 minutes.

Frances Hood, Pres.
Preceptor Theta XP-1054
Birmingham, Alabama

NUT TORTE

12 extra lg. eggs, separated
2 c. sugar
1 tsp. vanilla
1/2 c. cold black coffee
1 c. ground nuts
1/2 tsp. black walnut flavoring
2 c. sifted cake flour
4 tsp. baking powder

Beat egg yolks in large mixing bowl until lemon-colored. Add sugar, vanilla, coffee and nuts; beat at high speed until light and creamy. Add black walnut flavoring, flour and baking powder; mix well. Fold in stiffly beaten egg whites. Grease and flour bottoms of two 13 x 9-inch baking pans; place flour mixture in pans. Bake at 350 degrees for 30 to 35 minutes; cool. Remove from pans. May be baked in three 9-inch layer pans.

Frosting

1 c. shortening
1 c. butter

1 1/2 tsp. vanilla
2 1-lb. boxes powdered sugar

Mix shortening and butter in large mixing bowl until creamy. Add vanilla; beat in powdered sugar until desired thickness is obtained. Spread between layers and on top and sides of cake. Extra frosting may be stored in airtight container in refrigerator for several weeks.

Judy Kurucz, VP
Xi Beta Beta X880
Lorain, Ohio

VIENNESE PECAN-CHOCOLATE TORTE

6 eggs, separated
1/2 tsp. salt
1 tsp. vanilla
3/4 c. sugar
1 c. sifted all-purpose flour
Chopped pecans
Chocolate Creme Filling
Chocolate Satin Frosting

Combine egg yolks, salt and vanilla in mixer bowl; beat with electric mixer until lemon-colored. Beat in 1/2 cup sugar gradually; continue beating for about 5 minutes at medium speed until light and fluffy. Stir in flour and 1 cup of pecans. Beat egg whites until soft peaks form. Beat in remaining sugar gradually; continue to beat until glossy and stiff. Fold egg white mixture into egg yolk mixture. Divide batter equally between 3 greased and floured 8-inch layer pans. Spread just enough to level. Bake at 300 degrees for 20 to 25 minutes. Cool in pans on rack for 10 minutes; remove from pans. Cool thoroughly. Place layers together with Chocolate Creme Filling, using 1/3 of the filling on each layer. Sprinkle top with chopped pecans. Chill in refrigerator until filling is firm. Scrape excess filling off torte. Cover sides of torte with Chocolate Satin Frosting. Chill and serve.

Chocolate Creme Filling

1 6-oz. package semisweet chocolate bits
3/4 c. cold butter or margarine

1 1/4 c. sifted confectioners' sugar
1/8 tsp. salt
1 egg
3 tsp. rum

Melt chocolate bits in double boiler; cool, stirring often. Whip butter until fluffy with electric mixer; mix in sugar and salt. Beat at medium high speed for about 6 minutes or until light and fluffy. Add egg; beat for about 2 minutes or until mixture is fluffy and smooth. Fold in rum and chocolate carefully and quickly. Cool in refrigerator until slightly stiffened. Two teaspoons vanilla may be substituted for rum.

Chocolate Satin Frosting

1 c. sugar
1/4 c. cornstarch
1/4 tsp. salt
2 sq. unsweetened chocolate, melted
3 tbsp. butter or margarine

Combine sugar, cornstarch and salt in saucepan; mix well. Add 1 cup boiling water gradually, stirring constantly. Place over low heat; cook until smooth and thickened, stirring constantly. Add chocolate and butter; cook, stirring, until smooth and thick. Chill over ice water until cool and thick enough to spread, stirring frequently during cooling.

RUM CREME DELIGHT

1 1/4 c. flour
Sugar
1 1/2 tsp. baking powder
3/4 tsp. cardamom
1/2 tsp. salt
2 1/4 c. milk
1/3 c. shortening
1 egg
1 tsp. vanilla
2 tbsp. water
3 tbsp. dark rum
1/4 c. chopped raisins
1 3 1/4-oz. package vanilla
   pudding
1/3 c. flaked coconut
Sliced almonds

Preheat oven to 350 degrees. Mix flour, 1 cup sugar, baking powder, cardamom, salt, 3/4 cup milk, shortening, egg and vanilla in large mixing bowl; blend for 30 seconds at low speed, scraping bowl. Beat for 3 minutes at high speed; pour into greased and floured 8 or 9-inch square pan. Bake for 45 to 55 minutes; cool. Heat water and 1 tablespoon sugar until sugar is dissolved. Stir in rum and raisins; remove from heat. Let stand for 30 minutes. Prepare pudding according to package directions, using remaining milk. Stir in coconut; cool. Split cake in 2 layers. Drain raisins; reserve liquid. Stir raisins into pudding mixture. Prick cut side of layers with long-tined fork; drizzle with reserved liquid. Spread bottom layer of cake with 1/2 of the pudding mixture. Add remaining cake layer; spread remaining pudding mixture on top. Sprinkle with almonds; refrigerate for several hours.

Sue Chase, VP
Xi Alpha Eta X3444
Waukesha, Wisconsin

RUM CAKE

1 c. butter
2 c. sugar
4 eggs
1/2 tsp. baking powder
1/2 tsp. soda

1/4 tsp. salt
3 c. flour
1 c. buttermilk
1 tsp. vanilla
1/2 tsp. rum extract

Cream butter and sugar until smooth. Add eggs, one at a time; beat until fluffy after each addition. Mix dry ingredients together; add to creamed mixture alternately with buttermilk. Mix well. Stir in vanilla and rum extract. Pour into greased and floured 10-inch tube pan. Bake at 325 degrees for 1 hour.

Alice Fae Jones, Rec. Sec.
Xi Mu X-664
Fairmont, West Virginia

CHOCOLATE-CARAMEL TORTE

1 frozen loaf pound cake
4 oz. semisweet chocolate
1/2 c. butter or margarine
1 tsp. vanilla
1/2 c. unsifted powdered sugar
2 egg yolks
1/3 c. sugar
1/2 c. heavy cream, whipped

Let cake thaw until partially frozen. Melt chocolate in top of double boiler over hot water; cool to room temperature. Cream butter until light; beat in vanilla and chocolate gradually. Add powdered sugar and egg yolks; mix well. Slice top crust layer off cake; reserve. Slice cake horizontally into 6 or 7 layers; spread chocolate frosting between layers, reserving about 1/2 cup to coat sides. Place layers together. Melt sugar in small pan until amber-colored. Place reserved layer on sheet of waxed paper; pour hot caramel syrup over layer quickly, coating layer evenly. Place on top of cake. Heat blade of wooden-handled knife or spatula in gas flame; mark caramel topping into serving-sized slices immediately. Frost sides of cake with reserved frosting. Pipe border of whipped cream around top and bottom edge of cake; chill. May be made day or 2 ahead of serving.

Sharon Satkowski, City Coun. Pres.
Beta Pi No. 5175
East Brunswick, New Jersey

POT DE CREME AU CHOCOLAT

4 eggs, separated
Sugar
1/4 c. triple sec or Cointreau
6 sq. semisweet chocolate
1/4 c. strong coffee
3/4 c. butter, softened
Pinch of salt
Whipped cream

Beat egg yolks and 3/4 cup sugar in small mixing bowl until pale yellow and thick; beat in triple sec. Place bowl over hot water; continue beating for 10 minutes or until mixture is foamy. Place over cold water; beat until cool and consistency of mayonnaise. Melt chocolate in coffee over hot water. Remove from heat; beat in butter, 1 piece at a time; beat until smooth. Beat chocolate mixture into egg yolk mixture. Beat egg whites with salt until soft peaks form. Add 1 tablespoon sugar; beat until stiff peaks form. Stir into chocolate mixture. Turn into individual serving dishes; chill for at least 2 hours. Serve with whipped cream. One-fourth teaspoon instant coffee dissolved in 1/4 cup boiling water may be substituted for strong coffee. Yield: 8 servings.

Helen M. Davis, W and M Chm.
Xi Omega X3216
St. Louis Park, Minnesota

BROKEN GLASS TORTE

1 3-oz. package lemon gelatin
1 3-oz. package lime gelatin
1 3-oz. package cherry gelatin
1 env. unflavored gelatin
1 c. pineapple juice, heated
2 c. heavy cream
1/2 c. sugar
1 tsp. vanilla
1 1/2 doz. ladyfingers, halved

Dissolve each gelatin in 1 1/2 cups hot water; pour each into separate cake pan. Chill until firm; cut into cubes. Soften unflavored gelatin in 1/4 cup cold water; dissolve in hot pineapple juice. Cool. Beat cream until stiff, adding sugar gradually; add vanilla. Fold in unflavored gelatin mixture and gelatin cubes. Line springform pan with ladyfingers; place gelatin mixture over ladyfingers. Chill for 6 to 12 hours or until firm; slice to serve. Crushed pineapple, other fruits or nuts may be added before adding gelatin cubes, if desired.

Margaret N. Poston, Pres.
Xi Beta Lambda X-1915
Tampa, Florida

MARASCHINO BAVARIAN CREAM

1 8-oz. jar red maraschino
*   cherries*
1 env. unflavored gelatin
4 egg yolks
Sugar
1/4 tsp. salt
2 c. milk, scalded
2 drops of red food coloring (opt.)
2 tsp. vanilla
1 1/2 c. heavy cream
Stemmed red maraschino cherries
*   (opt.)*

Drain cherries, reserving 1/4 cup syrup. Chop cherries coarsely; drain on paper towels. Set aside. Soften gelatin in reserved syrup. Beat egg yolks in saucepan until light. Add 1/2 cup sugar and salt; blend in milk slowly. Cook over low heat, stirring constantly, until mixture comes to a boil; remove from heat. Add food coloring, gelatin and 1 1/2 teaspoons vanilla; stir until gelatin dissolves. Cool, then chill until mixture mounds slightly when dropped from a spoon. Whip 1 cup cream until soft peaks form. Beat gelatin mixture until fluffy; fold in whipped cream and cherries. Pour into oiled 1-quart mold; chill for 4 hours or until set. Unmold onto plate. Whip remaining cream with 1 tablespoon sugar and remaining vanilla until soft peaks form. Place whipped cream in center of gelatin mixture; garnish with stemmed cherries.

Carolyn Morgan
Epsilon Rho No. 2571
Springfield, Ohio

VANILLA MOUSSE WITH STRAWBERRY SAUCE

1 1/2 c. milk
1 1/2 c. sugar
2 eggs, separated
2 env. unflavored gelatin
1 1/2 c. water
1 tbsp. vanilla
1 pt. heavy cream, whipped
1 pt. fresh California
  strawberries
1 tbsp. cornstarch
1/2 c. lemon juice
2 tbsp. butter

Scald milk with 1 cup sugar in top of double boiler. Beat egg yolks lightly; stir in milk mixture gradually. Return mixture to double boiler; cook until thick enough to coat a metal spoon. Soften gelatin in 1/2 cup water. Stir into custard until dissolved. Stir in vanilla. Chill until custard mounds when dropped from a spoon; beat until light. Beat egg whites until stiff but not dry; fold into custard. Fold in whipped cream. Turn into greased 2-quart mold. Chill until set. Unmold onto serving platter. Garnish with 1 cup whole strawberries and additional whipped cream, if desired. Force remaining strawberries through food mill or blend in electric blender. Strain to remove seeds. Mix remaining sugar with cornstarch in medium saucepan. Blend in remaining water gradually. Stir over medium heat until sauce thickens and boils for 30 seconds. Stir in lemon juice, butter and strawberry puree. Chill. Serve sauce with mousse.

ORANGE-HONEY MOUSSE

1 env. unflavored gelatin
3/4 c. honey
1 c. orange juice
2 tbsp. coconut
1 c. heavy cream, whipped
3 egg whites
1/8 tsp. cream of tartar
1/2 tbsp. white vinegar
1 c. sugar
1 tsp. vanilla

Sprinkle gelatin over 1 cup water in small saucepan; add honey. Heat, stirring constantly, until gelatin is dissolved and mixture is clear; remove from heat. Add orange juice and coconut gradually, stirring until well blended. Chill for 1 hour or until thickened to consistency of unbeaten egg white; fold in whipped cream. Chill. Beat egg whites with cream of tartar and vinegar until soft peaks form. Add sugar gradually; beat until stiff peaks form. Add vanilla. Drop from tablespoon onto brown paper on baking sheet; make indentation in center of each. Bake at 250 degrees for 1 hour. Cool on wire racks. Fill meringue shells with orange mixture; top with additional whipped cream and cherry. Chill for at least 3 hours. Yield: 4-6 servings.

Florence B. and Mabel V. Seibert
Honorary Members
Beta Sigma Phi International
St. Petersburg, Florida

RASPBERRY-PEACH CHANTILLY

2 pkg. frozen raspberries, thawed
1 tbsp. kirsch
4 tbsp. sifted powdered sugar
1 lg. can peach halves, chilled
1/2 pt. whipping cream
1 tsp. vanilla
1/4 c. chopped pistachio nuts

Drain raspberries. Press raspberries through fine sieve, using back of large spoon; mix raspberry puree, kirsch and 2 tablespoons powdered sugar. Cover; refrigerate until chilled. Drain peaches. Arrange peach halves in sherbet glasses; fill each peach half with raspberry mixture. Whip cream until light. Sprinkle with remaining powdered sugar and vanilla; beat until stiff. Place whipped cream in pastry bag; pipe ring of whipped cream around each peach. May be spooned over peaches. Sprinkle pistachio nuts over whipped cream. Yield: 6-8 servings.

Margaret Wischmeyer, W and M Chm.
Xi Alpha Psi X3252
Dunwoody, Georgia

BUTTERSCOTCH BROWNIES

1/4 c. butter
1 c. (packed) light brown sugar
1 egg, slightly beaten
1/2 c. sifted flour
1 tsp. baking powder
1/4 tsp. salt
1/2 tsp. vanilla
1/2 c. coarsely chopped walnuts

Melt butter over low heat; remove from heat. Add brown sugar. Stir until blended; cool. Add egg. Sift flour, baking powder and salt together into separate bowl. Stir into butter mixture; add vanilla and walnuts. Spread in greased and floured 8 x 8 x 2-inch pan. Bake at 350 degrees for 20 to 25 minutes. Cool to lukewarm; cut into squares.

Marlene A. Fasel, Pres.
Theta Rho No. 6771
Crown Point, Indiana

SUNFLOWER SEED COOKIES

1 c. butter
1 c. (firmly packed) brown sugar
1 c. sugar
2 eggs
1 tsp. vanilla
1 1/2 c. unsifted all-purpose flour
1/2 tsp. salt
1 tsp. soda
3 c. quick-cooking rolled oats
1 c. shelled salted sunflower seed

Cream butter and sugars together thoroughly. Add eggs and vanilla; beat to blend well. Add flour, salt, soda and oats; mix well. Blend in sunflower seed. Shape into long 1 1/2-inch thick rolls. Wrap and chill well. Cut rolls into 1/4-inch thick slices. Arrange on ungreased cookie sheet. Bake at 360 degrees for 10 minutes. Cool on wire racks; store in airtight containers. Yield: 9 dozen cookies.

Janet Sprotte, Ext. Off.
Gamma Epsilon No. 8673
South Pasadena, California

OLD-FASHIONED WALNUT BALLS

1 c. butter or margarine
1/3 c. (firmly packed) brown sugar
1 tsp. vanilla
2 c. sifted all-purpose flour
1/2 tsp. salt
2 c. finely chopped California walnuts
Confectioners' sugar

Cream butter, brown sugar and vanilla together until fluffy. Sift flour and salt together; add to creamed mixture. Mix well to make soft dough. Stir in walnuts. Break off pieces of dough the size of a walnut; shape into balls. Place on ungreased cookie sheet. Bake at 375 degrees for 12 to 15 minutes. Remove from cookie sheet with spatula or pancake turner; cool slightly. Roll in confectioners' sugar. Yield: 4 dozen.

ANGELICA

1 1/2 c. sugar
1/2 c. water
2 egg whites
1/8 tsp. salt
2 tbsp. sherry
3 c. heavy cream, whipped
Candied cherries
Angelica

Combine sugar and water in saucepan; cook until syrup reaches 230 to 234 degrees on a candy thermometer or spins a thread when dropped from a spoon. Combine egg whites and salt in small bowl; beat until stiff. Pour hot syrup over egg whites in slow stream, beating constantly. Cool; add sherry. Fold in whipped cream. Turn into melon-shaped mold; freeze. Turn out on silver tray; decorate with candied cherries and angelica.

Lianne Dinwiddie, Pres.
Alaska Xi Mu X3631
Eagle River, Alaska

CHERRIES JUBILEE

1 tbsp. cornstarch
1 tbsp. sugar
1 1-lb. can pitted black cherries
3 or 4 strips of orange peel
Dash of lemon juice
1/2 c. warm brandy
Vanilla ice cream

Mix cornstarch and sugar together in saucepan. Add liquid from canned cherries and the orange peel. Cook until thick. Discard orange peel. Add cherries and lemon juice. Add warm brandy at the table; ignite. Serve over vanilla ice cream.

Patricia Carl, Pres.
Epsilon Eta No. 6914
Nashville, Tennessee

CHERRY CREAM FREEZE

1 15-oz. can sweetened condensed milk
1/4 c. lemon juice
2 1/2 c. cherry pie filling

3/4 c. crushed pineapple, well drained
1/4 tsp. almond extract
2 c. heavy cream, whipped

Combine milk, lemon juice, pie filling, pineapple and extract in large bowl; mix well. Fold in whipped cream until evenly blended. Turn mixture into 9 x 5 x 3-inch pan. Cover tightly with aluminum foil. Freeze for 24 hours or until thoroughly firm. Unmold onto serving tray. Yield: 2 quarts.

Mary Kay Brown, Pres.
Xi Chi X2161
Benton, Arkansas

MILK CHOCOLATE MOUSSE WITH CANDIED ORANGE SLICES

1 sm. seedless orange
1 c. sugar
1 6-oz. package semisweet chocolate pieces
1/3 c. water
1/8 tsp. salt
2 eggs, separated
1 tsp. vanilla
1/2 tsp. lemon flavoring
2 c. whipping cream

Cut orange into 12 slices; halve each slice. Sprinkle 1/2 cup sugar on large, flat plate; place orange slices in single layer on sugar. Let stand at room temperature, turning 2 or 3 times, for 2 hours or until glazed. Remove from sugar; place on waxed paper to dry. Combine chocolate pieces and water in small saucepan; place over low heat, stirring constantly, until chocolate melts and mixture is smooth. Stir in 1/4 cup sugar and salt; heat, stirring, until sugar dissolves. Remove from heat. Beat egg yolks slightly; beat in hot chocolate mixture and flavorings very slowly. Cool. Beat egg whites until foamy; beat in remaining sugar, 1 tablespoon at a time, until meringue stands in firm peaks. Beat cream in medium bowl until stiff. Fold chocolate mixture into meringue, then fold in whipped cream until well mixed. Pour into 8-inch springform pan; cover. Freeze for 6 hours or until firm. Loosen around edge with knife. Release spring; lift off side of pan carefully. Place dessert, on metal base, on serving plate. Garnish top and side with candied orange slices cut in wedges.

Sharon Moroni, Co. Coun. Pres.
Xi Theta Psi X-2315
Fullerton, California

ITALIAN STRAWBERRY WATER ICE

2 c. sugar
4 pt. fresh California strawberries
1/4 c. lemon juice
1/3 c. orange juice
Pink California champagne

Combine sugar and 1 cup water in medium saucepan. Heat, stirring, until sugar dissolves.

Boil for 5 minutes; cool. Force strawberries through food mill or blend in electric blender; strain to remove seeds. Blend strawberry puree and lemon and orange juices into syrup. Pour into ice cube trays. Wrap trays in aluminum foil; freeze until firm. Remove from freezer 20 minutes before serving time; let thaw slightly. Serve in sherbet glasses; pour champagne over ices. Yield: 8-10 servings.

TANGERINE ICE

3 peeled sectioned tangerines
2 c. sugar
3 c. tangerine juice
1/4 c. lemon juice
Grated rind of 2 tangerines
Chopped pistachio nuts

Chill tangerine sections until ready to use. Boil 1 quart water and sugar together for 5 minutes. Add tangerine juice, lemon juice and tangerine rind; mix well. Remove from heat; cool. Pour tangerine mixture into ice trays; freeze until ice crystals form. Beat thoroughly; return to freezer. Freeze until solid. Serve tangerine ice garnished with tangerine sections and nuts. Yield: 8 servings.

Virginia L. Crom, Ext. Off.
Xi Kappa Zeta X2556
Bishop, California

FRESH CRANBERRY ICE

4 c. cranberries
2 c. sugar
1/2 c. orange juice
1/4 c. lemon juice

Combine cranberries, sugar and 3 1/2 cups water in saucepan. Bring to a boil; simmer, stirring occasionally, for 10 minutes. Cool; press through wire strainer. Discard pulp. Add juices; pour into loaf pan. Cover with foil; freeze. Scoop out balls of cranberry ice several hours before serving; arrange in small serving dishes. Place in freezer until served.

Evie Reiss, Pres.
Xi Mu Kappa X2937
Chula Vista, California

HOMEMADE ICE CREAM

7 or 8 eggs
3 c. sugar
1/2 tsp. salt
3 tbsp. vanilla
1 pt. whipping cream
Milk

Combine eggs, sugar and salt in electric mixer bowl; beat with mixer until blended. Add vanilla. Spoon egg mixture into ice cream freezer container. Add whipping cream, stirring with wooden spoon. Fill freezer container with milk to 1/2 inch from top; freeze to desired consistency. Flavorings other than vanilla may be added, if desired.

JoAnne Hall, Pres.
Beta Delta No. 962
Sidney, Ohio

CANDY CRUST ICE CREAM PIE

2/3 c. semisweet chocolate bits
1/4 c. butter or margarine
1/4 c. milk

2 3 1/2-oz. cans flaked coconut
1 qt. cherry vanilla ice cream
Sweetened whipped cream

Combine chocolate, butter and milk in small saucepan. Place over low heat; stir until chocolate is melted. Remove from heat; blend in coconut. Spread on bottom and side of greased 9-inch pie plate. Chill until firm. Fill pie shell with ice cream; place in freezer until ready to serve. Place in refrigerator 20 minutes before serving time for easier slicing. Garnish pie with whipped cream.

LEMON CRUNCH ICE CREAM

2 c. milk
1 c. sugar
1/2 c. fresh lemon juice
1 tsp. grated lemon peel
2 egg whites
2 tbsp. sugar
1 c. whipping cream
1/2 oz. bitter chocolate, shredded

Combine milk, sugar, lemon juice and peel; freeze until firm. Beat egg whites until stiff peaks form, adding sugar gradually. Whip cream until soft peaks form. Remove frozen mixture to chilled bowl; beat until fluffy. Fold in egg white mixture and whipped cream. Add chocolate. Spoon into cake pan or ice cube trays; freeze until firm.

Michelle L. Schmidt, Treas.
Xi Nu Xi X-4071
Kaukauna, Wisconsin

EASY FRUIT SHERBET

3 1/4 c. sugar
2 env. unflavored gelatin
Juice of 4 lemons
Juice of 4 oranges
4 bananas, mashed
1 sm. can crushed pineapple

Bring sugar and 4 cups water to a boil. Soften gelatin in small amount of water. Add to sugar mixture, stirring constantly until gelatin is dissolved; cool. Combine lemon juice, orange juice, bananas and pineapple with gelatin mixture in ice cream freezer container. Water may be added to bring mixture to within 1 inch of top. Freeze according to manufacturer's directions.

Dorothy A. Isdell, Pres.
Lambda Zeta No. 7751
Bolivar, Missouri

APRICOT AND LEMON SHERBET

1 No. 2 can pitted apricots
1 3-oz. package lemon gelatin
1 c. sugar
1 c. whipping cream

Drain apricots, reserving 1 cup liquid. Force apricots through sieve. Bring 2 cups water to a boil; add gelatin, stirring to dissolve. Cool; add sugar, reserved juice, apricots and cream. Mix well; freeze in ice cream freezer according to manufacturer's instructions. Garnish

each serving with sprig of fresh mint, if desired.

Barbara Africano, Parliamentarian
Gamma Psi No. 906695
Falls Church, Virginia

CREME DE CACAO CHIFFON ANGEL PIES

3 egg whites
1/2 tsp. vanilla
1/4 tsp. cream of tartar
3/4 c. sugar
1 env. unflavored gelatin
1/2 c. water
1/2 c. semisweet chocolate pieces
Dash of salt
2/3 c. milk
1/4 c. creme de cacao
1/2 c. whipping cream

Bring 2 egg whites to room temperature. Add vanilla and cream of tartar; beat till soft peaks form. Add 1/2 cup sugar gradually, beating till very stiff peaks form. Cover baking sheet with brown paper; draw 6 circles 3 1/2 inches in diameter on paper. Spread each circle with meringue; shape into shells with back of spoon, making sides higher. Bake in 275-degree oven for 50 minutes; turn off heat. Let meringues remain in oven without opening door for 1 hour. Soften gelatin in water in small saucepan; stir over low heat till gelatin is dissolved. Add chocolate pieces, remaining sugar, salt and milk; cook till chocolate is melted, stirring constantly. Remove from heat; mixture will be chocolate-flecked. Beat with rotary beater till smooth; add creme de cacao. Chill till partially set, stirring frequently. Beat remaining egg white till stiff peaks form; fold into chocolate mixture. Whip cream till soft peaks form; fold into chocolate mixture. Place in meringue shells; chill till firm. Garnish with meringue topknots, if desired.

Carol Elias, Pres.
Theta Iota No. 6253
Indianapolis, Indiana

SPICY WALNUT MERINGUE SHELL

3 egg whites
1/4 tsp. cream of tartar
1/8 tsp. salt
1 c. sugar
1/2 tsp. cinnamon
*1/2 c. plain or toasted finely
  chopped California walnuts*

Beat egg whites with cream of tartar and salt in medium deep bowl until soft peaks form. Beat in sugar gradually, about 2 tablespoons at a time, until meringue stands up in stiff glossy peaks. Beat in cinnamon and any remaining sugar. Fold in walnuts gently. Pile meringue in lightly greased 9 or 10-inch pie plate. Spread over bottom and up side to form crust. Bottom of shell should be about 1/4 inch thick and side about 1 inch. Bake at 275 degrees for 50 minutes to 1 hour or until light tan in color. Turn oven off; leave meringue to cool with door closed. Meringue will crack and fall in center but this is normal. Press center lightly to level before filling. Spoon meringue into 8 mounds on lightly greased baking sheet for individual shells, shaping as for pie shell; bake for 45 minutes.

Chiffon Cranberry Filling

1 1/2 env. unflavored gelatin
1 c. sugar
1 c. whole cranberry sauce, sieved
2 egg whites
1/4 tsp. cream of tartar
1/8 tsp. salt
1 c. whipping cream
Red food coloring

Soften gelatin in 2 tablespoons water in saucepan. Add 2/3 cup sugar and cranberry sauce. Bring to boiling point, stirring constantly. Remove from heat; cool. Chill until mixture begins to thicken. Combine egg whites, cream of tartar and salt; beat until soft peaks form. Beat until stiff, adding remaining sugar gradually. Beat cream until stiff. Fold meringue and whipped cream into cranberry filling. Tint with food coloring. Turn into large baked shell; chill until firm. Garnish with walnut halves and whole cranberries, if desired.

Chiffon Pumpkin Filling

1 env. unflavored gelatin
1/4 c. sherry or orange juice
2/3 c. (packed) brown sugar
1/2 tsp. salt
1 tsp. cinnamon
1/2 tsp. nutmeg
1/2 tsp. ginger
3 eggs, separated
3/4 c. milk
1 c. canned pumpkin
1/3 c. sugar
1 c. minced California walnuts

Soften gelatin in sherry in saucepan; add brown sugar, salt, spices, beaten egg yolks and milk. Cook, stirring, for 5 to 10 minutes or until mixture thickens. Remove from heat; add pumpkin. Cool; chill until thickened. Beat egg whites until soft peaks form; add sugar gradually, beating until stiff peaks form. Fold meringue into pumpkin mixture; add 2/3 cup walnuts. Spoon filling into individual baked meringue shells; sprinkle remaining walnuts over top. Chill until firm.

Photograph for this recipe on page 160.

FRESH PEACH CUSTARD PIE

2 c. sliced peaches
1 unbaked 9-in. pie shell
3 eggs, beaten
1 c. sugar
Cinnamon to taste
2 tbsp. butter

Arrange peaches in pie shell. Beat eggs; add sugar, blending well. Pour egg mixture over peaches. Sprinkle with cinnamon; dot with butter. Bake at 400 degrees for 10 minutes. Reduce oven temperature to 350 degrees. Bake for 35 minutes longer. Frozen fruit may be used when fresh fruit is not in season.

Delores L. Haug, Pres.
Xi Alpha Nu X1851
Myrtle Point, Oregon

BANANA ANGEL PIE

16 graham crackers, crushed
1/2 c. melted butter
4 egg whites
1 tsp. vinegar
1/4 tsp. salt
1 c. sugar

Combine crumbs and butter; mix well. Press firmly into pie plate. Beat egg whites until frothy; add vinegar and salt. Add sugar, 2 tablespoons at a time; beat until stiff. Spread on crumb crust. Bake at 275 degrees for 1 hour to 1 hour and 15 minutes. Cool on rack.

Filling

1 c. coconut
1 1/2 c. whipping cream
2 tbsp. sugar
1 tsp. vanilla
1 c. sliced bananas

Toast 1/2 cup coconut; set aside. Whip cream; fold in remaining coconut, sugar and vanilla. Arrange bananas on meringue; top with whipped cream mixture. Sprinkle with toasted coconut.

Ann L. Clemens, City Coun. Pres.
Preceptor Kappa XP0430
Salem, Oregon

PIECE DE RESISTANCE BLACK BOTTOM PIE

1 1/2 c. vanilla wafer crumbs
6 tbsp. confectioners' sugar
6 tbsp. melted butter
1 tbsp. unflavored gelatin
1/4 c. cold water
2 c. half and half
3/4 c. sugar
4 tsp. cornstarch
4 eggs, separated
1 3-in. piece of vanilla bean
1 1/2 oz. chocolate, melted
1/4 tsp. salt
1/4 tsp. cream of tartar
1 c. heavy cream
1/2 oz. shaved chocolate

Combine crumbs, 4 tablespoons confectioners' sugar and butter; press into pie pan. Soften gelatin in cold water; set aside. Scald half and half; set aside. Combine 1/2 cup sugar and cornstarch; set aside. Beat egg yolks until light; stir in half and half slowly. Add sugar mixture and vanilla bean. Cook in double boiler, stirring occasionally, until custard coats spoon heavily. Remove 1 cupful custard; add chocolate. Beat until cool; pour into crust. Add gelatin mixture to remaining custard. Allow to cool but not stiffen. Remove vanilla bean. Combine egg whites, salt and cream of tartar. Beat until stiff; add remaining sugar gradually. Fold egg whites carefully into custard. Spoon vanilla custard over chocolate custard; chill until firm. Whip cream; add remaining confectioners' sugar gradually. Cover custard with whipped cream. Sprinkle shaved chocolate over top.

Linda Forman, Rec. Sec.
Xi Psi X582
El Paso, Texas

CHOCOLATE-PECAN PIE

2/3 c. evaporated milk
2 tbsp. butter
1 6-oz. package chocolate
* semisweet morsels*
2 tbsp. flour
Salt to taste
1 c. sugar
2 eggs
1 c. chopped pecans
1 tsp. vanilla
1 9-in. unbaked pastry crust

Preheat oven to 375 degrees. Combine milk, butter and chocolate morsels in 1-quart saucepan; stir over low heat until chocolate melts. Mix flour and salt in 1 1/2-quart bowl. Add sugar and eggs; mix well. Stir in chocolate mixture; stir in flour mixture. Add pecans and vanilla. Mix well; pour filling into pastry crust. Bake for 35 minutes or until firm. Cool before serving. Serve warm or cold; top with ice cream, if desired.

Doris Miller, Pres.
Xi Mu Delta X2892
Merced, California

HEAVENLY CHOCOLATE CHIFFON PIE

1 env. unflavored gelatin
1 c. sugar
1/4 tsp. salt
1/2 c. cocoa
6 eggs, separated
1 c. milk
1 tsp. vanilla
1/2 tsp. cream of tartar
1 baked 9-in. pastry shell

Mix gelatin, 1/4 cup sugar, salt and cocoa in top of double boiler. Beat egg yolks and milk together; stir into gelatin mixture. Have boiling water 2 inches deep in bottom of double boiler. Place gelatin mixture over boiling water. Cook, stirring constantly, for about 10 minutes or until gelatin dissolves and mixture thickens slightly. Remove top of double boiler from bottom; stir in vanilla. Chill, stirring occasionally, until gelatin mixture mounds slightly when dropped from a spoon. Combine egg whites with cream of tartar in large mixer bowl; beat with electric mixer until egg whites begin to form soft peaks. Add remaining sugar gradually, beating until stiff peaks form. Pour gelatin mixture over egg white mixture; fold in until completely blended. Chill until partially set; spoon into pastry shell. Chill pie for several hours or until filling is set. Garnish with whipped cream and chocolate curls, if desired. Yield: 8 servings.

STRAWBERRY SPONGE CREAM PIE

1   10-oz. package frozen
*   strawberries*
3 tbsp. cornstarch
Sugar
2 tbsp. flour
1/4 tsp. salt
2 eggs, separated
1 1/2 c. milk
1 tbsp. butter
1 tsp. vanilla
1 baked 9-in. pie shell

178

Thaw strawberries; drain well, reserving liquid. Add water to reserved liquid to measure 1/2 cup liquid. Combine 2 tablespoons cornstarch and 1 tablespoon sugar in small saucepan; add liquid gradually, stirring to make a smooth paste. Cook, stirring constantly, over low heat until mixture is clear and thickened. Remove from heat; stir in strawberries. Set aside. Combine 1/2 cup sugar, flour, remaining cornstarch and salt in top of double boiler. Beat egg yolks slightly. Blend in milk gradually, stirring with wooden spoon; stir in egg yolks and butter. Place over rapidly boiling water, having water just touching bottom of boiler top. Cook, stirring constantly, until mixture is smooth and thickened. Remove from heat; stir in vanilla. Pour mixture into prepared shell. Beat egg whites until frothy; add 3 tablespoons sugar gradually, beating until stiff peaks form. Fold strawberry mixture into meringue. Spread evenly over hot filling, sealing edge to crust. Bake at 350 degrees for 30 minutes. Cool before serving.

Ruth Ann Rihel, Pres.
Gamma Upsilon No. 6437
Weirton, West Virginia

PUMPKIN MOLDS WITH MINCEMEAT SAUCE

1 1/2 c. cooked pumpkin
3/4 c. (packed) light brown sugar
1/2 tsp. salt
1/2 tsp. nutmeg
1 tsp. vanilla
2 tbsp. butter
1 tall can evaporated milk
2 env. unflavored gelatin
1/2 c. cold water
2 eggs, beaten
1 c. prepared mincemeat
1/2 c. apricot nectar
2 tbsp. lemon juice

Combine pumpkin, sugar, salt, nutmeg, vanilla, butter and milk in heavy saucepan. Heat, stirring, until butter melts. Soften gelatin in cold water. Add to pumpkin mixture; stir until dissolved. Stir small amount of pumpkin mixture into eggs; stir back into pumpkin mixture. Cook for 1 minute over low heat; cool. Pour into individual molds rinsed in cold water; chill until firm. Unmold onto serving dishes. Combine remaining ingredients; heat through. Serve with pumpkin molds.

Elsie E. Williams, Honorary Member
Beta Sigma Phi International
Millsboro, Delaware

DANISH RUM PUDDING

3 egg yolks
6 tbsp. sugar
2 tbsp. rum
Salt to taste
1 tbsp. unflavored gelatin
1 c. whipping cream, whipped
Sweetened raspberry juice
Cornstarch

Beat egg yolks and sugar well; add rum and salt. Soften gelatin in 3/4 cup cold water; dissolve over boiling water. Add to egg mixture. Chill until thickened; fold in whipped cream. Combine raspberry juice and small amount of cornstarch in double boiler. Cook, stirring constantly, until thickened. Serve sauce over pudding.

Sharon R. Edmundson, Pres.
Beta Alpha Delta No. 6243
Sutter Creek, California

BUTTER-RUM SAUCE

2 tbsp. cornstarch
1/2 tsp. salt
1 c. sugar
2 tbsp. butter
1 tsp. rum flavoring
1 oz. rum
Juice of 1/2 lemon

Combine cornstarch, salt and sugar in saucepan; add 2 cups boiling water gradually, stirring constantly. Bring to a boil; boil for 5 minutes. Remove from heat; add butter, rum flavoring, rum and lemon juice. Serve warm over ice cream, if desired.

Paula J. Palmer, Pres.
Xi Gamma Tau X1273
Sacramento, California

CRIMSON SAUCE

1   10-oz. package frozen red
      raspberries
1 1/2 tsp. cornstarch
1/2 c. currant jelly

Thaw and crush raspberries; mix all ingredients in saucepan. Bring to a boil; cook, stirring constantly, until mixture is clear and slightly thickened. Cool. Serve over peach half filled with vanilla ice cream.

Ann Dagnon, VP
Xi Delta Omicron X2728
Hollywood, Florida

LEMON SAUCE

1 egg
1/4 c. lemon juice
2 tbsp. butter
1/4 tsp. salt
1/2 c. sugar

Beat egg lightly; add remaining ingredients. Cook in double boiler until thickened, stirring frequently. Chill.

Ruth Penhallegon, Corr. Sec.
Xi Alpha Pi X2316
Albuquerque, New Mexico

ELEGANT STRAWBERRY CREAM ROLL

4 eggs, at room temperature
3/4 c. sugar
3/4 c. sifted all-purpose flour
3/4 tsp. baking powder
1/4 tsp. salt
1 tsp. vanilla
Sifted confectioners' sugar
1   16-oz. package frozen
      strawberries
1 c. heavy cream
1/2 c. chopped blanched almonds
4 tbsp. orange liqueur
1/2 tsp. grated lemon rind
2 tsp. cornstarch
1/2 tsp. cardamom

Grease 15 1/2 x 10 1/2 x 1-inch jelly roll pan. Line with waxed paper; grease again.

Beat eggs in large bowl until foamy; add sugar gradually, beating constantly. Beat for 5 minutes longer. Sift flour, baking powder and salt together. Add to egg mixture; blend at low speed until well mixed. Stir in vanilla. Pour into prepared pan. Bake in preheated 350-degree oven for 15 to 18 minutes or until surface springs back when touched. Invert onto towel dusted with confectioners' sugar; remove waxed paper carefully. Roll as for jelly roll; cool. Thaw strawberries according to package directions. Drain well; reserve liquid. Crush strawberries with fork. Combine cream and 1/4 cup confectioners' sugar in chilled bowl; beat until stiff. Combine whipped cream, strawberries, almonds, 2 tablespoons orange liqueur and lemon rind. Unroll jelly roll; fill with strawberry cream. Reroll; place on serving tray, seam side down. Chill. Combine 3/4 cup reserved strawberry liquid, cornstarch, remaining orange liqueur and cardamom; bring to a boil. Reduce heat; cook for 4 minutes. Cool. Add several drops of red food coloring, if desired. Spread over chilled roll just before serving; garnish with whipped cream, fresh strawberries and sliced almonds. Yield: 12 servings.

Alta Smith, Pres.
Xi Alpha Psi X3527
Lenoir City, Tennessee

STRAWBERRY CREPES

1 c. sifted flour
1 egg
2 egg yolks
1/4 tsp. salt
1 tbsp. sugar
2 c. milk
4 tbsp. melted butter, cooled
2   8-oz. packages cream cheese,
      softened
1   1-lb. carton sour cream
2 qt. frozen strawberries, thawed
Cornstarch

Combine flour, egg, egg yolks, salt, sugar, milk and butter; beat with rotary beater until smooth. Grease 6-inch skillet; heat over moderate heat. Pour about 2 tablespoons batter into center of skillet. Lift skillet to spread evenly over bottom; batter should form paper-thin layer. Brown on both sides. Remove from skillet; cool. Combine cream cheese and sour cream; beat until smooth. Drain strawberries; reserve liquid. Add strawberries to cream cheese mixture; mix well. Place 2 tablespoons filling in middle of each crepe. Fold over edges; fasten with toothpicks. Place on baking sheet; broil until top begins to brown. Mix reserved syrup with enough cornstarch to thicken; cook over medium heat, stirring, until thickened. Serve with crepes.

Juanita Southard, Treas.
Iota Omicron No. 7908
Elkhart, Indiana

BRANDY BALLS

3 tbsp. honey
1/3 c. brandy
2 c. vanilla wafer crumbs
1/2 lb. milk chocolate, grated
1 6-oz. package butterscotch bits
Dash of salt
1/2 c. coconut (opt.)
Confectioners' sugar

Combine honey and brandy; combine with remaining ingredients except sugar. Chill overnight. Shape into balls; roll in confectioners' sugar. Place in sealed container; store in refrigerator. Roll in confectioners' sugar again before serving. May be refrigerated for 2 to 3 weeks.

Rebecca Moore, Pres.
Delta Rho No. 8641
Charleston, West Virginia

DATE-NUT ROLL

4 c. sugar
1 1/2 c. milk
3 tbsp. butter
1 7-oz. package pitted chopped
   dates
1 1/2 c. chopped pecans

Combine sugar, milk, butter and dates in heavy saucepan. Cook, stirring occasionally,

over medium heat to soft-ball stage; remove from heat. Fold in pecans. Beat by hand until very stiff. Place mixture on damp cloth in strip 1 1/2 inches in diameter; roll cloth around mixture. Cool; cut into 1/2-inch slices.

Gaye Scheffel, Past VP
Xi Alpha Iota X3432
Wallace, Idaho

GLAZED NUTS

1 1/2 c. sugar
1/2 c. sherry
1 tbsp. light corn syrup
Dash of salt
4 c. pecans

Combine sugar, sherry, corn syrup and salt in saucepan; cook to soft-ball stage. Remove from heat; stir in pecans, stirring well to coat. Pour pecan mixture onto sheets of foil; separate with fork. Cool; store in airtight container. Walnuts may be substituted for pecans, if desired.

Marjorie Davis, Corr. Sec.
Epsilon Sigma No. 8394
Chesapeake, Virginia

TURTLES

1 lb. soft caramels
3 tbsp. evaporated milk
1 1/2 c. chopped pecans
2 tbsp. margarine
1 pkg. milk chocolate chips
1/2 bar paraffin

Heat caramels and milk in top of double boiler over simmering water, stirring until mixture is smooth and creamy. Add pecans and margarine; mix well. Drop from teaspoon onto well-greased cookie sheet or waxed paper; chill until firm. Melt chocolate chips and paraffin in top of double boiler over hot water; stir well. Dip caramel drops into chocolate mixture; let cool on greased cookie sheet or waxed paper. Yield: 72 candies.

Barbara Amerin, Pres.
Epsilon Kappa No. 4616
Plains, Kansas

Beverages

Beverages can warm the body, calm the soul, arouse the senses,
set or break a mood, start a meal or finish it. With so much potential,
beverages should never be a mere afterthought to the menu.

When there's a thirst to be quenched, why not make the beverage
a scene-stealer, unusual to the taste and pleasant to the eye?
You might top your drink with a sprig of mint or even a lovely
spring blossom. Float fresh citrus sections and colored ice in a fruit
punch. Or serve the drinks in pretty frosted glasses.

Beta Sigma Phis think the beverage should be as special and appetizing
as the entree. In this section you will find their favorite recipes
for punches, eggnogs, slushes, and coffee and tea variations.

CHAMPAGNE PUNCH

1 6-oz. can frozen orange juice
1 c. lemon juice
2 1/2 c. pineapple juice
1 c. sugar
1 fifth sauterne
2 fifths champagne

Mix orange juice, lemon juice, pineapple juice and sugar. Chill for several hours. Combine juice mixture with sauterne and champagne in punch bowl. Float fruited ice ring in punch. Yield: 3 1/2 quarts punch.

Jeanne Twenge, Pres.
Delta Zeta No. 6652
Monmouth, Oregon

BELGIAN COFFEE

1 egg white
1/8 tsp. cream of tartar
1/8 c. sugar
1/4 tsp. chocolate flavoring
Coffee

Combine egg white, cream of tartar, sugar and chocolate flavoring in small mixer bowl; beat well until satiny. Place spoonful of egg mixture into heated cup; top with strong coffee.

Carolyn Princehouse, Pres.
Alpha Chi No. 3813
Hood River, Oregon

MEXICAN COFFEE

3/4 tsp. cinnamon
1 1/2 c. strong black coffee
Sugar to taste
1/2 c. whipping cream
1/4 tsp. nutmeg

Stir 1/2 teaspoon cinnamon into coffee; pour into 4 demitasse cups. Sweeten to taste. Whip cream with remaining cinnamon and nutmeg; top each cup with dollop of whipped cream. Yield: 4 servings.

Carol Traster, Pres.
Xi Rho X444
Fort Wayne, Indiana

TEMPTING TOPPERS

Iced coffee
Frozen non-dairy creamer, thawed
Frozen non-dairy creamer, whipped
Chocolate syrup
Cinnamon to taste
Whiskey

Pour equal amounts of coffee and thawed creamer into stemmed glasses. Top with whipped creamer.

Variation 1

Combine iced coffee and chocolate syrup to taste. Pour into tall stemmed glasses. Stir in whipped creamer. Top each serving with a dollop of whipped creamer.

Variation 2

Combine coffee and cinnamon; pour into tall glasses. Top with whipped creamer.

Variation 3

Pour coffee into 8-ounce glasses. Stir 1 jigger whiskey into each glass. Top with whipped creamer.

CRANAPPLE-CHAMPAGNE PUNCH

Orange slices
Lemon slices
Maraschino cherries
3 pt. cranapple juice
2 c. orange juice
1/4 c. lemon juice
2 fifths champagne

Combine orange slices, lemon slices and cherries in mold; fill with water. Freeze overnight. Combine cranapple juice, orange juice and lemon juice; chill well. Pour into punch bowl; add champagne and ice mold just before serving. Serve in champagne glasses. Yield: 20 servings.

Carol Mason, Pres.
Pi Delta No. 4568
Redwood City, California

COFFEE EGGNOG SUPREME

6 eggs, separated
3/4 c. sugar
1/4 c. instant coffee
Milk
1 pt. light cream
1 pt. heavy cream

Beat egg whites; add sugar gradually, beating until stiff peaks form. Beat egg yolks until thick and lemon colored. Fold egg white mixture into egg yolks. Make a paste of coffee and small amount of milk. Combine light cream and 1 quart milk; add to coffee paste gradually, stirring until dissolved. Add coffee mixture to egg mixture slowly. Whip heavy cream; fold into eggnog just before serving.

Roberta Nelsen, Hist.
Xi Theta Gamma X2097
Upland, California

EGGNOG BRASILIA

4 eggs, separated
3 c. milk
2 c. light cream
3 tbsp. instant coffee
1/2 c. light corn syrup
1/2 c. brandy
Ground nutmeg

Beat egg yolks slightly in large saucepan; stir in milk, cream, coffee and 1/4 cup corn syrup. Cook over low heat, stirring frequently, to scalding. Remove from heat; stir in brandy. Combine remaining corn syrup and 1/4 cup water in small saucepan; bring to a boil. Simmer for 5 minutes. Beat egg whites until foamy; beat in hot syrup gradually until soft peaks form. Fold in egg yolk mixture. Ladle into punch bowl; sprinkle with nutmeg.

Wenda Robertson, W and M Chm.
Theta Sigma No. 8798
Boise City, Oklahoma

SPIRITED CHRISTMAS EGGNOG

12 eggs, separated
1 qt. bourbon
6 oz. dark rum
2 c. sugar
2 qt. milk
1 pt. whipping cream, whipped
Cinnamon
Freshly grated nutmeg

Beat egg yolks until light yellow; add bourbon and rum gradually, beating constantly. Add sugar and milk. Fold in whipped cream and stiffly beaten egg whites. Sprinkle with cinnamon and nutmeg to taste.

Carolyn L. Anderson, Sec.
Preceptor Xi XP395
Englewood, Colorado

SUPERB EGGNOG

3 eggs, separated
1/2 c. sugar
1 c. bourbon
1 c. heavy cream

Combine egg yolks and sugar in blender container. Blend for 1 minute or longer. Pour bourbon into egg yolk mixture with blender running. Mix well. Beat cream in chilled bowl with egg beater until soft peaks form. Combine egg yolk mixture and whipped cream. Pour into chilled serving bowl. Fold in stiffly beaten egg whites just before serving.

Carole Adiego, Sgt. at Arms
Psi Pi No. 5721
San Jose, California

FESTIVE WINE PUNCH

2 1/2 c. orange juice
1 c. unsweetened pineapple juice
1/2 c. sifted confectioners' sugar
2 tbsp. grated lemon peel
1 qt. dry white wine or champagne
1 tbsp. honey
6 whole cloves
1/2 tsp. cinnamon
1/2 tsp. nutmeg
2 trays ice cubes
1 1/2 qt. ginger ale, chilled

Combine juices, sugar, peel, wine, honey and spices; add 2 cups water. Refrigerate, covered, for 3 hours. Strain punch; pour into serving bowl over ice cubes. Add ginger ale; serve immediately. Yield: 20 servings.

Janet Shipe, Sec.
Epsilon Chi No. 8401
Chamblee, Georgia

FORMAL TEA PUNCH

4 c. sugar
2 c. strong black tea
6 6-oz. cans frozen lemonade
2 6-oz. cans frozen orange juice
1 lg. can pineapple juice
1 16-oz. package frozen
*   strawberries*
2 qt. ginger ale

Bring sugar and 4 cups water to a boil; boil for 10 minutes. Cool; add tea, lemonade, orange juice and pineapple juice. Thaw strawberries partially; add to sugar mixture. Just before serving, add 4 quarts of water and ginger ale. Pour into punch bowl over ice. Chablis may be added with ginger ale, if desired. Yield: 50-60 servings.

Mrs. James G. Lewis, Pres.
Kappa Theta No. 471
South Haven, Michigan

FRUIT SLUSH

2 c. honey
1 6-oz. can frozen orange juice

1 46-oz. can pineapple juice
1/4 c. lemon juice
3 ripe bananas, mashed
3 qt. ginger ale

Combine honey with 3 cups water in large kettle; bring to a boil. Prepare orange juice according to can directions. Stir orange juice, pineapple juice and lemon juice into honey mixture. Add bananas; blend thoroughly. Pour mixture into two 9 x 13-inch baking dishes; freeze. Remove from freezer 1 hour before serving. Chop into small pieces; place into punch bowl. Add ginger ale. Serve immediately. Carbonated lemon-lime beverage or sparkling water may be substituted for ginger ale, if desired. Yield: 36 servings.

Alice Barrett, Sec.
Eta Omega No. 6079
Albany, Indiana

GOLDEN WINE PUNCH

2 1-qt. bottles sparkling water,
*   chilled*
2 fifths Rhine wine
3/4 c. curacao
1 lg. orange

Pour 1 quart sparkling water into bowl; freeze. Combine wine and curacao 1 to 4 hours before serving. Cut long spirals from orange's thin outer peel with vegetable peeler. Extract juice from orange; add orange peel and juice to punch. Unmold frozen sparkling water in 4-quart punch bowl. Stir in chilled punch and remaining sparkling water. Yield: 25 servings.

Carol L. Pryor, ECC Chm.
Chi Phi No. 5521
Lompoc, California

CHERRY-PINEAPPLE FLIP

1 4-oz. jar red maraschino
*   cherries*
1 1-pt. 2-oz. can unsweetened
*   pineapple juice*
2 eggs
Dash of ground cloves

Combine undrained cherries, pineapple juice, eggs and cloves in electric blender container; blend until smooth. Pour into ice-filled glasses. Garnish with mint, if desired. Yield: 4-6 servings.

Photograph for this recipe on page 182.

HOT CRANBERRY TEA

4 c. fresh cranberries
2 1/2 c. sugar
Juice of 1 lemon
Juice of 3 oranges
1/2 c. red hot cinnamon candies

Combine cranberries with 4 cups water in a saucepan; cook berries until skins pop. Strain; return pulp to saucepan. Add 2 quarts water and sugar. Bring mixture to a boil; cook, stirring constantly, until sugar is dissolved. Add lemon and orange juice and red hots. Heat until candies are dissolved; serve. May be served cold. Yield: 1 gallon.

Betty John, Pres.
Preceptor Alpha Alpha XP733
Mt. Carmel, Illinois

HOT CRANBERRY ROSE CUP

1 qt. cranberry-apple drink
1 c. sugar
4 1-in. cinnamon sticks
12 whole cloves
Peel of 1/2 lemon, cut in strips
2 fifths rose wine
1/4 c. lemon juice

Combine cranberry-apple drink, 2 cups water, sugar, cinnamon, cloves, and lemon peel in saucepan; bring to a boil, stirring until sugar is dissolved. Reduce heat; simmer for 15 minutes. Strain; add wine and lemon juice. Heat through; pour into punch bowl. Garnish with lemon slices and fresh cranberries, if desired. Serve in preheated mugs or cups. Yield: 20 5-ounce servings.

Jean Lombardi, Soc. Chm.
Alpha Alpha Chi No. 6189
Santa Rosa, California

ANNIVERSARY PUNCH

1 12-oz. package frozen sliced strawberries
2 tsp. grated lime rind
Juice of 1 lime
1 bottle sparking Burgundy
1 bottle dry champagne
1 bottle sauterne

Thaw strawberries; combine strawberries, lime rind and lime juice in saucepan. Bring to a boil; reduce heat. Simmer for 10 minutes. Force through sieve; cool. Add wines to strawberry mixture in punch bowl. Serve immediately.

Joy Urschel, Pres.
Xi Alpha Beta X2434
Phoenix, Arizona

PARTY PUNCH

2 10-oz. packages frozen whole strawberries
1 No. 303 can pineapple chunks
2 oranges, sectioned
Mint leaves
1 6-oz. can frozen lemonade concentrate
1 6-oz. can limeade concentrate
2 6-oz. can orange juice concentrate
1 46-oz. can pineapple juice, chilled
1/2 tsp. salt
2 7-oz. bottles club soda

Thaw strawberries; drain pineapple, reserving syrup. Arrange fruits and leaves in ring mold. Add reserved syrup to partially cover fruit; freeze. Fill mold to the top with water and freeze until ready to use. Combine concentrates, pineapple juice, 6 cups water and salt in punch bowl. Stir well and chill. Stir in club soda before serving. Unmold frozen fruit ring; drop into punch.

Jean Sego, Pres.
Kappa Lambda No. 8603
Greenwood, Indiana

PINEAPPLE WASSAIL

4 c. unsweetened pineapple juice
1 12-oz. can apricot nectar
2 c. apple cider
1 c. orange juice
6 1-in. cinnamon sticks
1 tsp. whole cloves

Combine all ingredients in large saucepan. Bring to a boil; reduce heat. Simmer for 15 minutes; strain into large punch bowl or pitcher. Serve hot. Orange slices may be floated on top, if desired.

Shirley Berrard, Pres.
Xi Epsilon Pi X2539
Paris, Illinois

SPICED CIDER

1/4 c. (packed) brown sugar
6 cloves
2 cinnamon sticks
4 c. cider

Combine all ingredients in saucepan; bring to a boil. Reduce heat; simmer for 5 minutes.

Barbara Sellars, Pres.
Delta Gamma No. 4955
Lebanon, Tennessee

ORIGINAL SPICED TEA

3 c. sugar
2 to 3 cinnamon sticks
1 tsp. whole cloves
1 1/2 c. orange juice
1 1/2 c. lemonade
8 tea bags

Combine sugar, cinnamon sticks and cloves with 5 cups water in a saucepan; bring to a boil. Add juices; simmer for several minutes. Combine tea bags and 4 cups boiling water; steep to make strong tea. Combine tea with juice mixture. Serve in teacup mixed with equal amount of boiling water.

Elizabeth M. Belmont, Ext. Off.
Xi Omicron X0918
Roseburg, Oregon

EGGNOG PUNCH

1 qt. cold milk
1 pt. cream
1 c. cold strong coffee
1 c. bourbon
1 pt. vanilla ice cream

Combine milk, cream and coffee; pour into punch bowl. Add bourbon gradually; blend well. Add scoops of ice cream; serve in punch cups. Yield: 8 servings.

Natalie Hollis, VP
Xi Tau X2382
Lafayette, Louisiana

CHERRY FRAPPE

2 4-oz. jars red maraschino
   cherries
1 pt. vanilla ice cream, softened
2 pt. orange sherbet
Crushed ice

Combine undrained cherries, ice cream and half the sherbet in electric blender container; blend until smooth. Pour into glasses half filled with crushed ice. Top with scoops of remaining sherbet. Garnish with mint. Serve with straws. Yield: 6 servings.

Photograph for this recipe on page 182.

MAGIC QUENCHER

3 c. mixed fruit punch
Canned pineapple slices
Maraschino cherries
1 c. orange juice
1 c. unsweetened pineapple juice
Juice of 3 lemons
3 c. dry ginger ale
3 tbsp. honey
Red food coloring
1 qt. ice milk

Partially freeze mixed fruit punch. Arrange pineapple slices with cherries in centers in ring mold. Spoon fruit punch over pineapple; freeze until ready to use. Combine orange juice, pineapple juice, lemon juice and ginger ale; stir in honey and desired amount of food coloring. Mix well; chill thoroughly. Combine juice mixture with ice milk; mix thoroughly. Add ice ring; serve immediately.

Dorothy Scott, Sec.
Xi Epsilon Zeta X3708
Sikeston, Missouri

FROZEN CHOCOLATE MALTS

3 c. chilled chocolate milk
1/2 c. malted milk powder
1 qt. vanilla ice cream, cubed

Mix milk, malted milk powder and 1 pint ice cream quickly with hand mixer or in blender until smooth but still thick. Add remaining ice cream; mix quickly. Pour into 4 chilled 10 or 12-ounce glasses. Freeze for 2 to 3 hours or until firm. May be served immediately; garnish with whipped cream and shaved chocolate or crushed peppermint candy, if desired.

SOUTHERN COFFEE PUNCH

2 qt. strong cold coffee
1 pt. cold milk
2 tsp. vanilla
1/2 c. sugar
1 qt. vanilla ice cream
Nutmeg to taste (opt.)

Combine coffee, milk, vanilla and sugar in punch bowl; stir until sugar is dissolved. Chill thoroughly. Add scoops of ice cream. Sprinkle lightly with nutmeg. Yield: 20 servings.

Janie Carpenter, Treas.
Gamma Lambda No. 3436
Sanford, Florida

KATIE'S PUNCH

3 oranges
3 lemons
2 oz. citric acid
5 lb. sugar

Grind oranges and lemons finely; combine with citric acid and sugar in stone crock. Pour 2 quarts boiling water over fruit mixture. Let stand, covered, for at least 12 hours. Combine 1 gallon mixture with 3 gallons water. Serve in punch bowl. Basic mixture may be refrigerated or frozen for several months. Mixed fruit punch or champagne may be substituted for 3 gallons water, if desired. Yield: 50 servings.

Norma G. Bauer, Past Pres.
Xi Eta Phi X3521
Effingham, Illinois

OUR PICNIC PUNCH

*1 can frozen orange juice
    concentrate
1 can frozen lemon juice
    concentrate
1 can apricot nectar
1 No. 2 can pineapple juice
Ginger ale*

Dilute frozen fruit juices with half the water recommended on cans. Combine with apricot nectar and pineapple juice in gallon thermos bottle; add half as much ginger ale as fruit juices. Serve over ice.

*Joyce Randall, Prog. Chm.
Xi Gamma Phi X1607
Bedford, Ohio*

ROSE PUNCH

*1 pt. concentrated mixed fruit
    punch
1 lg. can grapefruit juice
1/2 c. sugar
2 tsp. grated orange peel
2 qt. rose wine
1 qt. sparkling water
Fresh strawberries*

Combine all ingredients except strawberries in punch bowl over ice; float strawberries on top. Fruit or ice ring may be used, if desired.

*Mary Lee Hunt, Pres.
Xi Xi Theta X3264
Palos Verdes Peninsula, California*

SANGRIA

*1/4 c. sugar
1 c. sliced peaches
2 qt. red wine
1   6-oz. can frozen orange juice
1/2 c. lemon juice
1 c. lemon-lime carbonated
    beverage*

Add sugar and peaches to red wine; let stand for 24 hours. Stir in orange juice and lemon juice; let stand for 24 hours longer. Chill. Place in a punch bowl. Add carbonated lemon-lime beverage. Sparkling water may be substituted for lemon-lime beverage, if desired. Yield: 8-12 servings.

*Judeen M. Knott
Beta Eta No. 3397
Merrill, Wisconsin*

FROSTY GOLDEN PUNCH

*1   6-oz. can frozen lemonade
    concentrate
1   6-oz. can frozen orange juice
    concentrate
1   6-oz. can frozen pineapple
    juice concentrate
1   12-oz. can apricot nectar,
    chilled
1/2 c. lemon juice
1 qt. lemon sherbet
2 lg. bottles ginger ale, chilled*

Add water to frozen concentrates according to can directions; add chilled apricot nectar and lemon juice. Spoon in sherbet just before serving; add ginger ale. Pineapple or orange sherbet may be substituted for lemon sherbet, if desired. Yield: 20-25 4-ounce servings.

*Mary Schreiner, VP
Theta Zeta No. 3409
Tiffin, Ohio*

SPIRITED PUNCH

*Juice of 10 lemons
Juice of 6 limes
1/4 c. sugar
1/4 c. grape juice
4 tbsp. grenadine
3/4 c. dark rum
6 oz. light rum
6 oz. brandy
1 fifth bourbon
3 lg. bottles soda*

Combine all ingredients except soda; pour over ice cake in punch bowl. Add soda; serve immediately.

*Betty Clarke, Corr. Sec.
Xi Beta Epsilon X1812
Lakeland, Florida*

Index

COLOR ILLUSTRATIONS

PHOTOGRAPHY CREDITS: South African Rock Lobster Service Corporation; Florida Citrus Commission; American Lamb Council; National Kraut Packers Association; California Strawberry Advisory Board; Procter & Gamble Company: Crisco Division; International Tuna Fish Association; Accent International; Olive Administrative Committee; McIlhenny Company; Knox Gelatine, Inc.; United Fresh Fruit and Vegetable Association; The Borden Company; Brussels Sprout Marketing Program; California Apricot Advisory Board; National Cherry Growers and Industries Foundation; Pickle Packers International, Inc.; Carnation Company; California Artichoke Advisory Board; National Macaroni Institute; R. C. Bigelow, Inc.; Processed Apples Institute, Inc.; National Association of Frozen Food Packers; Pineapple Growers Association; Keith Thomas Company; DIAMOND Walnut Growers, Inc.; California Avocado Advisory Board; Canned Salmon Institute; U. S. Department of Commerce: National Marine Fisheries Service; National Dairy Council; California Raisin Advisory Board; Evaporated Milk Association; General Foods Kitchens; National Pecan Shellers & Processors Association; Apple Pantry; Pet, Inc.; Pillsbury Company.

Complete Your Cooking And Entertainment Library With Beta Sigma Phi Cookbooks!

Gourmet Cookbook – Apple Crêpes, Beef Braised in Red Wine, Charlotte Russe, Vichyssoise . . . here are hundreds of elegant recipes guaranteed to add special flair and imagination to your dining pleasure. Gourmet recipes are fun and easy . . . and are the pièce de résistance of every meal! **Party Book** – Beautiful, full-color covers hold hundreds of party plans that make every gathering a big success! Complete with themes, invitation designs, decorating hints, entertainment suggestions and menu tips. A must for everyone's party planning. **Fondue and Buffet Cookbook** – Hundreds of fondue, chafing dish and buffet recipes, sure to delight the most discriminating hostess. Colorful photographs and complete instructions give you great ideas for small and large parties, or even family fondue for two. **Meats Cookbook** – The way to a man's heart . . .? Nothing beats roast beef, lamb, pork, veal . . . or any other meat dish. Plain or fancy, mouth watering main dishes for every occasion and taste are included in this valuable recipe book. **Desserts Cookbook** – Flaming crêpes to frosted cakes . . . desserts are the crowning complement of every meal. And this marvelous book contains hundreds of tempting desserts . . . sure to bring smiles of delight from young and old alike. **Casseroles Cookbook** – From poultry to sirloin tips, here are hundreds of delicious and timesaving casseroles. Mix and match vegetables, meats, pasta, seasonings . . . and come up with a scrumptious meal – all in one dish. Fun to prepare and a breeze to serve. **Holiday Cookbook** – Prepare delicious and festive meals for all those special holiday events. Recipes are included for not only Christmas, Thanksgiving and New Year's Eve or Day . . . but for Halloween, the Fourth of July, St. Patrick's Day . . . every occasion throughout the year. **Salads Cookbook** – Tasty and tempting recipes for fresh salads are presented in this practical cookbook. There are recipes for every occasion, and hints on how to make sensational salads the hit of any meal.